ven After All This Time

ven After All This Time

STORY OF LOVE, REVOLUTION, AND LEAVING IRAN

Afschineh Latifi

with Pablo F. Fenjves

10 ReganBooks
Celebrating Ten Bestselling Years
An Imprint of HarperCollinsPublishers

Some names have been changed to protect the privacy of the individuals.

HarperCollins books may be purchased for educational, business, or sales promotional use. For information please write: Special Markets Department, HarperCollins Publishers Inc., 10 East 53rd Street, New York, NY 10022.

FIRST EDITION

Designed by Laura Blost

Printed on acid-free paper

Library of Congress Cataloging-in-Publication Data

Latifi, Afschineh.
    Even after all this time: a story of love, revolution, and leaving Iran / Afschineh Latifi, with Pablo F. Fenjves.—1st ed.
        p. cm.
    ISBN 0-06-074533-9
    1. Latifi, Afschineh. 2. Iranians—Biography. 3. Women—Iran—Biography. 4. Iran—Politics and government—1979–1997. 5. Latifi, Mohammad Bagher, 1938– 1979. I. Fenjves, Pablo F.   II. Title.

CS1419.L382A3   2005
955.05′42′092—dc22
[B]
                                                                                2004051461

05   06   07   08   09   10   9   8   7   6   5   4   3   2   1

In memory of my father, who gave his life for his country.

And for my mother—my heart, my rock, my inspiration.

Even after all this time

The Sun never says to the Earth

"You owe me"

Look at what happens with a love like that

It lights the whole sky.

—Hafiz

PERSIAN SUFI, FOURTEENTH CENTURY

Contents

سلام جان عزیز زرین‌دخت

۱- حال من خوب است و سلامتیم ...

...

سلام من عزیز زرین‌دخت جان بودم

...

...

زینب میرزا خطیبی
۱۴۱۶

لطفی عزیز ... در تاریخ ۷۸/۴/۱۹

...

زینب طیبی

CHAPTER ONE
The Arrest

BABA JOON

On February 13, 1979, my father, Colonel Mohammad Bagher Latifi, was detained at his barracks in the Farah Abad section of Tehran. A group of enlisted men stepped into his office, relieved him of his weapon, and informed him that he was under arrest. Less than an hour later, three men arrived at the barracks, escorted my father into the back of an open jeep, and drove away.

As the jeep approached the main gate, on its way out of the facility, my father asked if he could leave his house keys behind for my mother. The jeep stopped in front of the kiosk, and my father turned to the guard. "Please," he said, pressing the keys and his checkbook into the man's hands, "give these to my wife when she comes to fetch me."

The guard took the items, and the jeep pulled away.

When my mother arrived that afternoon, the guard told her that her husband had been taken away. She wanted to know who had taken him and why, but the guard shrugged and pursed his lips. He did not know, he said apologetically. He knew nothing. But he had two items for Khanoom Sarhang, Mrs. Colonel. He turned and retrieved the keys and the checkbook and put them into my mother's shaking hands, and she thanked him and drove home to tend to her four children.

At dinner that night, my older sister, Afsaneh, asked about my father, and we were told that Baba Joon was away on military business. This was not unusual, so we sat down to eat, oblivious, and we went to bed that night, still oblivious.

The next day, my mother drove from one Tehran jail to the next, looking for my father, and everywhere she went she was met with insults and abuse. "Look at you, you filthy slut! Have you no self-respect? Can't you dress like a decent woman?"

My mother had never worn a chador in her life—she was a thoroughly westernized Iranian: her head exposed, a hint of makeup on her eyes and lips, even a full-time job—but with the Shah recently deposed and Ayatollah Khomeini newly in power, the country was in upheaval.

"Please," she begged. "His name is Latifi, Sarhang Latifi. If you would just let me know he's here, it would mean the world to me."

"You are wasting your time," she was told. "We've probably executed him already."

The next day, she tried again, crisscrossing the city, driving from one prison to the next, but there was no sign of him, only more insults and abuse. And when we returned home after school, she was still out in the streets, searching, and her sister, Mali, was waiting for us by the front door.

"Where's Mommie Joon?" I asked.

"She's running errands," Khaleh Mali said. "She'll be back later."

I turned to look at Afsaneh. We both knew something was very wrong.

That night, we confronted our mother, asking her to tell us the truth. Afsaneh was eleven years old; I had just celebrated my tenth birthday.

"Baba has been arrested," she told us. "But it's okay; it's nothing to worry about, just a little misunderstanding. Still, you mustn't tell the boys. They are too young. They might get upset."

I had never seen my mother cry, and she didn't cry then, either. But she came close.

"So where is he?" I asked.

"I don't know," she said. "They're holding him somewhere. I'm still looking."

Afsaneh fell apart—she was very close to Baba—but I tried to be strong.

"Maybe I can help you find him," I said. "I'll go with you tomorrow, and we'll look together."

My mother's eyes grew moist, but still she didn't cry. "I don't want you girls to worry," she said, her voice harsher than usual to mask the pain. "Everything is going to be fine."

The next day, when I got out of school, my mother was waiting for me on the sidewalk. She had decided to take me up on my offer, hoping the authorities might take pity on a child. I felt like crying—I often cried over little things, like being late for school or misplacing one of my dolls—but I didn't cry this time. I knew my mother needed me, and I was determined to make myself useful.

For the next two days, we drove from prison to prison, searching for my father.

"Look," she would tell the guards, pointing at me. "He has children. There are three others at home. We are just normal people, like you." But they showed no mercy.

✢ ❁ ✢

When we arrived home that night, my aunt suggested that we broaden our search. She had heard from friends that many of the more important prisoners were being kept in government buildings, and that some of the religious schools had been transformed into holding facilities.

The next day, after class, my mother was again waiting for me in the street, and we tried anew. We visited half a dozen government buildings and another half-dozen schools with no luck. However, at our last stop, one of the guards took pity on us. He told us to try Madrese Alavi, one of the city's better known religious schools. "Many of the key people are there," he said.

I was exhausted and hungry, my feet hurt, and I didn't want to go. I was unable to get my young mind around the gravity of the situation, but my mother insisted. "This is the last place," she said. "I promise. Then I will get you a new Barbie."

That was different! A Barbie doll! I would do it for a new Barbie!

We drove to Madrese Alavi, and my mother left me in the car, near the entrance. The school had been turned into some sort of provisional headquarters, and members of the new regime were everywhere. I could see my mother at the front entrance, talking to two guards.

"Five days already?" they said, laughing. "It would be a miracle if he was still alive."

"Please," my mother said, turning to point me out, slouched in the front seat of the car. "We've been sleeping in the car. Tell him I need the house keys."

My mother didn't need the keys, of course, and she knew my father was aware of that. But if the guards came back with word that he had left his keys at the kiosk, then she would know that he was really there, and she could stop looking. She could focus her efforts on getting him out.

One of the guards went off, reluctantly, and my mother turned and waved at me, urging me to be patient. In due course the guard returned, and he said something to my mother, and I could see her light up and thank him, then turn and hurry back to the car.

She climbed behind the steering wheel, almost giddy with joy.

"What happened?" I asked.

"He's here!"

She started the car and pulled away.

"So why are we leaving?" I asked.

My mother didn't answer. She was lost deep within herself, full of hope and terror. We drove to a nearby drugstore and stocked up on soap, toothpaste, and a new toothbrush and returned to the Madrese Alavi. She made me wait in the car and delivered the purchases and hurried back.

"I don't understand," I said. "Why can't Baba come home with us?"

I was so naive. I thought the whole point had been to find him and to bring him home, and when my mother said he couldn't come, not just yet, anyway, I fell apart.

"I hate this!" I said, and I started crying. "I want Baba."

"You need to be strong," she said. "He'll be home soon."

But he didn't come home.

✷ ❧ ✷

In the days and weeks ahead, my mother kept going to the prison, trying to get in to see him, but she was rebuffed at every turn. So she began writing notes to him on small, unobtrusive slips of paper, and she would bribe the guards to slip them into his cell, hoping he would write back, praying for even a few words from him.

"Latifi azizam," she would write. "Latifi my love. We are well, and everyone says hello. Please advise me of your health as soon as possible. We are in the house, and we are lonely and missing you. All my love, Mommie."

Finally, he wrote back, using the same tiny square of paper on which she'd written, squeezing the words into the small space. He told us he was in good health and that there was nothing to worry about.

"Mommie joon'e azizam ghorbanat," he wrote. "My beloved for whom I would give my life. Please take care of the children. Console my mother until we find what God has in store for me. Do not worry about me. I am well."

From time to time, as the notes continued, back and forth, he would include vaguely coded messages for the wives of other imprisoned officers.

"Call Mrs. Mohri," he would write. "Tell her everything is fine." And my mother would do as she'd been asked, seeking out these women to bring them news. Their husbands were alive and well, she said. They were being held at the Madrese Alavi, along with her own husband.

In his notes, my father always closed by urging my mother to be brave. "Never forget," he wrote, "you are the wife of a soldier."

My mother never forgot, not for a moment. She kept the house running smoothly, as if nothing at all was amiss, and while we were away at school, she focused all of her efforts on Baba. She couldn't stand the thought of him in a soiled prison outfit, so she drove to the facility every day with freshly laundered clothes. She would send him shampoo and soap and toothpaste, on the off chance that some of it might actually reach his cell. She even sent him his tea flask, his pipe, and his favorite tobacco, suspecting that he would probably never see them, but hoping that these small "gifts," along with the bribes, might arouse a little sympathy in the guards.

In one note, dated March 19, 1979, just before Norouz, the Persian New Year and first day of spring, my mother wrote, "Latifi, my love, everyone is doing well. The children say hello. I am wishing you good health for this New Year. Please write me more details about your well-being."

And he wrote back, "*Hamsar'e azizam.* Beloved wife, I am doing well. Please don't worry about me. Please make sure the children don't feel lonely." And he closed with a coded message: "Please say hello to Mr. Hamidi and Mr. Pierhadi."

My mother did not know these men, but she made contact with them and learned that they had some influence with the new regime. They had been trying to help some of the other prisoners, but were so deluged with requests that they could do nothing for our family.

In time, my father's responses became increasingly pessimistic: "I am appreciative of your words and your visits to the prison, but please—there is no need to come every day. . . . Everything is good under the shadow of the Imam." This last part was for the benefit of the guards, who clearly read the notes.

At one point, Afsaneh wrote to him: "Dear Father, hope you are well. Don't worry about us. We are doing fine and send you our regards. Please take care of your health and have faith in God because you haven't done anything bad and don't need to worry." At the bottom of the note, in different ink, and at Mom's insistence, she had added, "All of us are thinking of you in our daily prayers." This, too, had been done for the benefit of the guards, so they could see that we were decent, God-fearing people.

Baba wrote back: "Thank you for your kindness. Kiss your sister and brothers. Make sure you study hard. God willing, I should be home soon."

Then there was a long period of silence, and Mom was horribly worried. She thought he might have been executed, but no one would either confirm or deny this, and she was forced to live in a state of perpetual, wrenching uncertainty. She heard rumors that some of the men had been moved to another facility, and many of them had been badly beaten by the guards, but all her inquiries amounted to nothing.

Finally, two weeks later, she discovered that the rumors were true. A number of prisoners, my father among them, had been moved to a regular prison, Zendan'e Shahrebani, and there was word that the families might be allowed to visit. My mother went early every morning and begged for admittance, but it was always denied. She would then hurry off to her job (teaching first grade at a local school, Haghigat) and return at the end of the day to try again. Many of the other wives and mothers fell apart, but not Mommie Joon. She was determined to be strong. She refused to become a victim. She would not be beaten.

On Fridays, when there was no school, she would take me and Afsaneh with her, begging for permission to see Baba, but it was always the same.

"Not today," she would be told, and the guards would laugh. "Keep trying, though! You never know!"

One day, we brought along my father's mother, Mammon Bozorgeh, and waited on the sidewalk for hours with the rest of the families. We were like sheep, as mute and docile as sheep. If anyone so much as grumbled, the guards would threaten them with arrest, or worse. Eventually, when it became clear that there was no hope of getting in, people would drift off, defeated, and return to their homes. We were the last to leave.

Two weeks later, my father was moved again, and again they wouldn't tell us where they'd taken him. It was a form of psychological warfare. Once again my mother searched the city, and she found him five days later, languishing at Zendan'e Ghasr, another prison. Once again she had to bribe the guards, and once again she begged them to pass along her small notes. "My beloved husband," she would write, "I cannot begin to tell you how much I love you and miss you."

This time, however, he did not respond. Nine, ten, eleven days passed—not a word from Baba. Mom kept writing, however, and the guards continued to deliver the notes, until at long last he responded. Strangely, the words were in an unfamiliar hand, and even the language seemed oddly stilted: "I am well. Do not worry. Everything is fine."

My mother was sure this was some kind of cruel joke—that my father had been executed, and that the guards were toying with her for their own amusement. Weeks later she discovered that he had only stopped writing because both of his wrists had been broken during an interrogation, and that he had been unable to pick up a pen.

Finally, after weeks of torment and frustration, we were waiting in our usual spot in front of the prison when the unexpected happened.

"Latifi!" It was one of the guards, calling our name.

We pressed forward, fighting our way through the crowd, but the guard stopped us at the door and said that only two of us would be allowed inside. Afsaneh, who had always been Daddy's girl, fell to her knees, weeping, and threw her small arms around my mother's legs. My mother didn't know what to do. She looked at me and at Mammon, as if to ask for our blessing, then took Afsaneh by the hand and disappeared into the building. I tried to console myself by looking on the bright side. Mommie and Afsaneh were going to see Baba Joon. We would soon have news.

Afsaneh bunched her head scarf at her throat, pulling it so tight that only her eyes showed. She was trying to make herself small, determined to sneak past even if the guards suddenly changed their minds. But they didn't change their minds. They led Mom and Afsaneh into the building and herded them into a large, airless room. It was separated into two equal halves by a narrow corridor. Each half served as a sort of holding pen, with a low, concrete wall in the middle and iron bars all the way up to the ceiling. Suddenly they saw Baba Joon in the distance, waving, and they hurried toward his side of the room. He was wearing clean clothes and smiling.

"How are you?" Mom asked, her voice breaking. She had to speak loudly in order to be heard above the din.

"I miss you," he shouted back, then turned to look at Afsaneh, gripping the iron bars. "And I miss *you*."

"When are you coming home?" Afsaneh asked, bursting into tears.

"Very soon," he replied. "Tell me about school. Tell me about your sister and your brothers."

"Everyone is fine," Mom said. "We are waiting for you to come home."

When they emerged from the building, less than twenty minutes later, my mother was smiling tightly. She said Baba looked well, and he expected to be home very soon. Afsaneh, however, seemed traumatized by the visit, and she refused to say a word about it.

The following week, it was my turn. My mother and I were led into the prison and taken to the same room. We were packed into one side, like penned cattle, and we waited for the prisoners to appear.

"Where is he?" I asked.

"I don't know," she replied. "Last time he was already here, waiting for us."

A few moments later, the prisoners began to shuffle in, and I saw my father among them, wearing clean clothes and standing tall but looking older than I remembered him, with a mustache even. He saw us and made his way over to the bars, smiling brightly. I felt the weight of my mother's hand on my shoulder and tried not to cry. "I love you, Baba Joon!" I called out. He waved and said he loved me, too, but in that cavernous space, with the iron bars and the narrow corridor between us and dozens of desperate voices raised in unison all around me, I could barely make out his words. I had so many things to tell Baba Joon. I wanted him to know that I was behaving and getting good grades and trying to be helpful around the house, but suddenly I was sobbing, and I called out that I missed him terribly and needed him to come home.

"I'll be home soon," he shouted back. "Tell your sister and brothers that I send my love."

Then it was all over, and I found myself clinging to my mother as we were ushered out of the room. The visit had been so brief and incomprehensible that for a long time I thought I must have imagined it.

The following week, Mammon went in to see him, and the week after that it was Afsaneh's turn. Then it was my turn again, but for some unexplained reason the guards weren't letting anyone in. We waited, hoping they might change their minds, but toward the end of the day my mother walked us back to the car and drove us home. No one said a word.

We went back the following Friday and the Friday after that, and the guards would make us wait for hours before turning us away. "There will be no visits this week. Maybe next week."

Finally, on the third Friday, they relented. My mother and I and a dozen other visitors followed the guards into our section of the room, and we again found the prisoners waiting on the far side of the narrow corridor. My father waved and smiled, and I waved back. But I didn't smile. I was crying. My mother placed one of her hands on my head and turned to a passing guard. "Please, sir," she said. "Do you think it might be possible to let our little girl hug her father? It would mean so much to her."

The guard looked at me for a long time—I held my breath—then nodded toward the small, wooden door at the far end of the room. I turned and fought my way through the crush of people and stepped into the corridor.

"No talking," the guard said. "Is that understood?"

I nodded.

As the guard watched, I ran to my father's side and hugged him through the bars. He lifted me clear off the ground and held on tight. I could feel his heart beating—both of our hearts, beating as one—and my eyes filled with tears. "Don't worry, Baba Joon," I whispered, bringing my lips close to his ear. "We are going to get you out of here."

All at once I was yanked from my father's arms. The guard scowled at me and literally dragged me down the narrow corridor, toward the wooden door. "*Behet goftam harf nazan*," he snapped. "I told you not to speak!"

☙ ❀ ☘

The prison notes continued into May. My mother would tell my father that she loved him more than ever, that the family was fine, and that we were all looking forward to the happy day when we would be reunited.

My father continued to say that he was being treated well, though clearly this was not the case, and that he was sure he would be home soon. And he always closed with words of caution and encouragement: "You are the wife of a soldier. You have to be strong. You are the children of a soldier. I ask that you be brave and that you look after your mother."

Then one morning in mid-May, without fanfare, my father was taken from his cell and marched into a makeshift courtroom. There were several mullahs seated in the front of the room, and one of them told my father that he was being charged with several counts of murder. The charges stemmed from a demonstration dating back to the previous September, when a number of antigovernment protestors were killed by gunfire. The mullahs accused my father of complicity in their deaths.

My father denied the allegations, noting that he hadn't even been in Tehran on the day in question. He then went on to tell the court that he didn't recognize their authority since he was a military officer and could only be tried by a military tribunal.

"So you are not only a criminal," one of the mullahs said, "but a stubborn criminal."

When my mother was finally told about the charges, she also remembered that we had been out of town on the day of the massacre, on a family vacation in Shomal, a resort on the Caspian Sea. And even *I* remembered the vacation because I had never seen my father sick. One evening he was struck by a stomach flu so severe that he had been hospitalized overnight. My mother contacted the hospital to ask for his records, then called the hotel and had them send her an itemized copy of the bill. Within days, she had put together an entire file—hotel bills, certified hospital records, restaurant receipts—showing that my father had been nowhere near the scene of the massacre, and she went to Zendan'e Ghasr to see the prison warden.

My mother was turned away, but she has an iron will and refused to accept defeat. She went back every day, and every day asked for a hearing, and, at the end of a week, the warden finally relented. She walked into his office with a dossier full of exculpatory evidence.

"My husband had nothing to do with the killings," she said. "He was in a hospital in Shomal at the time. The charges against him are false, and I have the documentation to prove it."

The warden accepted the file from her, feigning interest, then he took the pages, one at a time, and ripped them into tiny shreds. "You can bring me all the documentation you want," he said. "You can have your pages certified and recertified. But you are wasting your time."

My mother was finally beginning to understand the way things worked under the new regime. If they said Sarhang Latifi had orchestrated the massacre, it was as good as God's word: Sarhang Latifi had indeed orchestrated the massacre. Nothing else was even in the realm of possibility.

Every day my mother returned to the prison, begging to see my father, and every day she was refused.

"You *kaseef* slut," the guards said. "You run around with all sorts of men, like a common whore, and now at the last minute you remember that you once had a husband."

She would come home and keep the pain to herself, shielding us, and she would try to carry on as if everything were fine and normal. But it wasn't fine and normal. Baba hadn't been home in more than two months, and our house was crowded with frightened people: our aunt Mali; her son, cousin Nasser; and our maternal grandmother, Mammon Kobra. All of them were doing their best to help, but I would hear them talking at night, their voices low and furtive. *The streets are no longer safe. There is no established police system anymore. Every day there are more riots, more looting, more demonstrations.*

I don't remember much beyond a scattered demonstration here and there, glimpsed from the car on our way to and from school. When we returned home, we would park ourselves in front of the television, but we were no longer permitted to do so without an adult in the room. Our favorite programs were constantly interrupted by pro-Khomeini propaganda and almost-daily reports on the continuing arrests and executions, and Mom was determined to shield us from the bad news.

"Any moment now," I heard Mammon Kobra saying, night after night, "they will come to the house and drag us from our beds."

"Hush!" my mother said. "You will frighten the children."

In the morning, after a breakfast of freshly baked bread with butter and homemade jams and feta cheese, Mom would take us to school—Afsaneh to the French school, me to the German school—then she'd go off to teach her first-grade class. And every afternoon, without fail, she would drive to the prison and plead with the guards to let her see her husband.

She became a fixture there like so many others, but unlike the others she never wavered. The guards would laugh when they saw her coming, as if amused by her determination. "Here she is again. The Sarhang's whore."

On the evening of May 21, 1979, long after we children had gone to bed, the nightly newscast began with two dreaded words: *Ghasemel Jabarin*, "Enemies of God." This phrase, heard all too often in the months and years ahead, was always followed by the names of the military men who had been tried in the course of the previous days. On this particular day, the first name on the list was that of my father.

My mother pulled herself together and asked my cousin Nasser to drive her to the prison. She begged the guards to let her see Baba Joon, knowing there was very little time left, but they turned her away and she returned to the house. Khaleh Mali was chain-smoking, in shock, and Mammon Kobra was in her chador, praying and weeping. A moment later, the doorbell rang. It was the Etmeenans, along with several other neighbors. They, too, had heard the news, and when they saw my mother returning from the prison, they had hurried over to see if they could help. But what could they do? In a day or two, my father would be standing in front of a firing squad.

"We must go to Qom," my mother said, fighting tears.

Mom went into the bedrooms and woke us up. She told us to throw our coats over our pajamas and get in the car. The boys were crying.

"Why are you doing this?" I whined. "I have school tomorrow. I can't be late for school."

"Just do as you're told," my mother said.

The next thing I knew, we were speeding along in the car in the middle of the gloomy night. Mr. Etmeenan was behind the wheel, since Mom was too shaken to drive.

"Where are we going?" I asked.

"You'll see," my mother said tersely.

It was more than a hundred kilometers to the city of Qom and the roads were bad, so it took over two hours. We pulled up in front of the locked gate of a private home, and Mom and Mr. Etmeenan left us in the car and approached and rang the bell. I could see lights going on inside, and a moment later a man emerged from the house, silhouetted against the light, and moved toward the gate. The three of them stood there talking, and even from the distance I could hear an angry tone in the man's voice. In a matter of moments, Mom and Mr. Etmeenan returned to the car, and Mr. Etmeenan started the engine and pulled away.

"What happened?" I asked. Neither of them answered, and I knew better than to ask again. I didn't understand what was going on, but I knew there was worse to come.

Years later, I learned that she had been told that Ayatollah Khomeini himself lived in that house and that my mother was so desperate she had tried to appeal to him directly. Alas, she hadn't even made it past the servant at the front gate, who had strong opinions of his own. "You ought to be ashamed of yourself," he had said, scolding her. "A woman out in the middle of the night, with four young children!"

The next morning, my cousin Nasser returned to the house, looking devastated. There was a newspaper in his hand, with a photograph of my father on the front page. I was about to ask him if I could see it, but just then Mom emerged from the house and joined him, and they drove off together without a word.

MY FATHER (RIGHT) IN THE NEWSPAPER ARTICLE DESCRIBING
THE COURT PROCEEDINGS AND HIS ALLEGED CRIMES

"What's happening?" I asked my aunt.

"Nothing," she said. "Hurry up. You'll be late for school."

Nasser drove my mother to the prison, where she again begged the guards to let her see her husband one last time. "It's all over," one of them told her. "Go home." But she wouldn't leave. She stayed in the car all day, parked in front of the prison.

Finally, shortly before midnight, the guards relented. They ushered her into the prison, put a blindfold on her, then took her through a side entrance to the parking lot and helped her into a jeep. She was taken on a short drive, still blindfolded, and, at the end of it, she was helped out of the jeep and escorted into another building. When the blindfold was removed, she found herself in a classroom. The words *Mofsed'e Fel Arz* (Corrupt of the Earth) had been written on the blackboard.

"We will fetch your husband now," she was told.

My mother waited for a long time, but no one returned. Every so often, she could hear muted footfalls approaching on the far side of the closed door, and her heart would begin beating wildly, thinking she was about to see Baba, but he didn't come.

Suddenly she found herself thinking back to one of the last times that Baba had slept in his own bed. He had been in the kitchen earlier in the evening, with Ali, arm wrestling. Ali loved to arm wrestle—it was his favorite game—and of course Baba always let him win. On this particular night, after yet another marathon session, Mom finally broke up the little game and put Ali to bed, and when she returned to the master bedroom, she found my father in tears. She sat next to him on the bed, took his hand in both of hers, and asked him what was wrong. "Nothing," he said. "I am crying from happiness. I am happy that you have given me children. I am happy that I am a father, which is perhaps the greatest happiness of all. And at the same time maybe I am a little unhappy because I grew up without a father of my own."

Waiting there, in that little classroom, it suddenly occurred to my mother that her children would also grow up without a father. She bit her lip to keep from crying. Now she wondered if she herself would ever see Baba again. Maybe this whole thing was a cruel joke; maybe the guards had simply found a new way to torment her and were outside at that very moment, watching the door with wry amusement and wondering how much longer she would wait.

But just then the door opened, and my father stepped through. He was wearing a checkered shirt and his favorite beige suit. My mother, who had stood when he entered, went weak at the knees and found herself leaning against the wall for support. This was one of the outfits he used to wear when they went to fancy places, and it could only mean he was preparing for death. Baba Joon hoped to die in a good suit, with some small measure of dignity.

There were two guards at his side, both of whom were wearing checkered headscarves that hid everything but their eyes. Still, she could see that they were enjoying themselves, acting as if this reunion had been staged solely for their amusement. My mother turned away, looked directly at my father, and fought the urge to throw herself into his arms.

"How are you?" my father said stiffly.

She just nodded. She couldn't answer.

"And the children?"

She nodded again, feeling a rush of blood to the back of her throat.

"You know I've done nothing wrong," he said.

"I know," she said, her voice cracking.

"Please make sure the children know that I was guilty of nothing."

"They know it already," she said.

She wanted to reach out to him, to hold him in her arms, but the guards were still there, watching, and she could see that Baba wouldn't have approved.

"I love you," she whispered.

"And I love you," he said. "I have always loved you. More than you can imagine."

He stood tall and straight, the good soldier. And my mother knew in her heart, if not in her mind, that her husband of fourteen years, the only man she'd ever loved, was preparing to go to his death. That was the moment she fell apart. She turned to the guards, sobbing, and asked them how they could let this happen. Her husband was an honorable man. He had done nothing wrong. He had four small children at home.

One of the guards covered his eyes, which had suddenly filled with tears, and for a moment my mother thought there might be hope. After all, these men were human beings, weren't they? But a moment later they were leading my father out of the room, and the two guards who had driven Mom there stormed inside. They put the blindfold over her tearstained face, escorted her out, and walked her across the parking lot, toward the jeep. Just as they reached it, a shot rang out. It was May 23, 1979. Baba Joon was gone.

When I got up the next morning, I brushed my teeth, washed my face, got dressed, and walked into the main part of the house. Mom was sitting in a corner, dazed, dressed in black from head to toe, and I knew immediately that I would never again see my father. I turned and walked into the kitchen, and I looked outside and saw that it had begun to rain.

"Look," I told my aunt, "God is crying."

BABA JOON, MOMMIE JOON, AND HER
FATHER, AGHA JOON

MY MOTHER, FATHER, AFSANEH, AND ME

AFSANEH

CHAPTER 2
Family History

MY MOTHER, FATHER, AFSANEH, AND ME

MOM AND ME

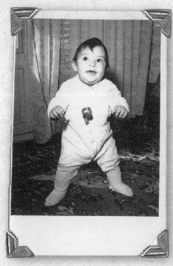

AMIR

THE DAY OF MY FATHER'S FUNERAL, my two little brothers, Ali, five, and Amir, three, were sent to the home of another aunt, and my sister and I, twelve and ten respectively, went across the street to stay with the neighbors, Maryam and Forood Kafi, a young, childless couple.

I could see the front door of our house from their kitchen window, and I sat there for hours, watching people come and go, paying their respects.

At night, Maryam fed us and put us to bed, and I would lie there, next to my sister, in a strange bed just across the street from our house, imagining that I could hear my mother wailing. The wailing would go on all night.

In the morning, if my mother had the strength, if she could face us without falling apart, she would come to see us. But the visits were brief, and she never said a word about my father.

When she left, I would hurry to the kitchen window and watch her shuffle across the street, back to our home. At thirty-four, she was a widow with four children and an enemy of the state.

❁ ❁ ❁

My father's full name was Mohammad Bagher Latifi Moghadam Tehrani. He was born on December 25, 1938, in Tehran. His father was a largely uneducated man who owned a small deli, and he died of a burst appendix when Dad was seven. The family struggled along, getting a little help from an older stepbrother, Shaban, who drove a taxi for a living.

In those days, Iran was still under the leadership of Reza Khan, also known as Reza Shah Pahlavi, who became prime minister in 1923 and tried to modernize Iran. He pushed for elections and tried to create a legislative assembly, and he overturned antiquated laws, like the one requiring women to be veiled in public—a decision that would eventually come back to haunt him.

On September 16, 1941, in the middle of World War II, after years of battle with religious hard-liners, Reza Khan was forced into exile by the British and fled to South Africa. He was succeeded by his son, Mohammad Reza Shah Pahlavi, who quickly regained absolute power, aligned himself with the West, and ruled for the next three decades.

This was the Iran in which my father grew up: a country dragging itself into the twentieth century. He lived in Dampezeshgi, a modest neighborhood in the western part of Tehran, with his mother, sister, and brother, and he committed himself to his studies. He enjoyed learning, but his reasons went beyond that: In books, there was escape.

All through high school, my father was at the top of his class. He felt that a man with an education was unstoppable, especially in the new Iran. On weekends, he would drive Shaban's taxi, to help pay the family bills, and there was talk, briefly, of getting a taxi of his own. But my father wanted more out of life, so at eighteen he enlisted in the military and went off to attend college at their expense. He got a master's degree in engineering and planned to use it in the service of his country.

"An education is the one thing no one can ever take from you," he used to tell me. To this day, I remember him in his study, surrounded by books, with his pipe next to him, preparing for the next test, preparing to tackle the next rung on the military ladder. He loved the military. He loved Iran. He was unabashedly patriotic.

"Doesn't studying end when you get older?" I once asked him.

"No," he said, laughing and taking me in his arms. "There's so much we don't know—so much we'll never know. One never stops learning."

He was always reading, advancing, bettering himself, working on his next degree.

"I don't care if you get a PhD and then decide to stay home and raise children," he would tell me. "But get that PhD first. The future is unpredictable. You must be prepared to stand on your own."

MY FATHER

MY MOTHER

My mother felt the same way. It had been her dream to become a doctor, and she would have done it, too. But she met my father, and it changed the course of her life.

Her given name was Fatemeh Jalilian. She was the last of seven children, born on January 27, 1945, as the war was drawing to a close. When her grandfather first laid eyes on her, he compared her beautiful round face to the moon. "*Shabeeh'e mah meemooneh,*" he said.

In Farsi, *Shabeeh meemooneh* means "looks like," and *mah* means "moon." But he said the words so quickly that they sounded like *Mommie*, and the name stuck.

Her family was originally from Hamedan, or Hekmataneh as it used to be called, an ancient city in the western part of Iran known for its towering mountains and rich farmlands. Her father was a very successful merchant who made a small fortune importing tea from India. The extended family lived in a huge house, which was divided into two parts, and was separated by a yard that was as wide as a New York City avenue. They owned a Russian-made car, something few people could afford in those days, and were tended to by nannies and servants.

Her grandfather, Haj Baba, lived with them. He was an extremely religious man, but also deeply enlightened. He owned several rock quarries on the outskirts of Hamedan and was one of the big suppliers to the construction industry, but he refused to sell to government officials. As he saw it, they earned their living through taxes, which was tantamount to theft. It would have been a crime to accept money that had been earned at the expense of the country's less fortunate citizens.

Haj Baba also loved poetry. Every night after dinner, children and adults alike were forced to sit through mandatory lectures, and he would hold court, reading poetry and literature and quoting long passages from the Koran. He often read from the works of Baba Tahir Oryan, a Persian mystic, whose poetry I enjoy to this day.

HAJ BABA, MY
GREAT-GRANDFATHER
ON MY MOTHER'S SIDE

22

I am that ocean now in foam and tide;
I am that sun, but now in rays abide.
I move and burn, and then reverse my course;
I shine and glow and then grow low and hide.

I am that sea now gathered in a tear.
I am that universe now centered here.
I am that book of destiny which seems
To form a lonely dot of hope and fear.

Most of my memories of Hamedan are vague, though I do remember playing hide-and-seek on the huge, sprawling property and the way I always discovered places there I hadn't even known existed. I also remember the stained glass windows and the way the sunlight would hit them in the late afternoon, filling the rooms with colored light.

Soon enough, alas, that chapter of her life came to an abrupt end. One of my uncles, Dai'e Hossein, had been working with my grandfather in his tea business, but he got into terrible debt, and before long everything was gone.

The family moved to a modest house in Tehran, the capital, a bustling city of millions, and started again. This is where my mother met my father, her future husband. It was a cool, September day in 1965, and she was on her way to the neighborhood grocery store to use the phone. She had just graduated from Aasemie College in Tehran, with a teaching degree, and her parents planned to throw a small celebratory dinner. She was going to invite a few close friends.

Mom walked into the grocery store, greeted the owner, Hossein Haghighat, and went off to make her call. She didn't notice that a young man had followed her into the store, nor how flustered he appeared. That young man was my father. He stood just inside the front door, staring at my mother, and emerged from his reverie only when Mr. Haghighat called out to him. "Can I help you?" he asked.

My father turned, startled. "Yes," he stammered. "Do you, uh—do you have a wrench?"

"A wrench?" Mr. Haghighat answered, and he grinned because he knew exactly why my father had walked into the store. "That, my friend, I do not have. In case you hadn't noticed, I sell groceries."

At that point my mother turned to face Mr. Haghighat, having lost her coin in the telephone box, and my father made a hasty retreat. It was only much later that she even knew he had followed her into the store. He had been working on his car, a blue Opel, when he spotted her crossing the street, and he had been so overwhelmed by her beauty that he simply had to find out who she was. That also explained the nonsensical request for a wrench: It had been the only thing that came to mind.

"My legs took on a life of their own," he said later, explaining why he had followed my mother into the store. "I was not in control."

As it turned out, my parents lived less than two blocks from each other, but they had never met. Fortunately, Dad knew Mr. Haghighat, and it was through him that he learned who Mom was and where she lived. He went home to Mammon Bozorgeh and told her he wanted to do his *khastegari*. His mother was surprised. Who was this woman he wanted to pay a call on? What did he know of her? Who were her parents?

Unfortunately, my father was unable to answer most of her questions, so she went off to investigate on her own. There was some confusion at first, since two unmarried women appeared to live in the house in question, but Dad provided a detailed description—based on his brief but memorable sighting—and off they went to make their visit.

A *khastegari* isn't just a simple, social visit. In Persian society, if you pay a call on a woman, it is with the intention of settling down, raising a family, and remaining together forever. You take your parents with you to show that your intentions are honorable, and you immediately get down to the business at hand. If you are found to be an acceptable suitor, the two of you become engaged, at which point you start dating and getting to know each other. It may seem a little backward, but how can one argue with tradition?

The following Wednesday, Dad arrived at Mom's house, wearing his khaki military uniform, with his sister and mother in tow. My mother had just returned from the hairdresser, and she was understandably flustered when her mother asked her to serve tea. This, too, is a Persian tradition. By serving tea, the hosts are not only acknowledging the reason for the visit, but showing that their daughter can serve tea with utmost grace.

The tea one serves is called *chay*. It is served hot, black, and very strong, in clear glasses—so that one can appreciate the reddish-brown color—and the eldest person is served first. Mom worked her way through everyone in the room, and finally got to my father, but she was so nervous that she promptly spilled the two remaining glasses in his lap. She did her best to stammer out an apology, but already Mammon Bozorgeh was on her feet. "We should leave," she said. "A girl who can't serve tea properly will obviously not make a good wife."

"On the contrary," my father replied, laughing. "She has already made me feel special. Everyone else got only one cup of tea, but I got two."

My mother had no intention of getting married, but she was deeply impressed by the way my father had stood up for her, and she decided to give him a chance.

By the following week, Dad was driving Mom to school every day. She already had her degree, and she had found a job as a teacher. Now that my father was in the picture, however, she suddenly found herself deeply conflicted about her future. She was twenty years old and hadn't so much as given a passing thought to marriage. It had been her hope to get her teaching degree and continue studying. She dreamed of becoming a doctor. Her most ardent hope was to teach medicine someday.

Now here she was, being driven around the city by a man who clearly had other plans for her. It made her very nervous. She was always pressed up tight against her side of the small car, as far from him as physically possible, worried that he might be so bold as to try to touch her hand—or worse. But my

25

father didn't try to touch her hand. He didn't try anything. He was an honorable man. All he knew was that he wanted to get to know the young woman beside him. He also knew that at any time she could break things off, and he wasn't about to let that happen.

"Why do you always sit so far away from me?" he asked wryly. "Do you think I'm going to bite you?"

"I'm more comfortable here," my mother replied, unamused.

"Please," he went on, "have a little mercy. God forbid the door opens, and you fall out! How would I explain that to your family?"

In time, however, she began to come around. He took her to visit the Golestan Palace and its manicured gardens and the National Museum of Iran and its trove of archaeological treasures dating back 6,000 years.

One weekend he took her skiing at a resort high above Tehran, in the Alborz Mountains. He was a good skier and wanted to impress her, but my mother had never skied in her life, and she spent the morning falling. Whenever my father tried to help her up, she shooed him away. She didn't want him to touch her. It wasn't proper. She would get up on her own.

Eventually, he wore her down. Within three months, he proposed. They were officially engaged on December 25, 1965, Dad's twenty-seventh birthday. Five months later, on May 14, they were married.

26

By Tehran standards, it was a small wedding. Fewer than sixty people attended, mostly relatives and a few friends. Mom and Dad sat on two small stools in front of a Muslim clergyman, with the engagement cloth, the *sofreh'e aghd*, spread out in front of them. Two silver candelabras and a silver mirror were laid out on the cloth, along with a copy of the Koran, a small dish of honey, almonds wrapped in white lace, a tray of bread and sweets, and fresh-cut flowers.

The cleric gave a speech about the importance of marriage and about standing by each other in good times and bad, and then, as is customary, turned to my dad and asked if he would take the woman at his side as his wife. My father said yes, nodding happily, at which point the cleric turned his attention to my mother. He asked her if she would take Dad as her husband, and she did not respond. But this, too, is in keeping with tradition. The woman responds only after the question has been put to her three times, at which point she replies, "With the permission of my parents, I do." This shows that she is not only modest, but that she respects her elders, which is a large part of Persian culture.

At this point in the ceremony, my mom and dad turned to look at each other, dipped their pinkies into the small bowl of honey, and fed the honey to each other. This, too, is a tradition: Honey at the start of the journey will sweeten the years ahead.

In the following month, they found a two-bedroom house, a rental, not far from the old neighborhood, and they got down to the complicated business of being husband and wife.

Generally, the role of the wife in Iran, especially during my parents' generation, was a subservient one. Iranian women were taught to marry as soon as possible, to obey their husbands, and to dedicate themselves to their families. In short, to have no life of their own. And while this sounds absolutely medieval to many people, it seems to work quite well for others.

My mother was not one of those others, however. She already had a career, she enjoyed it, and she wasn't about to drop everything to provide for her husband and perform her wifely duties. Fortunately, my father didn't expect her to. He was not only undemanding, but—unlike most of the Persian men my mother knew—actually enjoyed giving her a hand around the house. They

27

made the bed together, went shopping together, and he even tried to help her through those disastrous early stabs at cooking.

Soon enough, it dawned on my mother that she had chosen well. She was a happy woman. She was going to make a family with a smart, enlightened, loving partner. They were going to find a place for themselves in this uncertain world.

That June, they bought a modest, three-bedroom house in Shademan, a pleasant neighborhood within a few miles of their own families. But less than a day after they moved in, while they were still unpacking boxes, Mammon Bozorgeh and Dad's brother, Taghi, arrived, unannounced, at their front door.

My mother had never liked Mammon Bozorgeh—she was a cold, manipulative, unfriendly woman—and she didn't really know Taghi. He was a tall, handsome man, who was always chain-smoking, his fingers yellowed by nicotine. He was also a severe manic-depressive who still lived with his mother and who clearly would never make his way in the world.

"What are you doing here?" my father asked Mammon Bozorgeh, startled by the unexpected visit.

"Don't you have any shame?" his mother snapped. "Your brother is severely depressed. He needs to be in a pleasant environment, around decent people who care for him. You didn't have the courtesy to ask us, so we are doing it on our own."

MAMMON BOZORGEH, MY PATERNAL GRANDMOTHER

My father was about to question her further—he didn't quite understand what she meant—when he noticed a moving truck out front. They had arrived with all their things, and they proceeded to move right in. The entire house had to be reconfigured to make room for them, and Mom and Dad did their best to be accommodating. Alas, it didn't work out. Mammon Bozorgeh did nothing but create trouble for the young couple.

One time, at dinner, Mammon Bozorgeh tried one of my mother's early efforts at cooking and spat the food back onto her plate. My father was furious. He told his mother that she should either eat the dinner she'd been served or leave the table, and that if she wasn't happy with the food she could take over the cooking duties herself. "I am not going to stand by and let you criticize my new bride," he said.

Mammon Bozorgeh left the table, and right away my father knew in his heart that things would probably never work out between his mother and his wife. Unlike many men, however, he didn't need to choose between them. He had already made his choice.

It was—to understate the case—a very difficult time for everyone involved. My father was one of three children, the only one who had managed to create a real life for himself. One would think his family would have been proud and happy for him, but they resented his success and, more pointedly, his new bride. They didn't want him to have a life of his own. They didn't want to be left behind. After all, he had been taking care of them from the very beginning, and they needed him more than ever. They went out of their way to make life difficult for Mom, never passing up a chance to criticize her, whether about the quality of her cuisine or about the fact that she was away at work all day and neglecting them as a result.

To this day, my mother refuses to say anything negative about Mammon Bozorgeh, though much worse was to come. "Don't say anything bad about your paternal grandmother," she used to tell me. "Her blood runs through your veins." Still, I can't help myself. I heard the stories, from my father, her own son, and from other relatives. She was a horrible human being. Things started badly and only got worse.

Finally, my father decided they'd suffered enough. "I'm not going to let them destroy us," he told Mom one afternoon.

"What are we going to do?" she asked.

"Run," he said.

In short order, he had himself reassigned to Maragheh, in northwestern Iran. It was a remote, inhospitable town, and Father's engineering duties kept him away from home till all hours, but at least they had some privacy. And it paid off. On March 13, 1967, Afsaneh was born.

BABA AND AFSANEH   MOM AND AFSANEH

They were elated. This was the beginning of a real family, a family of their own. Mom kept working on her cooking skills, mostly through trial and error, and tried to make a real home for her husband and infant daughter. She also found work as a teacher, still very much on the career track.

The following year, the three of them moved to Mahabad, a city on the Iraqi border. My father had been promoted, working his way up, but in some ways it was a step back. The new house had no electricity or running water, and both the kitchen and the bathroom were outdoors.

Dad had the new barracks built—as the military engineer in charge, that was one of his principal duties—and they settled into their new home, but within a year they were transferred back to Maragheh, where he was kept busy on various military projects: designing bridges, building housing for the soldiers, and planning irrigation facilities.

As for Mom, she had her hands full, too. She had an infant daughter, she returned to her old teaching job, and, by the following year, she was pregnant again, with me. She told me that she'd been very worried about having a second

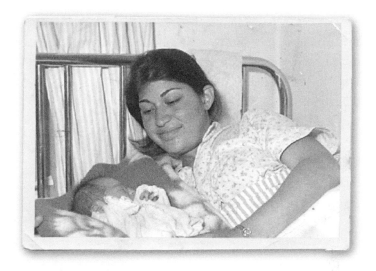

girl. In Iran, as in many societies, people tend to favor boys, and my mother didn't want to disappoint my father. But of course she had another girl, and she was crushed when he walked into the recovery room, empty-handed.

"Can you walk?" he asked her.

She nodded weakly. He helped her out of bed and guided her into the corridor.

"There was a bouquet of flowers on the floor so big it wouldn't fit through the door," my mother recalled. "I was so relieved I burst into tears."

The family stayed in Maragheh for the next four years, though I have no memory of the place, then moved to Kermanshah, a largely Kurdish city in the western part of Iran.

My first actual memories date back to Kermanshah, where we stayed until I was seven. For the first two years, we lived in a rented apartment, but then my parents found a modest home. It was small and quite rustic, but it had a huge yard. There was a small pond, or *hoz*, in the middle with a little fountain inside it, and Afsaneh and I would put floaties on our arms, squeeze into the tiny space, and splash around, with the fountain raining down on us. When my favorite cousin, Mojdeh, came to visit from

ME

31

Tehran, the three of us would sit under the fountain, bumping heads and laughing and soaking until our fingers began to look like prunes. On those lazy summer days, splashing around in the *hoz*, we felt we were in our very own Olympic-size pool. I couldn't have been happier.

I remember being an exceptionally well-behaved child, and I remember being sent off to kindergarten at age five, excited about the future. I don't remember what happened during those first two days in kindergarten, but at the end of the second day, when my mother came to fetch me, she was told that all I did was fight with the other children, and that my future at the school was in grave doubt.

CELEBRATING MY BIRTHDAY

My mother took me home, visibly upset. "What is wrong with you?" she asked. "What is this fighting business? Since when do you fight with other children?"

"I'm bored," I said.

Afsaneh, two years ahead of me, was already enrolled at Madrese Etehad, the private Jewish school—and reputedly the only good school for miles around. It was very hard to be admitted if you weren't Jewish, but Mom begged, cajoled, and used my father's military connections to get Afsaneh in. She was shameless when it came to the welfare of her own family. She had hoped to send me there, too, after kindergarten, but it seemed I was ready for first grade, somewhat prematurely, so she had to start begging and cajoling all over again. The school took me, probably because they'd already been through this once with my mother, and they knew she wouldn't give up till she got what she wanted.

I remember loving school. Everything was so new, exciting, and full of possibility. Once a day, however, the Jewish kids were sent to Hebrew class, and the few non-Jews at the school weren't permitted to attend. We were sent off to entertain ourselves for an hour. This only made me more curious, of course, and I pleaded to be admitted, promising that I'd sit quietly in the back of the class, listening intently but saying nothing. It didn't work. If it had, I might have been a real rarity in Iran: a Hebrew-speaking Muslim.

Come midmorning, we would be given a snack: a baguette, two hard-boiled eggs, a pat of butter, and a small carton of milk. It was the same snack every day, and for years afterward, I couldn't look at eggs without feeling queasy.

There was one incident at the Jewish school that left a big impression on me, which was the day a passing boy grabbed me on the stairs, kissed me on the cheek, then promptly ran away. I thought my life was over! I had been kissed by a boy. At the end of the day, when I found my mother waiting for me on the street, I jumped into her arms in tears and told her what had happened. "Don't be silly," she said, laughing. "That's just the way boys show they like you."

MY BROTHERS, ALI (LEFT) AND AMIR

33

My brother Ali was born on March 4, 1974, and Amir followed two years later, on May 30, 1976.

That summer, when we went back to Tehran for our annual vacation, I again found myself spending every possible minute with Mojdeh. She was the daughter of Dai'e Hossein, whose unfortunate debts had cost my grandfather his lucrative tea business. For a while, as a result of this bad luck, Dai'e Hossein had been the black sheep of the family, but he moved to Tehran, put the past behind him, and went to work as an electrical engineer for the government. Every penny he made went to support his family, and he didn't even begin to think about marrying until all his brothers and sisters—Mom included—had settled into comfortable lives of their own.

Whenever we visited Tehran, we generally stayed with Mammon Kobra and Khaleh Mali. At the time, Mali lived in a huge old house that seemed to go on forever, and the backyard was ablaze with fruit trees. Afsaneh and I used to climb the trees and bring fruit in for the entire family, except on those occasions when we couldn't resist devouring it ourselves.

At night, when it was warm, everyone would sleep under nets on the enormous roof, looking up at the starry sky, and, as we drifted off to sleep, my grandfather, Agha Joon, would sometimes tell stories about the "old days." In the morning, the adults would wake up early to say their prayers and to prepare breakfast, and the kids would moan and groan about having to get out of bed. But as soon as we caught a whiff of the freshly baked bread, fetched from the *noonvaie* (the local bakery), we would leap out of bed, rush off to the terrace where breakfast was served, and begin our day.

The best part of my day was the time I spent with my cousin Mojdeh. I only got to see her and her family two or three times a year—during that long stretch in the summer, in Tehran, and on the rare occasions when they came out to Kermanshah to visit. I was closer to Mojdeh than I was to my own sister, and the hours with her always made me giddy with excitement. I spent every possible minute in her company. We would play with dolls all day, pausing now and then to raid the kitchen for sweets. Or we'd go to the sports club and spend the entire day in the pool, laughing and talking.

"You are my favorite person in the world," I would tell her. "I wish we could be together all the time."

AT A PICNIC WITH (CLOCKWISE FROM LEFT) MOM, DAD,
MY UNCLE HOSSEIN, SHAMSI, AFSANEH, ME, AND MOJDEH

At night, I would call my mother and beg her to let me stay at Mojdeh's, and she often relented, wanting to be spared my tears. I would have dinner with her family, and afterward her father would take us out for ice cream. Dai'e Hossein was devoted to Mojdeh, and, by default, to me. He was my favorite uncle.

But this particular summer didn't turn out as planned. I discovered that Mojdeh and her family, along with my aunt Moneer, her husband and two children, and my uncle Reza with his wife and five children, were leaving for Shomal, on the Caspian Sea. The word *shomal* means "north," and it actually refers to the many beach towns that dot that section of the country. It is a heavenly place, with beautiful hotels, fine restaurants, and lovely beaches, and we were planning to go ourselves. But Baba was busy working, and we wouldn't be going till later in the summer. I was shattered. When it was time for Mojdeh to leave, I broke down in tears. But much worse was to come.

The three families had rented a big van so that all of them could travel together. Mom's brother Reza was behind the wheel. He was negotiating his way through a winding, mountainous road when he suffered a fatal heart attack and lost control of the van. It plummeted through the guardrail and over the side, flipping several times before coming to rest near a river.

Dai'e Reza and my aunt Moneer were killed instantly, and Dai'e Reza's daughter, Parya, age twelve, was paralyzed when broken glass from a rear window sliced through her back. Mojdeh's baby sister, Marjan, survived, discovered only hours later, hanging from a tree branch, unscathed. But Mojdeh—my dear, beautiful, loving cousin Mojdeh—had disappeared into thin air. She was found many days later, miles downriver, by a local fisherman, her little body so decomposed as to be virtually unrecognizable.

Mom lost a brother, a sister, and a niece, and another niece was paralyzed for life, and I lost my best friend in the world. I was sure I would never recover.

MOJDEH

PLAYING IN THE KOOCHEH WITH HALEH

ALI

AMIR

CHAPTER THREE
Tehran

MY SCHOOL PICTURE, AGE NINE

MOM AND HER COUSIN ENJOYING THE GARDEN AT OUR
HOME IN SALTANAT ABAD, TEHRAN

In September 1976, while the family was still struggling to make sense of the tragedy, Dad was told that he was being transferred to Tehran to take over as commander of the engineering unit of the *Guard'e Shahanshahi*, a prestigious division of the military. The news didn't undo history, but it made us focus on the future, and it helped us begin to get on with our lives.

In April, we returned to Tehran with all of our worldly possessions and arrived at the old house, in Shademan, where Mammon Bozorgeh and Taghi had been living all those years. It was their turn to make room for us, and they did—but not willingly nor with any measure of good grace.

Dad went off to the barracks to get to know his new men and to familiarize himself with his new duties, and Mom immediately found work as a teacher at a public school. In the early evening and on weekends, they drove around Tehran looking for a new home, and Mom finally found a place in Saltanat Abad, a very tony neighborhood in the northern part of Tehran. My mother instantly fell in love with the house—it had three bedrooms, a huge deck off the living room, and a spacious yard that was ablaze with cherry and apple trees—but my father felt it was much too much for them.

"We can't afford this," he said. "Let's keep looking."

"No," she replied, "this is perfect. Don't you want the best for your family?"

She could already picture herself puttering around the garden of that beautiful house, but my father, who was much more conservative about these things, was not ready for a commitment of that magnitude.

"Yes, I want the best for my family," he said, "but this we can't afford."

"You have to have more faith in yourself," my mother replied. "You have to have the courage to reach for bigger things."

At the end of the day, he deferred to her, wisely, and scrambled to finance our new home. Iran is not like America. The banks don't line up to give you loans. If you have most of the money, they might let you borrow a small percentage to close the deal, but they don't make it easy. Still, it was hard to ignore my father's credentials—he was a career military man with an unblemished record and a seemingly brilliant future—and even harder to ignore the iron-willed woman at his side.

In May, our parents took us to see the new house. We drove into Saltanat Abad and turned into a small, dead-end street, Koocheh Shahnaz, past a tiny kiosk where a man stood guard. He recognized my parents—the newcomers—and smiled and waved us through. We drove past half a dozen beautiful homes, and my father stopped the car in front of the most magnificent of them all. I was only seven at the time, and I know the house was no more magnificent than any of the other houses on the street, but to me it looked like a palace.

"This is really our new home?" I asked, breathless.

"It really is," my father said.

We got out of the car, stepped through the large iron gates, past the apple and cherry trees, and entered the large front doors. The house was on one level, very modern, very white, with lots of big windows, and it didn't seem to end. The foyer was huge, and there was an immense, open balcony off the formal living room. The kitchen overlooked a small backyard, which ended at a low wall. Beyond the wall, there was an endless, parklike garden—known as a *bagh*—which was privately owned, and there were several structures at the far end of the *bagh*, but they were a quarter of a mile away and not visible from the house.

Later that month, we moved in, and it was a happy day indeed. People say moving is stressful, but for a child nothing is more exciting. Everything is new. A new home. A new bed. New places to play. New smells. Relatives came over and oohed and aahed over the house and over the neighborhood. The name Saltanat Abad means "long-lasting monarchy," and it was apt: I felt like a princess.

"So suddenly you've become royalty?" my mother said, teasing.

"Yes," I said. "You may call me *Princess* Afschineh."

"Don't let it go to your head, princess," she said. "We are very lucky to have a home like this, and I never want you to forget it."

My mother didn't think there was anything wrong with striving for the good things in life—in fact, she encouraged it—but she also made sure we took stock of our blessings. "Never lose sight of your good fortune," she used to say, and she never tired of repeating it.

On the first day of school, my mother walked me inside to get me settled, and we went up to the bulletin board to find the name of the class to which I'd been assigned. I found it right away. It was right next to a name that had been crossed out with a black Magic Marker. It was Mojdeh's name that had been crossed out, and I almost fell apart. Mom took me in her arms and held me, and she stayed by my side until it was time for class.

39

I still missed Mojdeh, of course, and the news about her family was not good. Her mother, Zohreh, was inconsolable, and Dai'e Hossein had been plunged into a severe depression. Worse, when he first saw me after the accident, he was so convulsed by sobs that he had to be carried from the room. He was unable to look at me without thinking of his own daughter, so I was asked to keep my distance. My family never stopped reaching out to him, never stopped telling him that the door to their home was always open, but Dai'e Hossein seemed determined to grieve in private. He became a recluse, and it was many years before I saw him again.

Slowly but surely, I began to put the past behind me. In those first few weeks, I would come home after school and try to make myself useful around the house, which was still coming together. Our furniture had arrived from Kermanshah, and new items seemed to appear daily. Rugs. Chairs. Candelabras. Our crystal bowls.

"You make sure to keep the bowls filled with pistachios," my mother told me. "That's your job."

Every morning, Baba would go off to the barracks, Mom would go off to her new teaching job, and I would stand by the door, waiting for Afsaneh to drag her lazy self out of bed, so we could leave for school. We had a military driver, which was one of the perks of my father's job, and he'd wait by the door and listen to me scream at Afsaneh that I didn't want to be late for class.

The name of our school was Hadaf #2, and it was a private school because Mom thought public schools weren't sufficiently disciplined or demanding. But even Hadaf fell below expectations, so she transferred us to Pouya, a much stricter, more demanding school. I didn't mind, though. I liked the challenge. Afsaneh, however, wasn't even vaguely interested in academics. She was interested in gymnastics and in volleyball and excelled at both.

On weekends, we grew accustomed to the life of the leisure class, and I became a little corrupted by our good fortune. I really *was* turning into a bit of a princess. Dad would take us skiing in the Alborz Mountains, or, in warmer weather, to nearby parks to play soccer and volleyball. I could never keep up with either Afsaneh or my father. There were also piano and dance lessons, horseback riding, and—for the boys—karate.

Sometimes we'd just run around the garden while Mom and Dad tended to the vegetables, turning the dark earth, planting new seeds, and pruning the sweet-smelling roses. They loved that garden, and I loved seeing them in the dirt, on their knees, smiling and laughing and looking like a pair of happy, overgrown kids.

At the end of the day, we would play chess or backgammon, a big favorite, and have dinner as a family, and from time to time my parents would go off to some military function or other. I used to sit in my mother's bedroom as she got ready, watching her fix her hair and put on makeup. I couldn't believe how beautiful she was, and I couldn't wait to grow up.

On many weekends, especially in the summer, friends and relatives would drop by the house and stay for dinner. This is a big thing in Iran: People stop in unannounced and uninvited, and they expect to be fed. We had a huge freezer in the basement, stocked with enough food for a small army, and we bought fruits and vegetables by the crate.

MY PARENTS LOVED TO ENTERTAIN.

"The more friends and family you share a meal with," Baba Joon used to say, "the better the food tastes."

My mother had come a long way from those early days, when she didn't know enough to remove the innards from the chicken's cavity before setting it in a roasting pan and placing it in the oven. But Dad never found fault with her or her cooking. She would make the most atrocious meals, and he'd wolf them down happily, praising her, and she wanted to believe his kind words. But the rest of the family wasn't quite as tactful, and she herself knew that she was a terrible cook. Still, she was determined to learn. So she bought cookbooks, called friends and relatives, and asked for recipes, and by the time we were living in Tehran, many years later, she had turned into a regular gourmet chef. I loved helping her around the kitchen. "When it comes to food, don't be cheap," she would always tell me, and she tells me the same thing to this day. "You need to buy the very best."

I'd get home to find the house filled with the smells of my mother's cooking, and, by the time dinner was ready, I'd be ravenous. One of my Dad's favorite meals was *abgoosht*, a stew made with lamb, potatoes, chickpeas, tomatoes, and two or three kinds of beans. The ingredients are placed in a bowl and smashed to a pulp with a flat-bottomed *goosht-koob*, or tool. I enjoyed the smashing part more than the meal itself.

Another perennial favorite was *ghormeh sabzi*, a mixture of green herbs (*sabzi* means "green"), kidney beans, dried lemons, and beef or lamb, made as a stew and served over rice. And not just any rice, either. Persians are very particular about their rice, and rice dishes come in many forms, most of them quite complicated. But this is as it should be. In Persian society, to labor over a meal is a sign of respect: It shows that your guests are important to you. If you throw a shish kebab on the grill, it is considered inappropriate and perhaps even rude. That kind of cuisine is fine for your own family, but inappropriate for guests. Guests expect good, complicated meals, with lots of choices. A typical dinner should include three or four main courses and a variety of vegetables and side dishes. That is the price of entertaining.

During the week, the meals were far less complicated, of course, but equally good. On very cold winter mornings, we might have *haleem*, which I can only describe as oatmeal with turkey breast. It cooks overnight in a Crock-Pot and is served with cinnamon, sugar, and melted butter. If Dad was home, we might have a variety of kebabs. These were strips of meat, either steak, ground beef, or chicken, grilled on skewers with tomatoes, onions, and peppers. Of course, sometimes we just wanted grilled hamburgers, and Dad would oblige us, or we would order pizza from an American-style place near home. Mom did not enjoy fast food as much as we did, but she welcomed the occasional break from the kitchen. She was thoroughly westernized, as I've said, but she also believed in time-honored traditions.

My siblings and I, however, became more westernized with each passing day. There were two amusement parks in Tehran, Mini-City and Luna Park, and we begged our parents to take us until we wore them down. This became a once-a-month treat, unless we misbehaved.

And we absolutely loved movies. The so-called Bollywood movies from India were very popular, with all their high drama and wild, over-the-top theatrics, and a few racy foreign films actually made it past the censors. I remember watching *Z* by Constantin Costa-Gavras when I was barely nine years old. There was a torture scene in the film that remains with me to this day.

At home, we watched television. My all-time favorite program was *The Three Stooges*, which of course was dubbed. Curly and the others spoke fluent Farsi. From time to time, they would have a three-hour special with the Stooges, and nothing could keep me away. I also loved cartoons, especially anything from Disney.

On summer weekends, we spent a lot of time at Club Shahanshahi, a members-only club that was another military perk. It had tennis courts and a big swimming pool, and in the summer I could spend all day there without getting bored.

ME IN THE KOOCHEH (STREET)

We also enjoyed living on a dead-end street—or *koocheh*, as it is called in Farsi. Many of the neighbors had children, and they were always out there. To us, the word *koocheh* was practically a verb: You went outside "to street." We'd play jump rope or another game called *kesh*. A *kesh* is a rubber band, only this particular rubber band was several feet long. There were two people at each end of the *kesh* and one player in the middle, and the player in the middle would attempt to clear the *kesh* as it climbed ever higher. Other big favorites included *haft sang,* or "seven stones," our very own version of dodgeball, and hide-and-seek, or *ghayem mooshak.*

It was here that I met Haleh, who lived on the same street and would later become one of my closest friends. Her father, Mohsen Sepasi, was a colonel in the military, like Baba, but he was in another division, so they mostly only knew each other as neighbors. I liked Haleh, but I was still recovering from Mojdeh's death, and I think I was too frightened to get close to anyone. I was only comfortable with my own family.

❦ ❧ ❦

One summer evening my father took us to see a movie called *Vooroojak.* It was about a meddlesome little boy who couldn't keep his nose out of other people's business. That became my father's nickname for me: Vooroojak. I was small and meddlesome, and I had a hard time keeping my opinions to myself. If I was sitting at the dining room table, doing my homework, and there were two adults across the room, talking, that's where my attention went. And if anyone said anything I didn't agree with, especially about my family, I just couldn't bite my tongue.

Once my Dad's sister, Maheen, said something mildly critical of my mother, and I immediately started arguing with her. "You have no right to talk that way about Mom!" It turned into a big family feud, with Maheen screaming at my mother that she wasn't bringing her kids up properly, especially me, the bigmouthed meddler. I didn't care. The Latifis came first. People soon realized that they'd be in serious trouble if they said one bad word about my family, so—in my presence, anyway—they learned to keep their opinions to themselves.

Still, the fact is that I was one of those kids who needed to be seen and heard, and I know there were times when I behaved inappropriately. There's a Persian expression, *bozorgtar az senesh harf meezane,* that, loosely translated, means "she speaks older than her age." Well, that was definitely me. You didn't want to get into an argument with me. I had no qualms about expressing my opinions. However, I knew where to draw the line. If there was one thing my mother wouldn't tolerate, it was rudeness and disrespect. If I was in the middle of a heated debate with an adult, and I found her giving me that special squinty look of hers, I knew I was in danger of crossing the line, and

I would retreat. I didn't want to make my mother angry. She was the disciplinarian in the family, and when you were in trouble, she made sure you knew it. There was no getting her to change her mind, either. I never got spanked in my life, but I was always losing privileges. No movies. No TV. No Club Shahanshahi for the entire weekend. If I was really bad, I couldn't even go out to the *koocheh*.

So I learned to control myself around the adults. I pushed the envelope, certainly, but I didn't cross the line. I only ever crossed the line with Afsaneh, but that's only because I couldn't help myself. We were radically different, and she had no patience for me. She was a big tomboy, very athletic. I was a girly girl with braids and my collection of dolls. I had a *huge* collection of Kens and Barbies. I got every doll I ever asked for. What can I say? I was spoiled.

We also had beautiful clothes. My mother would order them from Marks & Spencer in London, and twice a year she would take us to this posh local boutique that only carried the finest American and Italian clothes.

"You get what you pay for," my mother used to say. She would show us the quality of the stitching, the way a dress was hemmed, the solid zippers, and high-grade buttons.

She also bought nice things for the house, and she began collecting fine Persian rugs. My father approved. They both wanted us to appreciate the good things in life, whether it was art, music, food, clothes, or school, knowing we would work hard for those same things when we were older. They both believed in living well, and my mother believed in it a little more than my father. Not for herself, though; never for herself. It was always about the children, Dad, the house, the guests, the relatives. She always thought of herself last, as if she were an afterthought. I honestly don't remember a single instance of my mother shopping for herself, and whenever my father bought her something—anything at all—she would always protest that it was much too much.

Once, on her birthday, he bought her a platinum-and-emerald jewelry set—necklace, bracelet, ring, matching earrings—and even *I* thought it was too much. Another time he came home with a beautiful gold bracelet. It had a small gold coin hanging from it, and he kept adding coins over the years. She never took it off, and you could hear her rattling her way through the house.

We lived a life of privilege, and, like privileged children everywhere, we didn't always appreciate it. So my mother kept reminding us: "You are very lucky. All of this you owe to Baba Joon, who came from nothing and worked hard, studied hard, and made something of himself."

She never took credit for anything, though Dad never tired of reminding us that she had been his Rock of Gibraltar. Many of his stories would start with, "If it wasn't for your mother . . . ," and then he'd tell us how she had always believed in him and how her faith had made him believe in himself. "I never once heard her complain about anything," he said. "Even when we lived out in the country, in the middle of nowhere, without so much as a proper bathroom, she remained cheerful and optimistic and made me feel good about the future. I tell you, if it wasn't for your mother, I never would have managed."

Every two or three months, much to my horror, Mom would drag Afsaneh and me to the worst shantytowns in Tehran. There was an area known as Joonoob'e Shahr, which means, literally, "south of the city." We would fill the trunk of the car with bags of rice, tins of oil, and other essentials, and we would deliver them to families who lived in abject poverty. I absolutely hated it. The visits always came without warning, and always on Fridays, when we were off from school.

"Why are we doing this?" I would whine. "I know there are poor people in the world! I saw them already."

I wasn't a complete brat, but I was a borderline brat. "Great!" I'd say. "It's 'Pain in the Ass Friday' again."

My mother would threaten to take away my privileges, and I'd get in the car, sulking, and sulk all the way there. She didn't care. She would lecture us en route, and it was always a variation on the same theme: "Just because you don't see the poverty, don't assume it's not there."

"I know it's there," I'd say. "I told you already: I've seen it."

"Most of the people in the world are not as fortunate as you," she would continue, ignoring me. "You have to be grateful."

"I'm grateful! I'm *super* grateful!"

The fact is we lived in splendid isolation, shielded from most of the population. Most of our relatives were fairly comfortable, too, but few of them had homes as nice as ours, and none of them had military drivers and people who helped around the house.

We were different in another significant way. When people think of Middle Eastern households, they picture a domineering patriarch ruling with an iron hand. This was certainly the case in many homes, but not in ours. In our home, Dad would come home with his paycheck and hand it to Mom. She was in charge, and he knew it.

One time they *almost* argued. Mom had gone to look at a new car, a big, beautiful BMW, and she wanted him to have it. My father thought it was way too expensive, and he tried to argue against it, but Mom set him straight.

"You belong behind the wheel," she said. "It looks as if it was built for a colonel."

I loved it. I thought it was totally hot.

"What do you think, Afschineh?" he asked me.

"You *have* to buy it," I said.

And he did.

⁂

In 1978, Afsaneh and I were once again transferred to new schools. My mother was still determined to provide us with the best of everything, and she'd been hearing that Pouya was no longer up to snuff. Afsaneh was sent to Institut Maryam, a French Catholic school, and I was sent to the Deutsche Schule, the German school.

Initially, she was going to send us both to Institut Maryam, but she had gone to the German school to get an application for Ali, my little brother, and found the place intriguing. She was told that they couldn't make room for Ali, since neither of his parents was German, and she knew that no amount of politicking was going to sway these people, who were even more exclusionary than the administrators at the Jewish Madrese Etehad in Kermanshah. This only made her more determined, however, and she asked if there was any chance I might get in, based on academic merit, if not parentage.

"She'd have to take the test," she was told.

A few weeks later, armed with a pair of No. 2 pencils, I joined several hundred other kids in a convention center in Tehran to take a test, "for fun," as Mom put it. There were more than two thousand applicants for thirty spots, and students from every corner of the city were taking that same test on the same day. The top five hundred were invited back to take the second part of the test, and I'm proud to say I was among them. Several weeks went by, and we didn't hear anything. But one day I came home after school, and my mother was waiting for me out front, grinning from ear to ear. I had placed third out of two thousand applicants! There was definitely a spot for me at the Deutsche Schule, with a partial scholarship even!

MY CLASS AT THE DEUTSCHE SCHULE.
I'M IN THE BOTTOM ROW, SECOND FROM THE LEFT.

I loved it. I loved learning all sorts of new things in an entirely new language. I was an academic nerd. I would leap out of bed in the morning, looking forward to school, brimming over with excitement. There were only two things I dreaded: being late and bad grades. I could take care of the grades, but every single morning Afsaneh went out of her way to torture me. I would be showered, dressed, finished with breakfast, and standing by the front door, book bag in hand, eager to get going, and she would saunter in, sashay past me, and ask for her breakfast.

"Afsaneh!" I'd say, already near panic. "We're going to be late."

She didn't care. I'd beg her to hurry up, she'd ignore me, and the morning would always end with me crying.

Mom hated that. It really annoyed her. "Why do you cry over such silly things?" she asked.

But I didn't think they were silly.

I didn't think good grades were silly, either. I was very competitive. The highest possible grade in our school system was a twenty, and if I got nineteen and a half on a test, I would despair. I would come home, lock myself in my room, and cry for hours.

During all this time, my mother was teaching full-time and deeply committed to her work. She taught first grade. In Iran, this is a very demanding class. The children are only five or six years old, but they look to you for everything. The alphabet, art, storytelling. . . . It's a very big responsibility since this is where the foundations are laid, and she took it very seriously. Some of our relatives couldn't understand it. Her husband was doing well. She had a beautiful home. Why didn't she lead a more leisurely life? But she wasn't like that. She wouldn't have known what to do with herself if she'd been locked up in the house all day. She enjoyed wearing many hats: mother, career woman, wife, chef.

We had been back in Tehran for almost two years now, and we felt settled and happy. But in 1978, things began to change. That was the year the mujahideen began to riot, followed in short order by the students and the *bazaari*, who ran the city's markets and bazaars. They were demonstrating in the streets, burning the Shah's pictures, and spreading rumors that the Ayatollah would soon return to Iran.

I didn't know what was going on, of course. I was a girl of nine. But apparently the unrest had been brewing for many years. The Shah was being accused of running an increasingly repressive regime, all in the name of modernization, and resistance grew.

The fundamentalist mujahideen were said to be behind it. They are a radical religious organization, many of whom belong to Hezbollah, the Party of Allah. Most of them are intensely fanatical, and they believe their primary purpose in life is to implement the laws of God on earth. If you are not with them 110 percent, you are the enemy. And the Shah was most definitely not with them.

As the year wore on, they continued to organize marches, sabotage government buildings, and stage massive demonstrations, and the Shah's responses became increasingly despotic and violent. People seemed to grow angrier by the day, and they expressed their anger on the streets. I didn't see the demonstrations myself, but I heard about them on the news, and, whenever I was on my way to school, I would see men distributing anti-Shah pamphlets. The pamphlets accused the Shah of raping the country. They said he was taking

49

the oil profits and funneling them into private, overseas accounts, or lining the pockets of his friends and allies while the poor suffered through blackouts, oil shortages, inflation, and other problems. They noted that under the Shah the gap between rich and poor had grown wider than ever.

In our home, however, no one ever said a bad word about the Pahlavi regime. My father was committed to serving and defending his country, and he wouldn't allow anyone to criticize the Shah.

I was very confused. I had seen the shantytowns in Joonoob'e Shahr. Some of these people were working two and three jobs to feed their children, and they still couldn't make ends meet, while at the palace, as everyone could see from the evening newscasts, life remained as lavish as ever.

Up until that point, I had been as self-absorbed as the next nine-year-old, but now I was frightened. It was a crazy, scary time. The people had legitimate complaints, and the fundamentalists were turning their unhappiness into a political weapon. Before long, the population began to turn against everything the Shah represented and against anyone who had more than they did, which included people like us. As they saw it, they had nothing, and we had everything, and this made us the enemy. It was a familiar story: the haves versus the have-nots.

But the fanatical fundamentalists hated the Shah for an even deeper reason: In his quest to modernize the country, he had turned the people away from God.

❦ ❀ ❧

One afternoon, my father came home early and told us to pack a few things— we were going to stay with my mother's brother Dai'e Mammad and his wife, Robabeh. They lived in a condo on Pahlavi Street, and my father thought it would be safer than our house. We lived right on the edge of that sprawling, wide-open bagh, which made our house vulnerable. Worse still, the buildings on the far side of the park were said to belong to SAVAK, the Iranian secret police. My father was worried that the demonstrations might reach those buildings and spill over to our own property.

We liked Dai'e Mammad. He was a banker at Bank'e Melli, but he didn't act like a banker. He was mischievous, fun-loving, and a bit of a womanizer, and he was a good father to his four kids. We didn't much like his wife, though.

She was a bright, educated woman, but she had a very condescending manner. She made you feel as if nothing you could ever say or do would possibly be of any interest to her, and, as soon as we arrived, she made us sit quietly in the living room and told us to remain there until she sent for us.

When Mom finally showed up, I was hugely relieved. We spent the night and had breakfast there, then Mom went off to teach class, and the military driver took me and Afsaneh to our respective schools.

By the time school let out, things appeared to have heated up. The driver seemed a little nervous. He told us he was taking us to Khaleh Mali's house and that our parents would show up later. Mali also lived in a condo, with her husband; her daughter, Soosan; and Mammon Kobra. She made a quick snack for us, then parked us in front of the television to keep us distracted.

"Where are Mom and Dad?" I asked.

"They'll be here," she said worriedly. "Don't worry. There's nothing to worry about."

Two hours later, as night was falling, the buzzer rang. Mali hurried across the room and answered, and I heard my father's voice on the intercom. "Please," he said, "I need you to keep the children for the night."

I ran to the balcony, looked down, and saw my father hurrying away, back to his car. The top of his head was crusted with blood, and I could see blood on his khaki jacket. Later, I learned that he had been at the university, trying to restore order, when he was struck on the head by a brick. He hadn't even stopped at the hospital; he first wanted to make sure we were all right.

I called out to my father, near panic, but he was already in the car, racing off into the night.

DAD

DURING THE REVOLUTION, MY MOTHER WORE A HEAD SCARF.
SHE HAD NEVER COVERED HER HEAD BEFORE.

CHAPTER FOUR
Revolution

DAD

DAD CAME TO TAKE US HOME the next afternoon. He had a small bandage where he'd been injured on his forehead, and he was smiling, trying to allay our concerns. I told him that I had seen him from the balcony the previous night—"Why didn't you answer me?"—and asked him what had happened.

"It was nothing," he said. "A few silly students. It was an accident."

But it was more than an accident. The demonstrations were beginning to get out of hand. There were rumors that some of the military bases in Tehran had been stormed and ransacked and that armed thugs were on their way to the city.

"Are we going to be safe?" Afsaneh asked.

"Absolutely," he said.

He seemed to be the only one who thought so. In the days and weeks ahead, friends and relatives kept dropping by the house, urging him to leave Tehran.

"Latifi," they said—everyone always called him by his last name—"you need to get out until this blows over."

"But why?" he said. "I've done nothing wrong."

Things kept getting worse. Night after night, we would hear our parents talking to friends and relatives, trying to keep their voices low. There had been street battles in Tabriz. Six people had been killed and more than a hundred injured. There were reports of casualties in Qom. Rioting had erupted in the southern part of Tehran, among the *bazaari*. More than a hundred people had been injured by the police—many of them seriously.

In early May, the Shah postponed a scheduled visit to Hungary and Bulgaria to deal with the troubles at home. There was an explosion at the Maroun oil fields, in the southwest of Iran. The fire raged out of control for five days, and Red Adair was summoned from Texas to put it out.

In Esfahan, Orthodox Muslims stirred up the local people, condemning the Shah's liberal policies. The rioting lasted through the night, killing four and injuring dozens, and martial law went into effect. But the rioting spread. People took to the streets in Najafabad, Shahreza, and Homayunshahr.

In August, a movie theater in Abadan was burned to the ground. More than four hundred people perished, including many women and children. The anti-Shah forces blamed the deaths on the government, but the government said the theater had been burned down by the fundamentalists, which later proved to be true.

The unrest spread to Tehran. Tens of thousands of people marched through the city in white shrouds, declaring their readiness for martyrdom, and, during the Ashura events, several hundred thousand demonstrators took to the streets. They wanted the Shah gone; they wanted a new Islamic government.

One morning we woke up to find a black mark painted on the front of our house. My father blamed it on vandals and had the wall repainted. I only learned much later that we had been singled out as enemies of the people. My father was with the military, after all—one of the most prestigious units. He was part of the elite. He was rich. He was a liberal. He was corrupt. He was a nonbeliever.

The threatening phone calls began. It got so terrible that we stopped answering the phone.

Shortly thereafter, military discipline began to crumble. There were widespread defections, even in our own home. Sharifi, one of the men who had been assigned to my father, decided it was time to go.

"Sir," he told my father, "I am leaving. I feel I must give up my life in a meaningful way, and I wish to give it up for the Ayatollah Khomeini."

Sharifi had been working for us for over a year, and I had never liked him. Now here he was, decamping, going off to join the other side. "I am going to fight for the cause, and it is a worthy cause," he said. "I will gladly lose my head—*sarbaz*—for the cause." On its own, the word *sarbaz* means "soldier." But when broken down into two parts, as Sharifi had done, it means "to lose your head."

I was in the other room, listening, holding my breath, and I heard my father say, "If that is the way you feel, then do what you must do."

As soon as Sharifi left, I ran into the living room to see my father.

"What was that all about? What a stupid man! What did he mean he was going to 'lose his head'? He was going to lose his head over what?"

"It's nothing," my father said, stroking my face. "You're right. He's a very stupid man."

The next day, my father had another soldier brought to the house, a man he trusted. He was armed with a pistol. He was there to protect us. And later that same day, my father stored the BMW in a garage and borrowed a less flashy, Iranian-built Peykan from a close friend. "People know the BMW," he told my mother. "I don't want you driving it for the time being. I no longer know who to trust."

Mom was seriously worried now. She joined the chorus of voices urging him to leave the country. "It isn't safe here," she said.

"No, it isn't safe—for criminals," he replied. "But I am not a criminal."

He was a soldier and a patriot, and he had responsibilities to the country. He would not abandon it.

The rioting continued. There were many factions—the mujahideen, the *bazaari*, the students—and, while they were split along ideological lines, they all wanted one thing above all others: to topple the Shah.

In December, there was a huge, national strike. The city was paralyzed. The Shah responded with violence, and the United States found it untenable to continue to support his regime.

On January 16, 1979, the Shah and his family fled. Nobody knew exactly what was going on. Some people thought he was a coward. Others felt he was only leaving to prevent more bloodshed and that he intended to return when the army had regained control. My parents, right or wrong, belonged to the latter camp. I remember hearing everyone talking about the Shah and his family racing across the tarmac, toward a waiting plane—and wondering what was going on.

"Don't worry," my mother said. "He's coming back."

She had to believe that, of course. Without the Shah, we were finished.

But he didn't come back. Two weeks later, on February 1, Ayatollah Khomeini returned from exile to be greeted by adoring millions. He was an Islamic fundamentalist, banished in 1964, and he had returned to take the country back to its roots. Under his leadership, the clergy would soon become the dominant force in the new Iran, which would once again become a God-fearing, Islamic republic.

Slowly but surely, everything began to change. Women were told to cover themselves. Makeup was disallowed. If a girl so much as licked an ice-cream cone on the street, it was grounds for arrest. Men were no longer permitted to wear short-sleeved shirts, and ties were banished—a symbol of the decadent West.

My mother's best friend, Sabi, lived just down our street. Her husband was an engineer for the water authority and very proper in both dress and manner. One morning, arriving at work in a coat and tie, he was summarily dragged into the office of the new security chief, who'd been given the job by the new regime.

"Why are you wearing a tie?" the man barked.

"I have a cold," he said. "It keeps my throat warm."

The security chief took a pair of scissors and cut the tie in half, just below the knot, and made him wear what was left of it for the rest of the day as a form of public humiliation.

Suddenly everything was being interpreted in political terms. Civil liberties continued to erode. The so-called guardians of morality and culture were determined to bring their fanatical brand of religion to all Iranian citizens.

Ironically, religion played a very small role in our home and in the homes of most of the people we knew. We were Muslims, Shiites, but we didn't attend services or have a favorite mosque. There was a copy of the Koran in our house, but it was tucked away in a drawer, and I can't remember anyone so much as looking at it. The only practicing Muslim in our family was Mammon Kobra. We were often at Khaleh Mali's home on weekends, and Afsaneh and I would beg Mammon Kobra to let us accompany her to the mosque. It was all in good fun, for us anyway, devoid of any meaning, and my parents knew it, but Mammon was oblivious. She would actually light up, her smile adding wrinkles to her old face. She thought it was wonderful that two such modern kids would be interested in Islam.

Afsaneh and I loved putting on the chadors. It felt like Halloween. We would go off to the mosque and mix with the other women, completely shrouded, with only our eyes showing, and sometimes we would speak in funny voices and pretend that we were a pair of little old ladies. Then the service would begin, and we would do the prayer, the *namaz*, a form of chanting in Arabic, and race through it as quickly as we could, as if we were in competition. We would even make a pledge or two, called a *nazr*—"I will bring a box of dates to the mosque if I get a good grade on my next math test"—and after the service we would mingle with the shrouded women and eat delicious sweets. That was the main reason we loved going—the sweets and the plump, juicy dates. But the rest of it was completely foreign to us, and that's what made it fun for me: For a few hours I could be transformed and become someone else entirely.

But we were and still are Muslims. We were brought up with the belief that there is only one God and that it is the duty of the faithful to serve him according to the tenets of the Koran. We grew up believing that the God of Christianity, the God of Judaism, and the God of the Muslim faith are one and the same, though we were told that only Islam was wholly accurate and that only the Koran told the complete story.

Every religion has its own way of seeing things, of course, and Islam is no exception. Adam, Noah, Abraham, Moses, Jesus, and Mohammed are considered to be prophets. Mohammed was the last prophet and the one who "completed the book," according to Islam. No more prophets would come after him. His was the right way and the true way. Islam does not judge or condemn other religions, but—to borrow from George Orwell—it certainly posits that some religions are more equal than others. Then again, isn't this the way of all religion?

Still, Islam is in many ways a very polarizing religion, especially in some of its more radical interpretations. The central message in Islam relates to one's responsibility to the community, to the extended family, and to Muslim society at large. But in Islam there are no obligations toward non-Muslims. In this sense, it is deeply exclusionary. But in my family we were taught that there was no difference between one person and the next or one set of beliefs and another, and we were expected to behave accordingly.

When I asked my mother what God looked like, she said, "He doesn't look like anything. He is not a being with arms and legs. He's just light—a big, bright, powerful light. A light that fills the world and guides us."

That is how I've always seen God: as an immense light.

I would say to my mother, "Why don't we ever go to the mosque?"

And she would say, "What for? If you want to talk to God, you can talk to him from your own room. You can talk to him from the backyard. You can talk to him on your way to school. Wherever you are, that's where God is, and that's where he'll be always."

During Ramadan, when most of the country fasted, we didn't fast. Children were not expected to fast, and Dad didn't fast, but Mom hued to tradition. What's more, my father even drank liquor—the Islamic equivalent of a venal sin. Not a great deal, certainly, and never during Ramadan, but he enjoyed a little vodka now and then and a glass of wine with dinner. People would come over, he'd fix drinks, and it was the most normal thing in the world. However, my mother never touched a drop of liquor in her life—not on religious grounds, but because she wasn't interested. She claims my father actually chased her around the house once, caught her, pinned her down, and tried to pour a little wine down her throat. But they were both laughing so hard that he spilled it.

"Drinking is not for ladies or children," she would say. With her, it was not about religious conviction, but about proper etiquette.

At the end of the day, organized religion did not play a role in our family, and I was fine with that, but we were the exception—we were the westernized minority. For many Iranians, religion was and is a huge part of daily life. That is why Iran ended up with a fundamentalist Islamic government: because the people believe. But what is it they believe? That America is the Great Satan? That Jews are the enemy?

I don't believe the Koran espouses hatred. Not of countries, not of people. Still, like all religious texts, the Koran is a complex and contradictory book, open to interpretation. When the politicians become the interpreters, however, they and they alone decide what is meant, and what is meant usually has more to do with politics than with faith.

As a child, I didn't understand any of this. I thought the riots had been about poverty and hunger. I thought if we all chipped in, if we all tried harder, if we all gave more, the problems on the streets would end. I thought we could redistribute the wealth and make everybody happy, and I simply assumed there was plenty to go around.

But for the fanatics, it wasn't about hunger. For them, it was a religious war, and their religion was neither loving nor inclusive; it was hateful and exclusionary. The fundamentalists used religion to unite the masses against a common enemy, as people have been doing for thousands of years, and we were the enemy.

I didn't understand why they hated us, and my mother was hard-pressed to explain it. "People don't always understand why they behave the way they behave," she said. "But you don't have to worry about that. You just concentrate on being a good person. God is everywhere. The light is all around you, and it's inside your heart."

Everything was crumbling, but I never doubted. I never stopped believing.

SABI, MY MOTHER'S BEST
FRIEND, WITH MY MOTHER,
SABI'S CHILDREN, AND ALI AND
AMIR (CENTER)

WITH ME IS MRS. ETMEENAN, OUR
KIND NEIGHBOR WHO SAVED OUR
HOUSE FROM ARSONISTS.

ME AND AFSANEH WITH MAMMON KOBRA,
MY MATERNAL GRANDMOTHER

CHAPTER FIVE
Things Fall Apart

WITHIN A MONTH OF THE SHAH'S DEPARTURE, the military and the police were in disarray, the arrests began, and there was sporadic chaos on the streets. I would overhear stories about high-ranking officers being dragged from their beds in the middle of the night by the *pasdars*, Khomeini's self-styled enforcers, many of whom had come from Palestine to support the new regime. They were joined in short order by many of the lower-ranking enlisted men, who were defecting in ever larger numbers, and these bands of lawless men went around the city terrorizing people, vigilante-style.

My mother begged my father not to go to the barracks, but he was stubborn. He was the head of his unit, and he had his duties, he said. If everyone defected, there would be no turning back. "This is our *home*. The only home we have."

Friends and relatives also urged him to leave, repeating the wild rumors. A colonel had been arrested on his way to work. Another had been ambushed as he returned home, dragged off in front of his wife and kids. No one knew where they had been taken. No one knew if they were still alive.

"I haven't done anything wrong," he insisted. "They have no reason to arrest me. And if I did run, everyone would assume I had reason to run."

I think he was in denial. I think he was having a hard time believing what was really happening to his beloved country.

Still, despite everything, for a short time it was possible to continue as if none of it were real. These things were happening to other people in another part of town, not to us. So we carried on as usual. Mom drove Dad to the barracks, though not without complaints, and Afsaneh and I went off to our respective schools, with our military driver, Omidvaran, one of the sweetest men I had ever met. He was gentle and always in a good humor, and, on our way to school, he would assure us that there was nothing to worry about and that all of this would pass. We wanted to believe him because he was so good to us and so charmingly convincing, but even at school we couldn't help but notice that things were changing. Every day, there were more empty seats at the Deutsche Schule and at Institut Maryam; every day, more people were leaving. They were mostly foreigners, of course. They had homes to go to. We only had Tehran.

"What's happening to the city?" I asked Omidvaran one day on our way to school.

"I don't know what you mean," he replied.

"What are people so angry about? Why is everybody leaving?"

"I'm not sure," he said. "What do your parents tell you?"

"Nothing," I replied. "That's why we're asking you."

"It's just silly students demonstrating," he replied. "Students are like that all over the world. They don't realize how good they have it."

"Do you think my father is in danger?"

"No. Of course not! Why do you even ask?"

"Because I saw on television that the students were angry with the soldiers."

"You mustn't worry," Omidvaran said. "Your father is one of the kindest, most honest men I have ever met. No one could ever accuse him of anything. Nothing can happen to him."

But the news seemed to grow worse every day. There was fighting on the streets now, distant though it was, and there were so many factions involved that people didn't know who they were fighting for or even why. There were the *bazaari*, driven by religion; the students, rebelling against the established order; the fanatical mujahideen, who believed they were fighting for Allah; and Khomeini's mullahs, who had already taken control of the media, and—from need—of the prisons.

Then there were the executions. You would read about them in the newspaper. So-and-so had been shot for "crimes against humanity." There would usually be a photograph of the victim, but no further explanation. Nothing about the alleged crime. Nothing about the trial. Nothing about the men who had decided his fate, nor how they had come to that decision.

This became a regular staple of the evening news, which was also controlled by Khomeini's regime. "*Ghasemel Jabarin*," the announcer intoned. "Enemies of God." At this point, we, the children, would be quickly ushered out of the room, and the adults listened in terror for the names of the people who had been executed in the course of the day.

The victims were generally officers, like my father, but unlike my father, most of them belonged to fighting divisions. He was an engineer, not a soldier in the true sense of the word. He believed he was safe. After all, he wasn't a threat to the new regime. He wasn't the type of man who could stage a coup. He was an *engineer*, for God's sake—the country needed him.

On February 13, alas, he was arrested at work, and the next few months were hell on earth. The searching. The begging. The pleading. The bribes. The all-too-brief prison visits. The little notes back and forth.

Somehow, miraculously, my mother held it together. We went off to school every morning, she went off to teach, and at night there was dinner, homework, a half-hour of television, and kisses on the forehead as she put her four children to bed.

Then on May 23, 1979—after three months of uncertainty and torture, and after one final, heart-wrenching visit—my father was taken away and shot to death on the prison roof. He was forty-one years old. He hadn't lived half a life.

The days that followed were long, gloomy, and confusing. I sat in the kitchen of the house across the street, watching the mourners filing in and out of my own home, not understanding any of it.

My mother took her pain and rage into the city. "I don't even have money for a proper burial," she told a government clerk, fighting tears.

"He doesn't deserve a proper burial," the clerk replied. "Toss his body to the dogs."

Then it was over. We were back in the house. Without Father.

Mom took a second job, as a tutor, to keep a little money flowing. It was a lot to handle: four kids, two jobs, no Father, and no help. Omidvaran had left the military. He had no choice. At that point, if you were still in the military—which, under the Shah, had been a requirement for all young men in Iran—you were working for Khomeini, and Omidvaran had no interest in working for Khomeini. But he still stopped by the house once or twice a week to make sure we were all right and to see if we needed anything. "Khanoom Sarhang," he would say. "Mrs. Colonel, if there is anything you need, anything I can do for your family, anything at all, I am here for you."

One day, returning from school, with Mother, we were approaching the kiosk at the entrance to our dead-end street when an unfamiliar man stepped out and signaled for us to stop. He was a *pasdar*, wearing the familiar checkered head scarf that had become their trademark, and he had a rifle draped over his shoulder. He circled the car, and my mother rolled down the window. "Where is the regular guard?" she asked.

"Gone," the man said. "Things are changing. Or hadn't you noticed?"

He opened the trunk and searched it, and, finding nothing, waved us on.

My mother was understandably upset. I overheard her talking to Khaleh Mali that night. "That man was put there to keep an eye on us," she said. "Now we are the enemy."

From the point of view of a self-absorbed child, especially one who didn't want to deal with the loss of her father, this wasn't the real problem. The real problem was that we weren't having *fun*. There was no Mini-City. No Luna Park. No military club. No swimming. No shopping trips for nice clothes. It was over. Life had become joyless and regimented, and we were going through the motions because that's all we knew: breakfast, school, homework, dinner, bedtime. It was all about routine, and we came to appreciate the routine, even subconsciously, because anything that interrupted it was bound to be unpleasant.

The next day, when we returned from school, there were two men at the kiosk, and they made Mom stop the car and searched it. Less than an hour later, she and Afsaneh left the house, to go to the store, and they flagged my mother down.

"What do you want now?" she said.

"To search the car," one of them said.

"You just searched it," she said, and pulled away.

The car had almost reached the corner when shots rang out. My mother reached over, pushed Afsaneh down in her seat, and crouched low, next to her, and one of the bullets whizzed past Afsaneh's ear, missing her by inches. They could hear the men hurrying toward the car and were both too terrified to look up. The men flung open the doors and yanked them out.

"What do you want?!" my mother bellowed.

"What are you smuggling here?!"

"Nothing! You searched the car less than an hour ago! I am taking my daughter to the store!"

They searched the car, inch by inch, and, finding nothing, told Mom that she was free to go. But one of the bullets had struck a tire, and she could only turn around and drive back to the house. She called Dai'e Mammad. He came over to get her, and they went to the police station together to file a complaint.

"This is an outrage," Dai'e Mammad told the mullah in charge. "You've got two Palestinians stationed at the end of the street, and they fire on an innocent woman and child."

"Maybe not so innocent," the mullah replied. "Maybe there is something going on in the house, yes? Maybe they are hiding weapons. Maybe they are smuggling insurgents. Maybe you know things you aren't telling us."

"There's nothing going on in that house," my uncle replied. "Why don't you go see for yourself?"

The mullah took him up on his offer. He showed up at the house that very afternoon, with two Iranians and two Arabs, and they searched the house from top to bottom. At one point, one of the Arabs flushed one of the toilets. He seemed absolutely fascinated, and, when he flushed it again, my mother confronted him. "What's the matter with you? Haven't you ever seen a toilet?"

"I've seen a toilet," the Arab replied defensively. "I've seen plenty of toilets. How do I know you're not hiding weapons down there?"

Later that same night, shortly after eleven, when we were all in bed, the doorbell rang. My mother opened up and found the same mullah outside, with some of the same *pasdars* and two or three new faces.

"What do you want now?" she asked.

"We're here to search the house."

"You've already searched the house. And everyone's asleep."

"Then wake them up."

"No," she said.

"Fine," he replied. "We'll do it."

My mother had no choice. She roused us and made us throw coats over our pajamas and led us outside, and we waited there—Mom, Mali, Mammon Kobra, Afsaneh, Ali, Amir, and me—while they went through the house again, room to room. At one point my mother asked if she could take the children across the street, to the neighbors' house, but the mullah refused. "You just shut up and wait," he barked. "I'll tell you what to do."

They didn't let us back into the house until two in the morning, and even then they said they weren't through with us. "We know you are hiding people and weapons," the man said. "Rest assured, we will find them."

If they could have taken us out into the street and shot us, they would have done so and done it gladly. But there was still a small level of accountability, thank God. In the cases of my father and men like him, there was no justice, but the regime was intent on creating the *appearance* of justice. Similarly, with the families of the accused, they needed at the very least a pretense at law and order, and this was the only thing that kept the bloodlust from boiling over. It was as if the new regime were saying, "We are here to right wrongs, to redistribute the wealth, and to bring the country back to its glory days. But we are God-fearing men; we know the difference between right and wrong."

The psychological warfare, however, continued unabated. One morning, for example, as we were leaving the house, on our way to school, two *pasdars* emerged from the kiosk and stopped us. They searched the car, and Mom asked them to hurry because we would be late for school. This piqued their interest. They wanted to know where we went to school, and they insisted on getting into the car and accompanying us. I got in front with Afsaneh, and the two men rode in back. Nobody said a word the whole way.

When we arrived at the Deutsche Schule, my mother turned to them and said, "This is where my youngest daughter goes to school. Satisfied?"

But the men weren't satisfied. They wanted to see the inside of the school. They wanted to know what went on in that fancy school. At this point I began to cry. I couldn't handle the embarrassment—I didn't want to be escorted to class by a pair of gun-toting thugs—and my mother put her foot down. "If you want to walk to the front entrance, fine. But you'll have to leave your weapons in the car."

One of the men stayed behind, with the weapons, and the other followed us to the front entrance. I felt like a criminal. He didn't stay long, however. He looked through the front door without going in, then turned and walked off. My mother kissed me, and she and Afsaneh followed him back to the car.

The moment I stepped into class, my teacher asked me if I was all right, and I burst into tears. She was so kind and sweet that it was almost more than I could bear.

The neighbors were the same way. You would think that they would want nothing to do with us since we had been singled out as enemies of the new regime, but they went out of their way to be helpful. We had the young neighbors directly across the street, Maryam and Forood Kafi, with whom we'd stayed for a few days after Father was executed. Maryam was beautiful and stylish, and she was close friends with Googoosh, a famous pop star. Afsaneh and I thought she was the most amazingly perfect woman we'd ever seen: stylish, beautiful, and kind. "Anytime you need me, day or night, all you have to do is cross the street and ring the bell," she told us.

Just down the street, there was also Haleh—the girl I had started becoming friendly with after Mojdeh's death—and her family. Her father, Sarhang Sepasi, had resigned his post as soon as Khomeini took over. He did not want to serve the new regime, and he had no qualms about showing that his sympathies lay elsewhere. "It would be a disgrace to wear the uniform in front of the Latifi children," he had told one of the neighbors. He would often stop by the house to see if he could help in any way, and he would bring Haleh with him to try to cheer me up.

My mother's best friend, Sabi, also lived on our street, just a few houses up. Sabi was like a sister to my mother. She was a very energetic woman, and she had a successful career as a voice-over artist. In fact, she did all the voice-overs for Lindsay Wagner in both *The Six Million Dollar Man* and *The Bionic Woman*. She had two children: a girl, Mahsa, and a boy, Mahyar, almost the same age as Ali and Amir. She always included my brothers in everything they did.

All of these people showed their support for us in full view of the *pasdars*, which I thought was incredibly courageous, but that was only the tip of the iceberg. One afternoon, while we were out, some thugs showed up at the house, carrying cans of gasoline. Mrs. Etmeenan, another neighbor and wife of an engineer, saw these men and ran outside to confront them.

"What are you doing?" she asked.

"We are here to burn down the house of the traitor Latifi."

"Latifi? What Latifi? What traitor? No traitor lives here."

"You are a liar," the man said.

Mrs. Etmeenan, knowing that these were religious men, ran into her house and hurried back with a copy of the Koran. The men were getting ready to douse the property with gasoline.

"Stop!" she said. "I swear before God that you have the wrong man."

Still they did not believe her. "Step aside," they ordered. "We know the criminal Latifi lives here, and we intend to burn down his house."

"Then what does he look like? Is he a tall man?"

"Yes."

"Well, there! You see? You have the wrong house. This Latifi is barely five feet seven. You are making a mistake. I swear this to you on the Koran."

The men were very confused by this point, but they were also deeply religious men. This business with the Koran really threw them. They got in their car and left, and our house was saved. Later, when Mrs. Etmeenan and the neighbors told Mom the story, everyone commented on how far things had fallen, how chaotic life had become. "They could have asked the *pasdar* at the kiosk if this was the colonel's house, but these were Iranians, and they probably didn't trust the Palestinians. The left hand does not know what the right hand is doing."

I was comforted by the presence of these people in our house. They had become our new family. Everyone was extremely protective of us. Any time a stranger showed up on our dead-end street, they went out in force and asked questions. "Who are you people? What do you want with the Latifis? Why are you here?"

We had been there less than two years, new to the neighborhood, new to this life, but they rallied around us. Doctors, engineers, businessmen, mothers, wives. Every single one of them was a source of inspiration and support. Their kindness helped us survive.

But it couldn't save Baba Joon's life.

Twenty-five years later, as I began writing this book, my mother broke down and remembered that terrible morning when she saw my cousin Nasser pulling up in his car, looking devastated. The way he rested his head against his arm, to support himself. The newspaper in his hand—the newspaper that described my father as an "immoral on earth," a *Mofsed'e Fel Arz*, and noted, in a single, heartbreaking paragraph as if referring to someone of no value whatsoever, that he was scheduled to be executed by firing squad.

She remembered the drive to the prison, with Nasser next to her, behind the wheel, both of them mute with shock. She remembered the blindfold, the ride with the guards. And she remembered those heart-crushing final minutes with my father, who stood before her in his best suit.

"Please make sure the children know that I was guilty of nothing."

Her memories sparked memories of my own. I remembered sitting in the kitchen of Maryam and Forood's house, watching the people come and go, and I remembered the day a mullah showed up with his entourage to spy on my family and on the mourners.

Even at that distance, I could hear the guests shouting at the mullah, their words faint, indistinct, and full of rage. "Get out of here! Haven't you done enough? Let these good people mourn in peace!" I remembered the way the mullah and his men hurried back to their car, protesting, "But you don't understand! We're here to pay our respects!"

I don't really remember the grieving. I was just numb. I knew Baba Joon was gone, but I don't think I actually believed it. I would lose myself in my studies or at play with my dolls, and, when I went to bed at night, I half-expected to hear his approaching footfalls. I would drift off, picturing his gentle, smiling face, waiting for his kiss. But of course there would be no more kisses.

One day a gaunt man arrived at our house, clutching a brown paper bag. He had been released from prison that very morning. "Your husband asked me to give you this," the man told my mother, taking a familiar tea flask from the brown paper bag. "He said it was very important," he added. "He said you would understand."

Before the gaunt man left, my mother went to her room to fetch something. It was a small photograph of Ali, frayed around the edges. It had been among my father's personal effects, which had been turned over to my mother a few days after the execution. "Do you know anything about this?" she asked the man. "Do you know why the edges are worn away like this?"

"Oh, yes," he said. "The Sarhang would look at that picture every day. He would hold it in his hand and weep."

After the man left, my mother sat at the kitchen table and painstakingly took the tea flask apart. She found four pages hidden inside the rim of the lid. This was Baba's Last Will and Testament, written on the day of his execution. "Everything I am, I am because of you," he had written in his small, neat hand. "Everything I have, I have because of you. I owe everything to you, and I leave everything to you. . . . I love you more than you will ever know."

My mother locked herself in her room and remained there for two days.

✿ ✿ ✿

The following week, I returned to the Deutsche Schule. As we were assembling for class, an announcement came over the loudspeaker: "Attention please. We are now going to have a moment of silence for Sarhang Mohammad Bagher Latifi."

Even then it didn't seem real to me: all the children standing by their desks in silence, their heads bowed, paying homage to my father. Later I found out that they had done the same thing at Afsaneh's school.

It was many years before I realized how much the schools had risked through this act of courage. That at a time like that—in the midst of a revolution, when most people didn't know whether to trust their own neighbors or even members of their own families, when your best friend might turn you in because he saw you drinking alcohol—they had put themselves at considerable jeopardy by taking a moment to pay their respects to our father.

✿ ✿ ✿

I was in a daze for weeks. By this time, Khaleh Mali and Mammon Kobra were living with us full time, trying to help out, and my mother was working two jobs to compensate for the loss of Dad's income.

It was suddenly very crowded in our house. Afsaneh and I still had our own room, but Khaleh Mali was sleeping in the boys' room, and Mammon Kobra had squeezed in with Mom. Khaleh Mali spent a lot of time with the boys, who were five and three and didn't understand why Baba wasn't coming home, and Mammon did her best to help out in the kitchen, despite the fact that the fingers on both her hands had been practically destroyed by rheumatoid arthritis.

In the middle of this, as we tried to make sense of the loss and of our lives, Mammon Bozorgeh decided that everyone had mourned long enough. She called on my mother to ask for money. Under Islamic law, she was entitled to a portion of my father's assets, and although she lived comfortably, thanks to my father, who had helped her during the course of his entire life, she wanted more. My mother was shocked and tried to reason with her, going so far as to show her the will that had been smuggled out of prison in the tea flask.

"Look here," she said, reading from the crumpled pages. "'All my belongings, including all personal and real property, is left to my wife and children.... The title to my car to be transferred to my wife, whom I love more than life.... The title of the house to my wife.'"

"That won't stand up in court," Mammon Bozorgeh said, clearly unimpressed. "I know you have money, and I want my share."

We did have money, but not the fortune Mammon Bozorgeh imagined. Every week, my mother had to sell another item to make ends meet: a Persian carpet, a gold coin from her beloved charm bracelet, pieces of jewelry, household appliances.

In a matter of months, we had gone from a life of privilege—from private clubs, fine Italian clothes, dinner parties, and vacations on the coast—to a life of crushing uncertainty. Mom did her best to shield us from it, but it was hard to ignore the changes.

There are two incidents in particular that I remember from this period. The first involved Afsaneh. She had a girlfriend over one afternoon, and she asked Mom if they could help themselves to some fruit.

"Of course!" my mother said. "Why do you ask? It's in the kitchen."

Afsaneh went off to the kitchen and returned a moment later with a small, shriveled orange. She had tears in her eyes. "Now that Dad is dead, this is what we have to eat?" she asked.

"No, no, no!" my mother said, taking her in her arms. "That's a *juice* orange. The good oranges are in the big drawer."

The other incident involved my little brother Ali. He was visiting a friend just down the street, Vahraz, whose mother, Mrs. Etmeenan, had saved our house from arsonists, and he saw a VCR for the first time in his life. Ali was fascinated by the VCR. He rushed home, crying, and told Mom that he wanted one, and she felt so badly that she hurried off, sold a coin from her bracelet, and returned home with a brand-new VCR and a Disney movie to go with it. The next day, Ali was crying again—it seemed as if he hadn't stopped crying since Father's death—because he'd been to Vahraz's house again that afternoon, and Vahraz had "stacks and stacks" of movies. Mom went off and bought Ali several new movies, but it still wasn't enough.

"Vahraz has more!" Ali said the next day. "Vahraz has everything!"

"I don't understand," Mom said. "He has a VCR, I bought you a VCR. He has movies, I bought you movies."

"Yes," Ali said. "But Vahraz has a father, and I don't."

My mother was crushed. She went off to her room to deal with it privately. But the neighbors heard the story, and from that day on they told their children that they mustn't talk about their fathers in front of the Latifi children, or of the things they had done with their fathers, or of the stories their fathers told them. These were the kinds of heroic measures they took to protect us, and it certainly helped, but nothing was going to bring Baba Joon back, and the damage continued to manifest itself in all sorts of unusual ways.

Ali started chewing his nails, for example, and he chewed them until they bled. And he cried incessantly. Any little thing—poor reception on the TV, a spilled drink, no cake—would make him break down in tears.

Afsaneh was in even worse shape. There was a small bench in the foyer of the house, and, whenever people came to visit to see how we were getting on, this is where they sat to remove their shoes and where they left their bags. Afsaneh couldn't stand the clutter, and she would immediately disappear into the foyer and frenetically try to restore order. The shoes would be lined up just so, the coats hung up according to some mysterious formula, and the purses arranged according to size. The compulsion spread to other parts of the house: She was forever tidying, organizing, fixing, rearranging. I made fun of her at first, but when I saw that look in her eyes—the intensity with which she attacked even the smallest task—I realized how serious it was, and I stopped tormenting her. Mom did her best to talk to her about it, but the behavior continued unabated for months on end.

I was affected, too. I cried over my homework, over my dolls, over a missing button. And I developed some of that same obsessiveness, constantly checking and rechecking the yard to make sure I hadn't "abandoned" any of my toys.

In addition, I absolutely loathed our new car. It was a little Renault, a shoe box, and at times I found it so intensely claustrophobic that I would have trouble breathing. And, certainly, the car was small, a far cry from the luxurious BMW, which had been sold for cash, but I wasn't that much of a princess. The problem was psychological: I felt as if my world was shrinking, and I was terrified. I wanted things to be the way they used to be.

"If you get in the car, I'll take you to the American market," my mother said.

The American market! Well, okay. For this, I would do it. We drove to the market with Afsaneh and went inside to find that many of the shelves were empty, a direct result of the continuing unrest. But there were still treats to be found in the bins of candy. I loved the chocolate eggs with little toys in them. Afsaneh preferred the chocolate-covered caramel sticks. That afternoon, my mother spent a small fortune on junk, but she couldn't help herself. She was trying to do good things for us, and, if she could see us smiling for even a few minutes, it took a little weight off her heart.

❦ ❧ ❦

In those days, power outages were frequent, especially at night. We were lucky in that we had a generator in the basement, but it was dreadfully noisy. One morning, several men showed up, identified themselves as police officers, and told us they were there to inspect the basement.

"Why?" my mother asked.

"Because we heard the noises. We know you used to work with SAVAK. You have a torture device in the house."

My mother let them in. She couldn't believe these men were so naive. They actually thought there was a secret tunnel running all the way under the *bagh*, from our basement to SAVAK headquarters. They found nothing, of course, but that didn't keep them from trying.

I hated these people, and I know my mother hated them, but she never said a single bad word about them—not in front of us, anyway.

By this time, she had unwittingly started an ersatz support group, which included the wives of other military officers who had been executed or were still languishing in prison. She had met many of these women while my father was alive, in the days when he had been giving her vaguely coded messages for the wives of some of his imprisoned fellow officers. Others she met in front of the prisons, where they had congregated with such tenacity. And still others she met through some of our neighbors. These contacts eventually turned into friendships, based on their common losses, and they did their best to help one another.

I never heard any of these women talking politics, and I never heard them utter a single bad word about the Khomeini regime. I don't believe my mother would have allowed it. It wasn't just to protect us, her children, or because she was worried that the regime might be listening, but because she felt, as she had done her whole life, that hatred only fostered more hatred. She didn't want us to become bitter, angry people.

However, Khaleh Mali was extremely vocal about the new regime. She would curse them all day long, giving vent to her rage. "Those bastards! They call themselves religious, God-fearing people, but they are the worst kind of murderers! May God strike them dead, every last one of them!"

Mali was so open about her hatred of the regime that one afternoon, on her way home in a gypsy cab, as she was cursing them and wishing eternal damnation on every last member of Khomeini's entourage, the cab pulled up in front of a government building. "If you hate them so much," the driver said, "why not go inside and tell them yourself?"

Mom would argue with Mali, asking her to please exercise a little self-control, to show some restraint in front of the children, but I liked hearing it. She was saying everything I felt but wasn't permitted to express. I knew they had killed my father, and I hated them.

Afsaneh was also circumspect about her feelings. At home, anyway. We were still going to school at the time, trying to live as normally as humanly possible, and Mom picked us up in the Renault every day. She would come to get me first, then we would fetch Afsaneh. She was always the last one out, her uniform was always covered with chalk dust, and every day my mother would ask her how she had managed to get so messy.

"I don't know," Afsaneh replied curtly. "I just do. And I don't know why it bothers you so much. Before, I was too neat. Now, I'm too messy."

One afternoon, however, Mom finally got her answer. A nun emerged from the school, trailing Afsaneh, and asked my mother if she could have a word with her. My mother got out of the Renault and joined the nun on the sidewalk. She was told that Afsaneh had been writing dangerous slogans on the school chalkboards.

"Slogans?"

"Yes, Mrs. Colonel," the nun answered, lowering her voice. "'Death to Khomeini!' 'Down with the dirty murderers!' We've asked her to stop, but she won't listen. Your daughter is going to get us all killed."

When we got home, Mom took Afsaneh aside and told her she had to stop. "You are endangering yourself, the people at school, and your entire family."

"But I hate them!" she wailed.

"That won't help," my mother responded.

I know my mother hated them, too. And she was being tested every day.

One evening, a friend called to tell her that one of the women from the support group had been arrested. It was actually someone I knew, a woman who had come by the house from time to time with her little girl. The girl was five, Ali's age, but Ali never wanted to play with her, so I would take her to my room and let her entertain herself with my collection of Kens and Barbies. It turned out that the girl's mother had been involved with a group that was attempting to stage a coup. She and the others had been rounded up and summarily executed. A few days later, when the woman's elderly mother went to the morgue to claim her daughter, she saw that both her breasts had been cut from her body.

The support group fell apart. Many of the women left, to try to start anew, abroad, but, when word trickled back to Tehran, the news was seldom good. Life in these foreign places was hard and confusing, especially without a man. The children were having trouble adapting. Resources were finite. The women had no marketable skills.

They lived in relative freedom, to be sure, at least comparatively speaking, but they remained prisoners of the uncertain future.

Still, the exodus continued. Doctors, lawyers, businessmen—all the people society needed most, gone. As for the military families, they left in droves. If you had any connection to the Shah's regime, no matter how tenuous, you were the enemy. And doubtless some of these military men *were* the enemy—were, indeed, guilty of crimes against humanity—but in most cases guilt had nothing to do with it. Presumed guilt was enough; guilt by association was grounds for execution.

My mother was at a loss. Sometimes, at night, I could hear her crying, or *think* I could hear her crying, just as I had heard her wailing, or *imagined* I had heard her wailing, in the days following my father's death. And even though she still refused to cry in front of us, the signs of her inner torment were clear and unmistakable. She wasn't wearing makeup. Her hair was carelessly knotted at the back of her head. She wore the same drab, black clothes day after day. She was letting herself go, and it frightened me.

One afternoon, we had a visitor. It was the mother of the woman from the support group, the one who had been tortured and shot to death. She had brought her granddaughter along, and the little girl lit up when she saw me. I took her into the kitchen and got her an orange Popsicle, then we went to my room to play with the dolls.

Later, when they left, when I saw how old and beaten her grandmother looked as she shuffled down the walkway toward the street, with the little girl at her side, I remember thinking to myself that I was very lucky indeed. I felt immensely grateful because that little girl had nothing but her ancient grandmother, and I at least still had my mother.

Life was frightening and unpredictable, and horrible things happened every day. But we were not the only ones who suffered.

I went off to look for my mom. I needed her close.

MOM, MY COUSIN, AND MY AUNT (FROM THE RIGHT)

CHAPTER SIX
Flight

AT THE AIRPORT THE DAY WE LEFT FOR AUSTRIA
WITH COUSINS AND MAMMON KOBRA

In October 1979, the deposed Shah arrived in the United States for cancer treatment, and the Ayatollah promptly used the visit to stir up anti-Americanism at home. The Shah belonged in chains in an Iranian prison, the Ayatollah said and claimed that the United States was already working on a plot to restore him to power.

There were violent demonstrations across the country, demanding the Shah's return to face trial. America came to be known as the Great Satan.

Finally, on November 4, 1979, Iranian militants seized the U.S. Embassy in Tehran, taking fifty-two American hostages. The ordeal, the most profound crisis of President Jimmy Carter's presidency, would last more than a year. For the Khomeini regime, however, this was no crisis—it was cause for celebration.

The *pasdars* were out in full force, rounding up the country's enemies in even greater numbers. They banded into vigilante-style gangs and made their way through the city, looking for "infidels" and beating and torturing anyone who resisted. Some of them were mere boys, playing at war but carrying real guns.

Meanwhile, the mujahideen were very unhappy. Things weren't changing quickly enough for them. They talked incessantly of the *jihad*, the holy war that wouldn't end until the last non-Muslim had been wiped off the face of the earth. Amazingly enough, even Khomeini's supporters thought these fanatics were too radical.

At times it was impossible to tell who was running things. The man who used to pick up your trash was suddenly in charge of public transportation. Everything was based on access to the regime. One day, you were selling carpets at the bazaar. The next—thanks to your brother, who was a close friend of Khomeini's third cousin—you were in charge of security for the entire southern side of the city. Fanatical people with no common sense were thrust into positions of authority and power, and their fanaticism was seen as a measure of their commitment to the regime. Non-Muslims? Guilty. Military? Guilty. Rich people? Doubly guilty since money equals corruption, which equals not following the teachings of the Koran. The men operated under the cloak of religion, and they did so with complete impunity.

At about this time, Dai'e Mammad and Robabeh, his wife, decided they were going to leave Iran. Their daughter, Naheed, and their two older sons, Nader and Farhad, were already living in Norfolk, Virginia, where they were attending college, and Dai'e Mammad and Robabeh and their youngest son, Fareed, hoped to join them there. They appealed for help to Edwin J. Wasilewski, an American officer whom they had befriended during his short tenure in Iran. He was now back in Fort Ord, California, but he wrote a letter on their behalf to Cyrus Vance, who was Secretary of State at the time. In this letter, Mr. Wasilewski noted that my father had pulled some strings to supply him with heating oil and gasoline at a time when both of these were strictly rationed in Tehran, and that—as the political situation grew increasingly untenable—my family had even offered to hide him. "Since the fall of the monarchy, Colonel Latify [sic] was arrested by the revolutionary government, sentenced, and executed. . . . I feel the service he provided me . . . was brought to the attention of the revolutionaries. . . . I feel that I and this country have an obligation to this magnificent family, in assisting them in living their lives free from tyranny and oppression."

Meanwhile, Mammon Bozorgeh continued to badger my mother, on an almost daily basis now, demanding her share of my father's money. "Under Islamic law, when a son dies, the wife gets a portion and the surviving parent gets a portion," she kept repeating. "Where is my portion?"

We had never been close to my father's side of the family, but, while my father was alive, we had been dragged to see them from time to time. I know my father didn't enjoy those visits, either—Mammon Bozorgeh was a cold, hostile woman, and Dad's brother, Taghi, was a broken, depressed man—but it was his responsibility as a son and brother, and he took his responsibilities very seriously.

Now here was Mammon Bozorgeh, her son recently dead, still asking for money. I didn't understand it. She had a nice, comfortable house, already paid for, and plenty of savings. What more did she need? Couldn't she see that my mother was struggling? She had lost her husband, the only man she'd ever loved, and she was holding down two jobs and trying to raise four kids—Mammon Bozorgeh's grandkids.

But Mammon Bozorgeh remained unmoved. She wanted her "entitlement," and she wanted it now.

My mother again read from my father's will: "I repeat once again, all my belongings are to be disposed of under my wife's sole discretion and as she sees fit."

"I've told you before," Mammon Bozorgeh said. "That won't mean anything in court. Under Islamic law, I am entitled to part of the house, part of the furniture, and part of your savings."

"But I don't have any money!" my mother protested. "I am selling off our entire life, one piece at a time!"

"Then you will hear from the lawyers," Mammon Bozorgeh said, and she made good on her threat. She called her daughter, Shaheen, my father's half sister, who was a lowly clerk at the courthouse, and enlisted her help. This was very upsetting to my mother. Under normal circumstances, the wheels of justice turned at an excruciatingly slow pace, and this would have served her well, since she had neither the money nor the energy to deal with a lawsuit. But Shaheen used her influence to speed things along, and in no time at all my mother was in the middle of a bitter court battle.

❀ ❀ ❀

As the school year drew to a close, there was more bad news. The Deutsche Schule and Institut Maryam were being shut down and converted into regular schools. My mother went to see someone in the Department of Education about this, and she was told that I would have to repeat grades four and five. Afsaneh, on the other hand, had been studying in Farsi, so she would have been spared the same fate.

"Why?" my mother asked. "Afschineh has been receiving an excellent education, too. She graduated near the top of her class."

"In a *German* school. What do the Germans know about education? This is Iran. Your girl needs a proper *Persian* education."

Mom was at a loss. She had no faith in the public school system, and, even if she had, she didn't understand why they were intent on holding me back. That would cost me two years of my life. Plus she had heard the horror stories about the admission procedure to the university: All applicants were carefully screened, and those with even a hint of antigovernment activity in their pasts were denied admission. We didn't stand a chance.

In April 1980, the Carter administration tried to rescue the hostages. The mission was a fiasco. There were celebrations in the streets of Tehran.

That spring, Mom flew to London with Ali. He had finally stopped biting his nails, but he had become severely depressed, and she thought that a trip to Europe, far from the sad memories at home, would help him get over Baba's death.

But that was only part of the story. She was also in London to try to find a good school for Afsaneh and me. After all, she had promised my father that his children would get the best possible education, and she wasn't going to let him down.

She didn't have much luck with the schools—those she visited were neither sufficiently strict nor sufficiently demanding—but Ali responded well to the short vacation, and when they returned home he was greatly improved.

My mother remained deeply concerned about our uncertain future, however, and she began to make inquiries, discreetly, about sending us abroad. She heard about a place near Vienna from the mother of an older girl, Roshanak, whom I knew in passing from the Deutsche Schule. The school was academically demanding, and it was run by nuns. It sounded perfect. My mother was convinced that it was just the place for her two daughters.

She wrote the school to make inquiries—with the help of a translator and without telling us—but even as she waited for their reply, she began to have second thoughts. Suddenly she couldn't imagine sending us off to Austria on our own. She was still grieving, we were still grieving, and she couldn't picture life at home without us.

But one day, a strange encounter gave her the strength to do what needed to be done. We went to visit Ezatollah, one of my father's elderly uncles, on the outskirts of Tehran. We hadn't seen him in several months, and my mother thought we should look in on him. When we got to his house, we found an older man there with his young son. He was the Kadkhoda of a distant village. A Kadkhoda is the head of a village, and any disputes between the locals are usually taken to him for resolution. To the villagers, he is an important man. But to us, he was the type of person one might call, less than generously, a *dahati*, a peasant. He and his son were dressed in ragged clothes, and both of them looked horribly unkempt. The father had a stack of freshly baked bread under one arm.

"Who are these *dahati* people?" Afsaneh whispered.

My mother didn't know, but she found out soon enough. Uncle Ezatollah had a little land in this man's village, which is how he knew them. And this Kadkhoda had come all the way from his small farm to the big city because he had heard that one of Ezatollah's nephews, my father, had passed away. He had further heard that the man had two lovely daughters, and he was hoping that the eldest daughter, Afsaneh, who had just turned thirteen, would become his son's bride. The bread was a token of his esteem for my family.

"What do you think?" Ezatollah asked my mother.

"What do I think?!" My mother was deeply offended, but she didn't want to insult the old *dahati*, so she took Ezatollah off to the far side of the room. "My children may have lost a father," she whispered angrily, "but they aren't orphans yet!"

Alas, this was the mentality she was being forced to deal with. The ancient villager thought he was doing my mother a favor by taking Afsaneh off her hands. And it seemed like a pretty good deal for him, too. "I'll get my son a city girl," he had told my great-uncle.

My mother turned to look at the old villager, who smiled at her from across the room. "I am here to ask for your daughter's hand," he said brightly. "Look! I have brought fresh bread."

Mom again turned to Ezatollah, fuming. "When he approached you, you should have slapped him," she said, keeping her voice low. "That you even come to me with this proposal is both insulting and embarrassing."

She grabbed us, hustled us out to the car, and off we went.

"What happened?" I asked.

"This country has become medieval overnight," my mother snapped. "There are people who haven't made an inch of progress in four hundred years and just as many who seem to have regressed."

When we got back to the house, Mom told us that we were going to go to Europe. "Isn't that wonderful?" she said. "It's going to be the adventure of a lifetime!"

It *was* wonderful. Afsaneh and I could barely contain our excitement. We were going to Europe! We were going to see the world! We were going to travel, buy nice clothes, and visit fancy places!

As word of my mother's plans filtered out, the rumors started. She was getting rid of the girls because she wanted to find a new husband. My mother was outraged by these stories. She was a widow at thirty-five, and she had her whole life ahead of her, but the last thing on her mind was another man.

But they came anyway, all the hopeful suitors—including Shareef Ashraf, the husband of her own sister-in-law, Maheen. He would visit often, always arriving with chocolates and other special treats. My mother didn't really understand what was going on, and, worse, she couldn't bring herself to believe it. So she ignored it. But after a few visits, Shareef made his intentions clear. He said that he was trapped in a miserable marriage, and that under Islamic law, recently implemented, he could have more than one wife, and he told my mother that he was madly in love with her.

"I'm sorry," my mother said. "You've come to the wrong house."

He was taken aback. Like the old *dahati* at Uncle Ezatollah's house, he thought he was doing her a favor. Everyone assumed that Mom needed someone to look out for her. After all, she was *bee sar va parast* (without guardianship).

"This family isn't up for grabs," she said. "Not while there is still breath in my old body."

Now she was more determined than ever to get us out of Iran. She told us about the school in Austria, the most wonderful school in the world, and she was such a great spin doctor that I thought I was about to embark on the adventure of a lifetime. Afsaneh fell for it, too. This was partly because Mom omitted a crucial element—the fact that she was going to leave us there, alone. When we asked about this, she worked her magic on us. "No, no, no," she said, "I'm leaving you there, yes. But it's only for a short time. I have to come back, sell the house, and get things together with Ali and Amir. And then we'll join you. And we'll be one big happy family again."

It sounded pretty good.

"One more thing," she said.

"What?"

"It would be better if you don't talk about the trip to people outside the family."

"Why?"

"These are strange times. You never know what might happen. Maybe someone in the government doesn't want us to go."

"Why not?"

"I don't know, *azizam*. I don't understand these people. But don't worry about it. I'll get you there, one way or another."

My mother was terrified, of course. And the thought of being separated from us was already breaking her heart. But as she told me years later, "There was no room for emotion. I had to be a purely rational person. I really had no choice in the matter."

This was completely lost on me. I was blissfully unaware and ecstatic. The little girl who had lost her father had become the little girl who was going to Europe. I kept picturing it in my mind: a big, life-size Mickey Mouse waiting for me at the airport. Lollipops the size of my head. Streets paved with chocolate. I thought Europe would be a giant, endless Disney World, a fantasy come to life. And there would be no mullahs there! I was tired of seeing those strange, frightening men. They had begun to invade my dreams—mullahs with turbans and fangs.

Every day, I would badger Mom. "Are we leaving? Is today the day? Are we going to Europe today?" And every day, with the patience of a saint, she would say the same thing: "Not today. Soon, though. And please stop thinking that we're going anywhere until we're on the plane and in the air."

"Why?"

"Because things can change. When we're in the sky, with our seat belts on—that's when we'll know we're really on our way. Understood?"

"Understood."

Her paranoia was not without justification. We would hear her talking to Khaleh Mali or to Sabi. The new regime kept lists. They might not let us leave the country. Our name was Latifi. Our father had been executed.

In those days, for me, anyway, the two scariest words in the language became *mamnoo'ol khorooj. Mamnoo* means "prohibited;" *khorooj* means "exit." I couldn't bear the thought of these vile men trying to stop me from meeting Mickey Mouse. Didn't they understand? He would be waiting for me at the airport, in person.

On August 27, 1980, Mom, Afsaneh, the two boys, and I got in the car with Khaleh Mali and Mammon Kobra and drove to the airport, followed by another aunt and several cousins in a second car, who were there to see us off.

We had packed lightly, clothes mostly, and I was carrying my little stuffed doll with the red pants. Mom was very conservatively dressed. She was wearing a head scarf, which was now required by law, and on her left wrist she had the gold charm bracelet my father had given her, though by this time she had sold off half the coins. The bracelet looked like a mouth with many missing teeth.

As we stepped into the terminal, Mom paused to take some pictures. "So that you always remember this important day."

Then we went to the ticket counter and on through, to customs. At customs, they checked our passports, and they went through our bags. Just as they were finishing up, one of the men noticed the gold bracelet.

"You can't take that with you," he said. "Nothing of value leaves the country."

"I'll have to give it to my sister," Mom said.

She made us stay there, alone, while she rushed back to the terminal, where Khaleh Mali and the others had promised to wait until the plane was in the air. She gave her the bracelet and hurried back, and we went through to the waiting area, and I was so excited that I couldn't contain myself. "You see!" I told my mother. "We really *are* going!"

"Don't say that," she said. "Wait till we're on the plane."

We went and joined the other passengers in the waiting area, and I looked out through the big windows and saw the buses coming to fetch us to take us to the plane.

"Look," I told my sister. "The buses!"

Just then, the loudspeaker crackled to life. "Fatemeh Jalilian, please return to security." In Iran, women retain their maiden names on all official documents even after they are married, but everyone knew Mom as Mrs. Latifi or Khanoom Sarhang.

For a moment, this didn't register. But then I looked at my mother and saw that all the blood had drained out of her face. I didn't understand what she was upset about. We didn't know anyone called Fatemeh Jalilian. Then I noticed that everyone in the waiting area had fallen silent. I looked at Afsaneh and then again at my mom, and it struck me: They were calling my mother. Fatemeh Jalilian was my mother. I felt suddenly ill.

Just then, two military men emerged from the back and approached us. It wasn't hard to figure out who we were. My mother was as pale as a ghost, I was practically shaking with fear, and everyone in the lounge was now staring at us.

"Passports," one of the men barked.

"We've already shown our passports."

He put out his hand and repeated it, somewhat more harshly: "Passports."

She gave him our passports, he turned, and both men marched out of the room. My mother didn't know what to do. The buses were pulling up out front, and it was time to go. She stood and hurried across the room, toward one of the airline employees, and told the woman that two military men had taken our passports.

"Why did you allow it?"

"I don't know," she said. "They asked. They had guns."

The loudspeakers crackled to life once again. They were about to begin boarding our flight. Mom returned to our side, at a loss, and just then I saw eight military men moving across the room, directly toward us. Afsaneh saw them, too. Mom turned around and watched them approach. I started crying.

"Come with us," one of them said.

"Where are we going?"

"You'll see."

We followed them back into customs, and they took us through a side door into a private room. Our luggage was laid out on a long, wooden table. Everything had been taken from the bags; every tiny item opened and inspected.

There was a tall man standing on the far side of the table, in front of the open luggage. He seemed to be in charge. "What is this?" he asked.

He was holding a copy of my father's will.

"Nothing," she said. "It is a note from my late husband."

"And why are you smuggling it out of the country?"

"I'm not," she said. "I brought it for my children. If you read it, you'll see that he talks about the importance of a good education. We are going abroad to look at some schools, and I wanted them to know how much it meant to their father to study hard and get good grades."

"You're a liar," the man said. "I know why you're taking this with you. You're going to give it to the foreign press so that they'll publish it and make us look bad."

"No," my mother said, and it was the first time in my life I had seen her look genuinely terrified. "That is not my intention at all. This is a private letter. A family matter. I don't need it. You can keep it."

At that point, a mullah stepped forward. He was wearing a white turban. He looked my mother up and down with such disapproval that it bordered on disgust. He had her passport in his hand.

"So," he said unctuously. "You were married to Sarhang *'ghod'* Latifi."

"No," my mother replied, not understanding. "His name was Mohammad Bagher Latifi."

"Maybe," the mullah said. "But he was very *ghod*."

Now my mother understood. The word *ghod* means "stubborn."

"Whenever we asked him a question, he refused to answer," the mullah said. "He told us that he didn't recognize us as a proper court of law. And he said he wanted his wife present, at his side." The mullah smirked. "Do you know what we did? We just laughed at him. That's what. We all laughed at him."

At that moment my mother realized that the mullah had been present at Baba's so-called trial, and it was all she could do to keep from falling apart. But even then the mullah wasn't done. "Are you still living in that big house you built with the blood money of the people you murdered?"

I started crying again. Afsaneh started crying.

"I don't know what you mean," my mother said, but her voice was barely audible, a notch above a whisper.

"Take them to the next room and search them," the mullah snapped.

We were herded into another room, where two women were waiting for us. As we watched, they slipped rubber gloves over their hands and submitted my mother to a full, physical search. My mother did as she was told. She didn't utter a word.

When they were done, they turned to look at us. "You're next," one of them said, addressing Afsaneh, and at this point my mother lost it. She was still only half dressed, but she leapt across the room and parked herself in front of us. "You are not going to touch my children with your filthy hands," she said ferociously.

The women backed off, visibly startled. We were ushered back into the neighboring room, our passports were returned to us, and in short order we were back in the lounge. But it was empty. Everyone was gone. Then we saw a bus parked at the distant gate. The driver waved from afar, urging us to hurry, and we ran across the lounge and climbed into the empty bus. He started it and raced across the tarmac, toward the waiting plane.

When we boarded, the entire cabin burst into wild applause. Everyone was cheering and clapping. I looked at my mother and saw tears streaming down her cheeks.

We worked our way to our seats and strapped ourselves in, with Mom in the middle, and then the clapping finally died down. The engines started, and the plane taxied into position.

We sat there stiff as boards, dead silent, still in shock. A good ten or twelve minutes had elapsed since we'd raced across the tarmac in the bus, but we hadn't exchanged a single word. And still we sat there, side by side, hardly breathing, mute, until at long last the plane roared down the runway and lifted off into the sky.

At this point, Mom reached for our hands, took a deep breath, and said: "*Now* we are on our way."

AFSANEH

I'M ON THE TOP RIGHT, AT THE SACRÉ COEUR GENERAL MEETING ROOM
DRESSED IN MY DECIDEDLY UNCOOL DUDS.

AFSANEH IN OUR DORM ROOM

CHAPTER SEVEN
Austria

WITH MOM, AT SACRÉ COEUR

I REMEMBER NOTHING about the rest of the flight. Only that phrase—*Now we are on our way*—and the feel of my mother's hand on mine.

When we arrived in Vienna, Mickey Mouse was not waiting for us at the airport, as I had hoped, but there wasn't a mullah in sight—and that in itself seemed cause for celebration. Plus I was in charge! Sort of. I had learned German at the Deutsche Schule, and my mother and Afsaneh depended on me for absolutely everything. When we got into a cab outside the terminal, it was up to me to tell the driver where we were going. And when we arrived to our destination, a modest bed-and-breakfast called the Kölping Haus, it was up to me to announce that the Latifis had arrived. I felt like an adult.

Vienna was my first experience with Western culture, and I loved it. We knew no one in the entire city, but that didn't stop us from exploring on our own. It was unlike any city I'd ever seen. Electric trams; elegant, helpful people; swanky sidewalk cafes along Mariahilfer Strasse; and lots of hole-in-the-wall shops that sold some of the best chocolate I'd ever had in my life—which is saying a great deal, since I've been a lifelong chocoholic.

This was also the first time I'd seen a real department store. We had two notable department stores in Tehran—Kourosh, where every kid went just before school started, to get his back-to-school supplies and ride up and down the escalator, an annual rite of passage, and Bozorg, for the boring basics: clothes, shoes, household items—but these stores were nothing like the ones in Vienna. These were so filled, they seemed to burst at their seams. If you wanted a blender, there were seventeen types of blenders, one more spectacular than the next. And if it was toys you were after, there were *miles* of toys. You could walk for hours and find new surprises at every turn.

I also had my first Big Mac in Vienna, not a life-altering experience, to be sure, but it felt like one—and I was instantly hooked. Every day, I would insist on going to McDonald's for lunch, and every day I would have the same thing: a Big Mac with fries and a hot apple pie for dessert. And of course a chocolate milk shake, which I always took with me when we left. Even if I was full, and I was usually pretty full, I wouldn't waste a drop of my chocolate shake.

On the third day, after too many Big Macs, too much shopping, and too much walking, feeling almost giddy with exhaustion, Mom decided it was time to visit Sacré Coeur, the boarding school, the reason we were there. It was out in Pressbaum, half an hour away by train. We took a shiny, high-speed U-Bahn to the station and found the connecting train to Pressbaum.

Mom kept smiling and smiling, but it was unlike any smile I'd ever seen on her. She knew what was coming—she knew she would soon be leaving us behind, in the care of nuns, to be sure, but still very much on our own—and she was struggling with the enormity of her decision. *How will they manage? Am I doing the right thing? When will I return? Can I really afford this?*

As for Afsaneh and me, we were oblivious. On some level, I'm sure we both knew we were about to be separated from Mom, but it hadn't really registered. And it's not as if we discussed it. Afsaneh and I had never been very close. My best friend in the world had always been Mojdeh, and since her death I had been reluctant to get close to anyone, least of all my sister, who had tortured me all those years by threatening to make me late for school.

When we got to Pressbaum, the train ground to a stop, and the announcer called out the name of the town, separating it into two distinct words, "Press . . . baum," as if he were about to break into song.

At the end of the platform, there were stairs that led down to the street, past a little ice-cream kiosk, and I insisted on stopping for ice cream. They had something called a Schokobanana, which was made with banana-flavored marshmallows, dipped in chocolate, and actually shaped like a banana. I ate it as we made our way through the underground walkway, toward the gate that led to Sacré Coeur.

SACRÉ COEUR

It was a half-mile up a hill. At the end of the long hike, an old church came into view, along with the cloisters and a second, smaller church. To our left, we saw a modern brick building, which housed the classrooms and the dorms. The place looked very beautiful. The surrounding trees and foliage were lush and green, but fall was just around the corner, and some of the leaves had already begun to turn.

We walked into the main building—the place was empty because classes hadn't started yet—and I approached the first nun we saw and told her who we were.

"Oh yes!" she said, smiling. "Schwester Belle is expecting you."

Sister Belle was an elderly, soft-spoken nun. She gave us a tour of the school and told us all about it, and I translated for my mother and sister. Sacré Coeur was divided into two parts, an upper school and a lower school, and it was home to three hundred students, two-thirds of them girls. Schwester Belle showed us the dorms, the classrooms, the kitchens, and the broad dining room, and she walked us through the lush gardens. With the exception of a nun here and there and the occasional groundskeeper, the place was solemn and empty. Schwester Belle said she was delighted we had chosen to attend Sacré Coeur and assured us that we would be very happy there. She said she was looking forward to seeing us the following week, when classes started.

"It's very nice," my mother said. "Isn't it?"

"Yes," we said. "Very nice."

We walked into town to look around. It wasn't much of a town, more a village really, with one main street and a dozen smaller streets snaking off into the distance, past the quaint houses. There were a few stores: a butcher's shop, a cleaner's, a small market, a bank—where we stopped so Mom could open an account. There were plenty of smiling, pleasant people going about their business, and my mother kept saying how wonderful it was, how marvelous, and describing everything in superlatives, as if trying to convince herself that she had chosen wisely. We had lunch at a small, local restaurant, where I was introduced to Wiener schnitzel and *kartoffel salat*. Things were looking up.

That night, we actually slept in one of the dorm rooms. It was unusual, but we had come from so far away, and they thought it might help us get used to the place. The next morning they even made breakfast for us, some kind of mush, and Mom wolfed it down and said it was wonderful, *"absolutely wonder-*

ful," though she'd only ever liked Persian food. Afsaneh and I, however, were less than impressed, but we kept our opinions to ourselves.

After breakfast we went for another walk through the property and came across an old walnut tree. Mom found a walnut, broke it open, and marveled about the miserable little walnut, along with everything else: "Excellent! The best walnut I ever had. And wasn't that older nun charming? Didn't she remind you of Mammon? And look how green the grass is! And such beautifully trimmed hedges!"

I looked around, and suddenly the school looked much less beautiful than it had only a day earlier. It felt lonely and remote, with its dark church and drab buildings and with those dour nuns making their way about in their habits. Still, I wasn't particularly troubled by it. This place didn't mean anything to me. It had nothing to do with me. I mean, I knew we were enrolled there, and I knew we would be starting classes in a week, but it didn't feel real—it felt as if this were all happening to another Afschineh, not to me.

Before we left to catch the train back to Vienna, we were told that we would need a guardian, someone the school could contact in case of an emergency. My mother immediately suggested her cousin Manouchehr Malek, who lived in Göppingen, Germany, and who in fact we were about to visit, but the school needed a local contact, which only added to Mom's worries. She was already completely stressed out—she was about to leave her two daughters in a foreign country, with some nuns, who were thoroughly pleasant women, certainly, but whom she'd only just met—and now she had to find someone to act as a legal guardian. It was almost more than she could bear, but she never wavered, never even let us know she was the least bit concerned. And I didn't notice. I was as blissfully self-absorbed as the next eleven-year-old, plus I still hadn't accepted that my sister and I were actually going to be left behind to fend for ourselves.

❁ ❁ ❁

We took the train back to Vienna at midday and made the connection to Stuttgart, en route to Göppingen, to visit cousin Manouchehr, the son of one of Mom's uncles. It was a seven-hour ride, and the first part was largely uneventful. I passed some of the time counting cows in the pastures and waving at farmers on tractors. But at one point I looked up and saw Mom crying.

"What's wrong?" I asked her.

"Nothing," she said. "This country is so beautiful."

The country's beauty had nothing to do with it, of course. She was worried about leaving us behind in a foreign land; she was worried about the tuition at Sacré Coeur; she was worried about Ali and Amir, back in Tehran with her mother and her sister; and she was worried about the future.

"What are you crying about *really?*" Afsaneh asked.

But just then the train began to slow, and we found ourselves pulling into Salzburg. Mom brightened quickly. She said we should get up and stretch our legs, and she took us into the terminal for sausages and Cokes.

It is amazing how quickly a young mind can be distracted.

❀ ❀ ❀

When we pulled into the station at Stuttgart, she spotted our cousin waiting for us on the platform—the handsome surgeon I hadn't even heard of until that week. He was with his German-born wife, Liz, who spoke fluent Farsi and turned out to be one of the sweetest women in the world, and their two young sons, ages eight and five.

Within half an hour we were at their beautiful home in Göppingen. Mom got the guest bedroom, and we took the boys' bedroom, much to their chagrin, and then we sat down to dinner like a regular family. Almost immediately Manouchehr began to talk about the school in Pressbaum, how far away it was, and didn't Mom think it would be better if the girls stayed in Germany, closer to them, closer to family. "That way they'll always get a home-cooked meal on the weekend," he pointed out.

My mother actually considered this. It wasn't a bad idea. And the next morning Liz made some calls and arranged for us to attend a day or two of classes at the local grade school, which was already in session. Everyone was hoping we would get a feel for the place and like it. This would make us a little late for classes at Sacré Coeur, but my mother felt it would be worth it, especially if it worked out. If it didn't, missing a day or two at Sacré Coeur was no big deal.

The following Monday we drove to school in Liz's car, and a woman from the principal's office escorted Afsaneh into one classroom and me into another. I remember being introduced to the students by the teacher: "This is Afschineh. She's visiting from Iran. Let's make her feel welcome." Then the teacher indicated an empty seat toward the middle of the room, and I walked toward it. And just as I was about to sit down, the girl at the adjoining desk pushed the chair in, letting me know she didn't want me there. I was absolutely crushed—I couldn't understand why she would do a thing like that—and I found another seat near the back.

I remember fighting tears and thinking, *I'm not staying here. If there's one child in this school who doesn't like me and who treats me like this, not even knowing me, there must be many more.* And I wondered how Afsaneh was doing in her class. The poor thing didn't even speak the language! But maybe that was a good thing: She wouldn't be able to understand the horrible things these horrible kids were saying.

At the end of that grueling day, the teacher told me there would be swimming the next morning and to remember to bring a bathing suit. I said I didn't have a bathing suit, and one of the other girls in class immediately volunteered to bring me one of hers. "We're about the same size," she said. "I'll bring you a nice one. I have lots." It was an incredible act of kindness, but I hadn't recovered from the earlier slight.

When we got back to our cousin's house, I tried hard not to be ungracious, but I told them that one of the little girls had treated me like a leper and that I didn't want to go back. At which point Afsaneh piped in: "I didn't like it, either."

But Mom said we had to give it another chance, that we couldn't judge the entire school based on one bad experience with one bad little girl. And Liz said, "There are uneducated people everywhere in the world. I'm sorry you had a bad time with that German girl, but I think you will find that she was the exception."

I still didn't want to go, but when Mom makes up her mind, there's no changing it. And in the morning, as we pulled up in front of the school, the other little girl, the nice one, was waiting for me, smiling brightly and holding up a bathing suit as promised. For some crazy reason, I started bawling. I refused to get out of the car. "I can't go!" I said. "I won't!" And no amount of cajoling was going to make me change my mind.

It didn't make any sense to anyone, me least of all. But in retrospect I think I was just beginning to get my young mind around the fact that I was really truly being sent away to a school in a foreign country, without my mother, and it was more than I could handle. So we didn't go to school that day. And the next day we returned to Austria and checked into a hotel, since it was too late to go directly to Pressbaum.

We were hungry, so we went out to find a place to eat. And as we were making our way along, we saw a Persian restaurant. We went in, sat down, and ordered shish kebabs, and, the moment the food arrived, my mother took a deep breath and started crying. She wasn't making a sound, but tears were spilling down her cheeks.

"Mom?"

"It's nothing," she said, but the words poured out of her in a regular torrent. "It's nothing. I'm homesick. I miss the boys. I'm worried about you. I feel so alone. It's so hard without your father."

She took another deep breath and through sheer force of will stopped crying. Maybe she thought she was scaring us, which, to be honest—speaking for myself, anyway—she was. But now the tears were gone, and she had pulled herself together, and, when the waitress returned to check up on us, Mom asked about the restaurant's owner.

"They're from Iran," the waitress replied. "The wife is in the back at the moment. Did you want to talk to her?"

"If it's not too much trouble," Mom said.

A moment later, the woman came out, and Mom introduced herself and explained that we girls would be going to school in Pressbaum, and that we needed a legal guardian. And before she could even finish her story, the woman cut her short. "Don't even think about it," she said. "I'll be glad to do it. What do you need from me?"

"Are you sure you don't want to discuss this with your husband?" my mother asked.

"No. It would be a pleasure. I'm happy to help. And you girls should know that you can come to see me anytime you want."

Mom had the appropriate document from the school in her purse, and the woman filled in her name and phone number and signed it then and there.

"I can't tell you how much this means to me," Mom said. "It has been weighing on me for a week."

"Don't even mention it," the woman said. "It's my pleasure."

The next day we took the train to Pressbaum, stopped for a Schokobanana at the small kiosk, then made the half-mile trek to the school. We were shown to our dorm, and Mom jotted down the number of the phone in the lobby and said she'd call us at seven that night, and that we were to wait for her call. Then she went back to the Kölping Haus, planning to spend a few more days in Vienna until we got adjusted.

We went to class, and it didn't seem that bad. Many of the students were new to the school, and there were even a few foreigners. Nobody did or said anything mean or unkind. So already it was a step up from Göppingen.

Late in the afternoon, we met our roommate, Monika, a tall, chunky, Austrian girl. She was a very sweet girl whose biggest joy in life was eating. She showed us to the room, which was at the end of the hallway. It had four single beds, each with a little built-in bookshelf and its own nightstand, and two small wooden desks at the far end of the room. The bathrooms were on the main floor—five bathrooms for fifteen girls, which of course was less than ideal. We didn't like the idea of sharing a bathroom with anyone, especially complete strangers.

At 6:45 that night, Afsaneh and I were already waiting by the phone. And when Mom called at seven sharp, I immediately began to whine. "We just found out that we have to take an extra hour of tutoring every day," I said, "to help us with our German."

"That's a good thing," Mom said.

"I guess," I said. "But it's hard."

"Just pay attention," she said. "Before long you'll speak fluent German, and you won't need any additional tutoring at all."

"What about the food?"

"What about it?" she asked.

"It's terrible. I hate it."

"Just eat what you can. When we're together, I'll make you lots of wonderful meals."

"I have one more thing to ask you, Mom."

"What?"

"Can you come see us tomorrow?"

101

"No."

The next morning we got up and went to breakfast, where our choices were limited to cereal, sweet rolls, jams, and butter. Then we went to class, and at ten o'clock, we got a break and were again herded into the dining room. This time we could choose between *wurstsemmel*, a kaiser roll with cold cuts, or *schneke*, a cinnamon bun shaped like a snail.

We got through the day and spoke to Mom again that night, and I again told her about the bad food. I also told her that I didn't understand why all the kids wore the exact same outfits two days in a row, down to their socks. "They're a little strange," I said. "But they seem nice."

Then Afsaneh took a turn on the phone. She said she didn't understand why we had to hang our comforters out the window to air them out. She could see doing this once a week, perhaps, but *every day*? And she hated getting out of bed so early. She was also frustrated because she didn't speak a word of German, so there was talk of giving her extra tutoring, and she wasn't wild about that, either. However, she had to admit that the kids at Sacré Coeur were a lot nicer than the ones in Göppingen.

Mom listened patiently, then said she would come to see us in a day or two and told us to behave ourselves and study hard. It was important to get good grades.

As it turned out, Mom stayed in Vienna longer than she had intended. On September 20, 1980, Iraq invaded Iran in a dispute over the Shatt al Arab waterway, and this was the beginning of an eight-year war. It was also the first time most Americans had ever heard of Saddam Hussein, the now deposed president of Iraq. Initially, the fighting took place far from Tehran, but Mom was understandably worried, and she kept calling home to make sure everyone was all right. She had been in the process of making plans to fly home, something she hadn't shared with us, of course, though in our hearts we already knew this, and she was having trouble booking a flight on account of the war. Many flights were canceled, and the rest were oversold. Everyone was desperate to get home to their families.

※ ❀ ※

On our very first Saturday at Sacré Coeur, in the middle of the day, a strange thing happened: The place emptied out. The courtyard was suddenly crowded with cars, and we saw kids piling in and going home to their families for the weekend. Within an hour, the dorm was like a ghost town, and it felt horribly lonely. We called Mom, and she came to get us and took us into Vienna for the night. The next day we went shopping, we had lunch at McDonald's, and Mom took us to the train station, still clutching our chocolate milk shakes, for the ride back to Pressbaum. "I will call you at seven o'clock sharp," she said, and she kissed us both good-bye.

We got back to the dorm to find that Sunday nights were a bit of a free-for-all. Most of the kids were just getting back from weekends at home, and they were running around wildly and playing loud music. I remember one song, "Funky Town," that was unlike anything I had ever heard before.

Gonna make a move to a town that's right for me
If time will keep me moving, keep me grooving with some energy

I would ask Afsaneh, "What is this music?" And she would just shrug: She didn't have a clue, either. We hadn't made much progress beyond the Bee Gees, and this was essentially the first time either of us had ever heard disco. We were basically dorks, to be completely honest about it, and we knew we didn't fit in with these people on any level. We weren't cool enough for them. And we certainly didn't look like any of them. I remember especially these two girls from Sweden, blond-haired and blue-eyed. To me, they were the epitome of beauty. They were the "It" girls, completely unapproachable, and I knew those girls would never want anything to do with me.

Three days later, on Wednesday, in the middle of class, one of the nuns came to get me. And I don't know what happened, but my heart just sank. I had this horrible feeling that something awful was about to happen. And, sure enough, Afsaneh was waiting for me in the hallway. We went outside, and Mom was there, standing next to a taxi. And she had a big smile on her face.

"Good news," she said, trying to put the old spin on it. "I got a flight to Ankara."

"Ankara?"

"Yes. I should be able to find a connecting flight from there to Tehran."

I didn't understand why this was good news, and I wasn't buying the big fake smile. I could feel tears welling in my eyes.

"Afschineh, you stop that right now!" my mother said. She was almost mean about it. "I need you to be strong—both of you. There's not going to be any crying here, understood?"

I couldn't compose myself enough to answer. I thought if I opened my mouth, I would completely fall apart. And I guess Afsaneh felt the same way.

"You are the children of a soldier," my mother said. "And soldiers are brave. They don't cry."

I couldn't believe she was saying that to me! Me, who cried over everything! Me, who cried if I thought I was going to be late for school.

"But why do you have to go?" I asked, fighting back tears.

"To look after your brothers," she said. "You are big girls. You need to be brave and look after each other, and I'll be back just as soon as I can."

"I don't want you to go," I whined.

My mother ignored me. "If you need a little money," she said, "don't forget the account at the bank in Pressbaum. Herr Razenberger has the savings book. You can ask him for help if you need a little extra cash."

She then reached into her purse, pulled out a small photo album, and crouched next to us near the steps. She opened the album and tore out one of the pages, and that's when I saw that it was actually two pages sealed together. When she separated the pages, about ten small gold coins dropped into her palm. "Here," she said, placing the coins in Afsaneh's hands. "You're the older one. Hide these in a safe place, for emergencies."

"I don't want them," Afsaneh wailed, and she threw the coins into the grass.

Mom again resorted to her mean voice. "Now look what you've done! Help me pick them up. Come on, girls. Both of you. Help me."

And so we got on our hands and knees and searched through the grass until we found all the coins. And Mom made Afsaneh put them in her pocket. Afsaneh kept crying, and I began to cry, too. I tried to hold my head up high so that the tears wouldn't spill onto my cheeks. I wanted to be brave for my mother; I wanted to be a soldier's daughter. But even with my face turned to the sky, the tears came pouring down my face.

"Girls, *please.* Please don't cry."

And I said, "I'm not crying, Mom. It's the rain, really."

But it was a clear, sunny day, and there wasn't a cloud in the sky.

Just then the taxi driver honked the horn twice, impatiently, and Mom gave each of us a quick hug. "I'll be back before you know it," she said. "I love you both, more than you can imagine. Don't forget to study hard."

And she ran and jumped in the taxi, and we stood there, sobbing, in shock. The driver started the engine and pulled away. We watched the taxi getting smaller and smaller, and, when it was almost out of sight, Mom turned once and waved. We both absolutely lost it. We were bawling and holding onto each other, and now the taxi was gone, and I had never felt so alone in my life. I felt completely and utterly abandoned. And that's the moment it hit me: that this girl next to me, my sister, with whom I'd never even been close—she was all I had left in the world.

And that's all I could think: *Now all we have is each other.*

DURING MOM'S VISIT

AFSANEH, MOM, AND ME, BEFORE OUR
FLIGHT TO AMERICA

MOM WITH MARYAM'S MOTHER IN VIENNA

CHAPTER EIGHT
Sacré Coeur

ON THE PHONE WITH MOM—SUNDAY NIGHT RITUAL

THE DAY MY MOTHER LEFT VIENNA, Afsaneh and I couldn't face going back to class. So we returned to our room and stayed there for the rest of the day, almost too numb to speak.

"I can't believe she's gone," I said.

"I can't believe it, either," Afsaneh replied.

She lay in bed, staring at the ceiling, and I sat by the big window, looking out at the driveway and at the woods beyond, as if I expected that Mom might return at any moment, having changed her mind about leaving us at school, alone.

We didn't go to dinner that night. The nuns gave us permission to stay in our room. And when it was time for bed, I felt hot and achy and had a hard time falling asleep.

In the morning I was very sick, and someone sent for the school nurse. I was running a temperature of 103 degrees, and nothing would bring it down. For the next three days, I remained feverish. The nurse was very concerned about me, and she sent for a doctor, who looked in on me and urged me to keep drinking lots of liquids. Afsaneh had to go to class, but she was given permission to come see me at intervals during the day. She would bring me food, and she would help me change the sheets and pillowcases, which were soaked with sweat and tears.

On the fourth day, the fever broke, and weak as I was, I pulled myself together and went to class. The other students were very respectful. They knew I had been ill, and they knew I was upset. They behaved very gently toward me. I don't suppose any of them really understood what it was like to know that your mother, your sole surviving parent, was suddenly thousands of miles away, but they were certainly empathetic.

Afsaneh and I never really discussed the situation. You would think we might have broached the subject—Mom is gone, this is the hand we've been dealt, let's deal with it—but it was more than either of us could bear. So we just pushed through, focused on our classes, did our homework, and tried not to think.

On Sundays, promptly at seven, we waited by the phone for her call, and the moment I heard the sound of her distant voice I would start to cry. She would tell me I had to be strong, and that I was in good hands, and that she never stopped thinking of us, not even for a moment. And she promised that she would come back to visit us as soon as humanly possible.

"*Meekh basheen*," she used to say. "Be like nails." This was her favorite saying. We had to be tough like nails. The harder one hammered a nail, the more deeply it became imbedded in its place, and it became that much stronger as a result. I understood the analogy, but I felt I'd been hammered a bit too hard.

Not three weeks after my undiagnosed fever, it was Afsaneh's turn. She came back to the room after dinner one night complaining of a stomachache, and I went with her to the school infirmary. The nurse found nothing wrong with her and sent us on our way, but in the days ahead, the pain persisted. At times it was so severe that Afsaneh literally doubled over and dropped to the ground. Finally, one of the sisters accompanied us to a hospital in Vienna. The doctors decided to keep Afsaneh there for observation, and, when I realized that I would be going back to the school without her, I was overwhelmed with fear and grief. Once again, I would be leaving someone behind. I felt more alone than ever.

The sister could see that I was near tears, but instead of comforting me she grew stern and distant. I imagine she didn't want to feed into my sadness. We left the hospital and began making our way back to the train station to return to school. It was an unusually cold afternoon, the kind of wet, bitter cold that cuts right through you, and we walked the whole way to the train station. It felt like miles and miles. I didn't understand why we couldn't take a cab—maybe it wasn't in the budget—and I found myself cursing Afsaneh every step of the way.

Three days later, Afsaneh was discharged from the hospital. They had found nothing wrong with her. The pain was purely psychological, the doctor said. "She misses her mother," he told me in German.

"So do I," I said.

Afsaneh was glad to be out of there. She said all the other children in the hospital picked on her because she didn't speak German, and that's what had cured her. The nasty kids and the unpleasant circumstances made for a speedy recovery, and, like magic, the stomachaches disappeared.

Every two or three days, I would sit at my small desk and write home to tell Mom how unhappy I was. I would write,

Dear Mom,
I miss you super bad. I hate school. The food is awfull.
Love, Afschineh

And she would send my letter back, marked up in red ink. She would note that I'd spelled "awful" wrong. She would say that "super" was not a proper adjective, and go on to suggest changes:

"A better choice would be, 'I miss you terribly.'" But she wouldn't address the fact that I missed her.

Another time, I wrote:

Dear Mom,
I can't believe it's been so long since I've seen you and I get up every day missing you and wanting to be with you so much.
Love, Afschineh

Again, she would focus on the grammar, not the emotion, pointing out that I was trying to squeeze too much information into one sentence. "Think before you write," she would suggest. "Organize your thoughts. Be clear."

Another time, Mom asked me for a picture of myself. I sent her one, but she didn't keep it. Instead, she returned it to me with a poem written on the back. Roughly translated from the Farsi, it said:

You asked me for a photo
A photo has no value
I would give my life so that you have a remembrance of me
A photo has no value

It was at this point that my relationship with Afsaneh started to change. She was my big sister, she was all I had, and now that I'd taken a closer look, I realized she was a pretty decent person after all. Vulnerable, too. Before long we started dealing with our new life, such as it was, and focusing on this strange new world into which we'd been thrust.

We still didn't fit in, and we began to wonder if we ever would. We had the wrong haircuts, the wrong clothes, and the wrong shoes. Most of the girls

THE PHOTO I SENT MOM,
WHICH SHE SENT BACK TO
ME WITH A POEM.

ON THE PHONE WITH MOM

wore leggings and long, large sweaters, and one of the big trends was cowboy boots or those furry après-ski boots. We didn't have tights, large sweaters, or boots of any kind. We wore little plaid dresses and mousy little shirts that buttoned all the way to the top, and we had argyle socks and girlish little patent leather shoes with buckles. We were wearing conservative, age-appropriate clothes, while all the other girls were too hip for words.

Weekends were especially hard on us. Parents would arrive in their fancy cars, and most of the kids would hurry off with their expensive overnight bags, squealing and laughing. We'd be left alone in that hauntingly empty dorm. It was strange, walking around the deserted campus or going into Pressbaum and looking in the shop windows at all of the things we couldn't afford, like those furry boots. We felt like orphans. We felt like all these other kids had wonderful, thrilling lives, with good food, fun vacations, and nice toys—all the things we'd had before Baba died.

One Sunday we took a long walk through the property. The leaves were turning, and the surrounding hills were alive with color, but it was lost on us. We were too depressed to appreciate it. And when we passed the walnut tree, where Mom had gone on at length about the wonderful walnut, the wonderful school, our new wonderful life, we both started to cry.

We returned to the empty dorm, which was as quiet as a morgue. There was nothing to do. They had a television in the upper school, in the common area, but lower-school girls were not permitted to watch television. The nuns thought it was a bad influence.

At 6:45 every Sunday night, without fail, Afsaneh and I would be waiting by the phone for Mom's call; and at seven o'clock, right on schedule, the phone would ring. She had taken to talking quickly, and she would press us for answers when we drifted because the calls were expensive and she was having trouble making ends meet. But if we were in particularly bad shape, she understood, and she was there for us. She listened for as long as we needed it.

In November, we had a falling out with Monika, our chunky roommate. Afsaneh and I kept a lot of snacks in the room, which Mom had gone out and bought for us before she left. There were tins of tuna fish, boxes of cookies, candy, chocolates, etc., and they were disappearing at an alarming rate. At one point we had asked Monika if she knew anything about the missing snacks, and she got a little huffy. "I can't believe you'd accuse me of such a thing!" she said.

"We're not accusing you of anything," Afsaneh said in her broken German. "We were just asking."

A few days later, while Monika was in the process of cleaning out her desk, a bag of trash tore open and spilled to the floor. And there it was—the evidence we needed to convict her: empty cans of tuna fish, candy wrappers, cookie boxes.

She moved out shortly thereafter, and two Turkish girls moved in. Nazli was thin, with beautiful green eyes, and Elvin was big-boned and big-breasted and had unruly, wavy hair. They had become our friends by default because they were foreign and far from home, just like us, and because they were just as uncool and as homely as we were. I guess people have bonded over less.

There were a few foreigners in the upper school, too, but we had no contact with them. One of them was Roshanak, the Iranian girl I'd known briefly at the Deutsche Schule in Tehran, the one whose mother had told Mom about Sacré Coeur. I only saw her once in the course of that entire first semester, in passing, and she just smiled and asked how I was liking the school and went on her merry way. There were also two Iranian boys at the school, about fifteen or sixteen years old, and I had also seen them in passing, but I'd never spoken to either of them. One afternoon, however, one of the nuns came to get me to ask me to talk to one of the boys, who was apparently having a nervous breakdown. By the time we got to the infirmary, he was mumbling and banging his head against the wall, and the nun realized that summoning me had probably been a bad idea. The next day, the boy left the school, and I never saw him again.

One weekend there was a terrible snowstorm, and a lot of the kids stayed behind. Among them were the two Swedish goddesses, who ended up hanging out with us in the common area. They turned out to be very nice girls. They told us that they had been curious about us, but found us unapproachable.

"We thought that you thought you were too good for us," one of them explained.

"Oh no!" I said. "We thought we weren't cool enough for you!"

We had a good laugh over this, but it taught me a valuable lesson. My own insecurity had played a big part in the misunderstanding. I had been intimidated by their poise and beauty, and as a result I had made myself distant and unapproachable.

The following weekend, the goddesses invited us for a day of skiing with their families, and we went. We were pretty good skiers, but we couldn't keep up, and our ski outfits left a lot to be desired. We were glad to have been asked, though, and we were polite and thankful. When we came back Afsaneh gave each of them a gold coin, completely unaware of their value. But we still felt like complete outsiders.

"Do you think we're always going to be nerds?" I asked Afsaneh.

"Absolutely," she said.

And we had a good laugh.

❦ ❦ ❦

That Christmas, we went to Göppingen to visit Manouchehr Malek, Liz, and their two boys. They showered us with beautiful gifts and took us skiing in Innsbruck and made wonderful, home-cooked meals. After dinner we'd eat cookies, play cards, and sit in front of the roaring fireplace. I felt like I had a family again.

Before we left, Liz took us to town to get haircuts. The woman did a terrible job on me. It was a bowl cut. I looked like John Lennon. I was horrified, but I couldn't say anything. Liz seemed to think it looked wonderful. Afsaneh's haircut wasn't much better. Her bangs were too short along the temples, leaving her with one narrow bang in the center of her forehead.

When we got back to Pressbaum, we felt lonelier than ever. And when that first weekend rolled around, and we found ourselves alone in that ghost town of a dorm, Afsaneh decided she couldn't take it anymore. She said we should go to Vienna for the day. It was only half an hour away. And Mom had left money for us at the bank in Pressbaum.

"What good is that money doing either of us?" she said.

"How do you mean?" I asked.

"It's just sitting in the bank. They don't need it."

So we went to see Herr Razenberger, and he said he couldn't allow it, but if our guardian gave us permission, he'd be more than happy to oblige; he knew how hard it must be to be locked away in the dorm on weekends while all the other kids were off with their families. We called our guardian, the lady from the Persian restaurant, but she didn't feel she could authorize such a thing. So she phoned Mom in Tehran, and when Mom called us that Sunday at seven, we begged, pleaded, and finally resorted to crying.

"Mom, you don't understand—we're all alone here," Afsaneh whined. "Don't you want us to be happy?"

Then it was my turn: "All the other kids have families, nice places to go, and cool things, but we have nothing."

It was blackmail, pure and simple. And it worked. In fact, if anything, it worked *too* well. Somewhere along the line, communications got a little murky. When we went to see Herr Razenberger on Monday, he simply handed over the bankbook, along with the blank checks. The following Saturday, we went into Pressbaum and waltzed into the bank, and Afsaneh wrote a check for the equivalent of one hundred U.S. dollars. The teller promptly cashed it, and we took our money and went to Vienna.

Thus began our long, slow slide into corruption. We started small, a hundred dollars here, two hundred there, but soon enough we were spending every Saturday in Vienna, acting like the Rockefellers. We would always start at Herzmonsky, the big department store on Mariahilfer Strasse, and check out the latest fashions. Before long we had cowboy boots, tights, and long, bulky sweaters. Then we each got a pair of those expensive, furry boots, more tights, and more sweaters. We would stop for lunch at McDonald's, say, for the usual, and then we'd shop some more. I bought Barbie pencil cases. Or stickers. I loved all stickers indiscriminately: Snoopy, Hello Kitty, every single Disney character. When we'd had enough of that, we'd stop at a café for Sacher torte and milk, and, feeling fortified, would go to Benetton to shop some more. It was crazy. Two girls, thirteen and eleven, on a wild shopping spree. We looked like game-show contestants! Finally, toward dusk, we'd hurry back to the train station, struggling under the weight of all our bags, and return to Pressbaum.

PRESSBAUM STATION

"Press . . . baum!" the conductor sang.

We'd stop at the little kiosk for a Schokobanana and eat it before facing that steep, half-mile walk. And we'd stumble into the dorm, exhausted, and collapse on our respective beds with our purchases.

At one point, Afsaneh decided that it wasn't enough to go to Vienna once a week. She was like a drug addict. She needed more. And having inherited my mother's iron will, she was able to convince Herr Razenberger to let us go into town on Wednesdays.

"Okay," Herr Razenberger said. "But the gate closes at eight. If you're not back by then, you'll be in big trouble."

It was during this period that Afsaneh and I truly began to bond. We lived for those trips to Vienna. They were our only moments of real happiness. And in some small way, they changed our lives. Gone were the plaid dresses and the mousy little shirts; gone the argyle socks and the patent leather shoes. We weren't exactly hip, but we were making progress.

That Easter, Manouchehr and Liz were driving through Vienna and stopped to see us. They brought all sorts of presents, including Easter candy in the shape of eggs and rabbits, books, and beautiful goose-down ski vests, which we both kept for years and years. After they left, we went to see Schwester Belle and asked her if we could have access to the upper school, so that we could watch a little TV in the lounge. She made the necessary arrangements, and the Latifi girls continued their slow, steady slide toward total corruption. We watched *Last Tango in Paris*, with Marlon Brando, and pretended not to be shocked. And the fact is, we weren't shocked: We didn't understand any of it.

On the day the students were due back from vacation, Afsaneh and I sauntered into Pressbaum to while away the afternoon. We found ourselves at the local grocery store, with the equivalent of about one hundred unspent dollars burning a hole in our pockets. So we spent it on candies and chocolate. And believe me, in those days, more than twenty years ago, a hundred dollars bought a lot of junk. I remember the two of us standing at the checkout counter, with the clerk processing our purchases. It took a very long time, and a line began to form behind us. I remember the way the people stared at us, these odd little girls, two dark-haired foreigners, spending all that money on bags of chocolate and candy.

When we got back to the dorm, we were very popular, and we remained popular for several days—until the candy ran out.

A few weekends later, we were invited to the home of a girl who lived about forty miles from Pressbaum. Her name was Gundula, and she was a little nerdy, with glasses and two long braids, but very sweet. Her mother owned a hair salon, which was attached to the house, and her grandfather was mayor of their little village. Her mother served pound cake with *schlage*, a very heavy whipped cream—quite delicious. We also drank cups of hot chocolate, and we put big dollops of *schlage* in that, too.

Before we left, Gundula's mother took me aside and asked me, very diplomatically, if she could trim my hair. I almost wept with gratitude. She took me to the salon and did what she could to fix it, and to this day I will never forget that kindness. She had heard a little something about our history and about our father's execution and, like some of the other parents, tried to reach out to us. Those acts of kindness made a world of difference in my life. They filled me with hope.

My mother still called every Sunday, and every Sunday we told her we missed her and cried and complained. We never stopped to think about her increasingly bleak circumstances. Day-to-day life in Iran was becoming impossible. There were regular bombings in and around the city. There were shortages of gas and food. Oil, sugar, milk, and rice were rationed, and you needed government-issued coupons to get them. At home, Mammon Kobra was sick and had to be taken to see doctors two and three times a week, at outrageous expense. Plus Mom was very worried about the boys. Clerics from the new regime were visiting the schools on a regular basis, trying to brainwash the students. At one point, they had all the boys shave their heads, military-style, and even lowered the enlistment age to thirteen, though boys as young as ten were being urged to sign up. Last but not least, Mammon Bozorgeh was pressing ahead with her lawsuit, and it appeared that the case would soon be going to court.

ALI'S SCHOOL PHOTO (SECOND FROM THE LEFT). THIS
WAS TAKEN AFTER THE REVOLUTION, AS CONFIRMED BY
KHOMEINI'S PHOTO DISPLAYED IN THE CLASSROOM.

Mom was paying lawyers and doctors and still selling off possessions, one piece at a time. More rugs, silverware, the last of her jewelry. And still she came up short.

She didn't say a word about any of this, of course. Everything was always fine. The boys were fine. Khaleh Mali was fine. Mammon Kobra was doing better. Everyone sent their love. "Don't worry about a thing," she said. "Just study hard, and get good grades."

She didn't say a word about her ongoing battle with Mammom Bozorgeh, either. But we found out later that she had taken Ali to court with her one morning, hoping to appeal to the old woman's better nature. It didn't work. Mammon Bozorgeh lifted her chador and placed it over her eyes, as if to suggest that neither my mother nor Ali even existed.

A short while later, seated in court, the judge noticed that Mammon had her back turned to her own family. "Madam," he said. "Won't you take pity on your own grandchildren?" And Mammon Bozorgeh replied, "It is not in my financial interest to do so. The price of steel is very high these days." My mother didn't understand what this meant. Had Mammon Bozorgeh gone into the construction business?

One Sunday, Mom reached us in the dorm, as always, and told us to expect a visit from Forood, who was going to be in Austria that week. Forood and his wife, Maryam, were the neighbors from across the street who had taken us in for a few days after my father's execution. They were leaving Iran—as far as they were concerned, the fanatics had already destroyed the country—and were thinking of opening a small import-export business in Austria.

Sure enough, Forood called a few days later, and we took the train to Vienna and met him at a very fancy hotel. He actually booked a room for us, and we were stunned: We had never stayed in such a posh place in our lives.

He took us out to dinner, and I had Wiener schnitzel, which made me feel very grown-up indeed, and, for dessert, I had a banana split, which was not particularly Austrian but excellent nonetheless.

When we got back to the hotel, there were chocolates on the pillow.

Forood took us to the station the next day, for the train to Pressbaum, and he said he would return soon, with Maryam, who missed us terribly. Sure enough, two months later they were back, and they bought a small house in a very tony part of Vienna, and, before they had even settled in, they asked us to come out for dinner. They told us we could bring some friends if we wanted, so we brought Nazli and Elvin, the two Turkish girls. They were like us—they didn't get away very often—and we knew they would enjoy it. We had a wonderful meal and camped out in their small house, and the next day we took the train back to Pressbaum. Afsaneh gave each of the Turkish girls a gold coin to cement the friendship.

Finally, at long last, Mom and the boys came to see us. It was late spring, and school was still in session, but we got permission to skip class and went to the airport to fetch them.

"I'm so happy they're coming," Afsaneh said as we made our way through the terminal. "Maybe we'll finally get to go home."

This was very much on my mind as well—to go back to Tehran and to be with my family again—and I was as anxious as she was about our uncertain future. The moment I saw them coming off the Jetway, however, the clouds parted. I let out a whoop of joy and practically knocked my mother down in my eagerness to get to her.

"You're here! You came!"

"You silly girl!" she said lovingly, wiping away my tears. "You didn't think I'd come?"

"I don't know," I said. "I guess I was a little worried."

We took a cab to the city, to the Kölping Haus, the little bed-and-breakfast we'd stayed at when we first arrived in Vienna, almost a year ago now. It had a double bed for Mom and bunk beds for the boys, which she had arranged in advance, and we bounced on the beds while she unpacked.

"You're going to get us kicked out of here," she said, laughing.

We went out for a bite to eat, and I remember clinging to her the whole way. Even when we sat down, I didn't want to let go of her hand.

"So how's school?" she asked.

"You always ask about school," Afsaneh said. "It's terrible. We hate it. We want to go home."

"Are you getting good grades?"

"We're both geniuses, Mom," Afsaneh went on, rolling her eyes. "The teachers can't keep up with us."

"I only wish that were true," she said. "I'm going to be talking to your teachers this week, and we'll soon see what kinds of geniuses you are."

When the food arrived, Mom grew serious. She said she had a great many decisions to make about the future. She had lost her battle with Mammon Bozorgeh, and the only way to pay her off was to move out of the house and find some wealthy tenants. In Iran, when people rent a place, they sometimes pay the full amount in advance, and Mom needed two years' worth of rent to cover her debt to her mother-in-law. She didn't have a choice. She, Khaleh

Mali, and Mammon Kobra were making arrangements to move in with Daï'e Hossein.

But she didn't complain. She was amazing. She was just happy to see us again, happy to see her four kids together in one place. She didn't have a bad word to say about anyone, not even Mammon Bozorgeh. Not a single angry word. She had lost the case against her own mother-in-law, she had sold off everything of value, she was still working full time as a teacher and tutoring five afternoons a week, and she had no idea how she was going to make it through the next six months. But she never wavered. Never doubted.

Until that one horrible day.

She had been in Austria for almost a week, staying at a modest bed-and-breakfast in Vienna, with the boys. We came and went every day, a big happy family once again, and every day she would say, "Tomorrow we'll come out to Pressbaum, the boys and I, and we'll go to the bank. I need to get some money out." And every day, we did our best to distract her.

The fact is, we had done a horrible thing. Mom had put the equivalent of fifteen thousand U.S. dollars in that account. She had painstakingly collected the money through the sale of our dwindling possessions and set it aside for our education, and we had managed to work our way through the bulk of it. We had spent our way through Vienna like a pair of spoiled princesses.

When there was no hope of putting it off any longer, she and the boys came to Pressbaum, and we accompanied them to the bank. And that was when Mom discovered that there was less than two thousand left in the account. She turned to look at us, in shock. "What happened to the money?" she said, tears welling in her eyes. "Who's been spending your money?"

She was looking at Afsaneh, not at me, because I was still a baby. Afsaneh shrugged and shook her head. "We had to take the money out," she said.

"Out?" she asked. "What for?"

"Well, you know, I was—I was in the hospital," Afsaneh said, stammering. "That cost a lot of money. A *lot*."

This was patently untrue. The hospital bill had been very reasonable, and it had been taken care of by the mother of Francesca Kirschner, one of the girls at school. Apparently, Francesca had told her mother all about us, the two near-orphans from Iran, and she had paid the bill without so much as telling us.

"What are we going to do now?" Mom said.

She looked at us, at Afsaneh and me, but we didn't know what to say. How could we answer such a question? We had never thought that far ahead. We had never considered the consequences.

Now she turned and made her way to the door and out into the street, and we followed like sheep, with Ali and Amir trailing. Mom had started crying by this time, which I found absolutely terrifying. We must have been quite a sight: four dark-haired Iranian children, on the streets of tiny Pressbaum, walking behind their crying mother.

I looked at Afsaneh. For the first time, we realized we had done something really bad, perhaps even irreparable. I'm sure that on some level we had known it when we were gallivanting from store to store, blithely spending money, but we had justified it, even subconsciously, because we felt we *needed* it. We needed something to fill the emptiness, and what better than nice things?

Now my mother turned around. She wiped the tears with the back of her hand. "What did you buy with all that money?" she asked.

We shrugged. We didn't know. Candy. Nice clothes. Chocolates. Stickers. Pencil cases. Boots.

"And the gold coins?"

"I gave them away," Afsaneh said.

My mother's knees seemed on the verge of buckling. She reached out and supported herself against a streetlamp. "You gave them away?" she asked, but her voice was barely audible.

"I'm sorry," Afsaneh said. "I didn't know."

"I'm sorry, too," I said.

She took a moment to process this new information, then turned, and we walked toward the train station.

"I'm sorry," Afsaneh repeated.

"Me, too," I said.

"Well, don't worry," Mom said, taking a deep breath and sighing. "It's only money. I'll think of something."

We took the train into the city, five unhappy mutes, and went to Maryam and Forood's house for dinner. They were like family, so Mom told them the whole story. She had come to spend a few weeks in Vienna with her children, but now she barely had enough money for the bed-and-breakfast.

"Then you'll just have to stay here," Maryam said.

"We couldn't possibly," Mom said.

"No, no," Forood said. "We insist. It's small, but we'll manage."

Forood drove Mom back to the bed-and-breakfast, and she fetched the bags and checked out. When they returned, we had dinner, all of us in a rather somber mood, and for the next few days, we tried to stay out of the way. Mom didn't want to impose on Maryam and Forood, so we spent most of our time away from their small house. We would go to local parks or to museums, where our student IDs got us in for free. Or we would window-shop along some of the city's fancier streets. Several times we had lunch at McDonald's, which for the boys was like a five-star restaurant, and in the early evening, during the week, Afsaneh and I would return to school.

SIGHTSEEING IN VIENNA   OUR FAVORITE SPOT—MCDONALD'S

At the end of the week, some of Maryam's relatives arrived from Tehran, and Mom and the boys had to move out for a few days. Afsaneh and I met them in Vienna, and went to a neighborhood of modest hotels, but none of them seemed to have any vacancies. When at last we found a place, the clerk told us that the room wouldn't be ready till nightfall, but that we could leave our bags with him and come back after dinner. Mom was elated. She took us out for Wiener schnitzel and even splurged on dessert, but when we got back to the hotel the clerk, looking guilt-ridden, told us that he had been mistaken; the room was no longer available. Mom was crushed. She suspected that the man had been told not to give the room to an Iranian woman with four young children, and now she was truly at the end of her rope.

We left in the middle of the night, dragging three heavy bags, and found a pay phone. Mom called Forood. It was a very difficult moment for her. In our culture, people always do their best to save face, and this was a crushing humiliation. But Forood was practically family, and Mom was completely honest with him about our situation, and he couldn't have been sweeter. He had a friend who owned a modest little hotel about an hour from Vienna, and he made a call. He phoned back to say that it had been arranged.

Afsaneh and I returned to school in Pressbaum, and Mom and the boys went off to their new quarters. The place was remote, surrounded by farmland, and there was nothing much to do. Mom and the boys went for long walks, and she read to them for hours on end. On that first weekend they came out to Pressbaum to see us. We were still in school, but classes were winding down for vacation, and we wanted to know what we would be doing for the summer.

"I don't know," Mom said. "I'm thinking about it."

On Sunday, they had to go back to their remote hotel, which almost defeated the purpose of the trip: The idea had been for us to try to spend some time together, as a family, but this had become geographically untenable.

The following week, when school finally let out, Maryam and Forood invited us back to their home. Their relatives had returned to Tehran, and Forood had to go away on business for a few days. Maryam made us believe that she longed for our company. She wouldn't take no for an answer. "I will be insulted if you don't come," she said.

"You see," Mom told us, "this is the way it is with Persian culture. Friendships are very important. Back in Tehran, these people weren't neighbors; they were family."

One afternoon, as Mom's vacation was winding down, I was in the living room, watching television, when I heard her asking Forood for directions. She was very formal. "*Bale . . . Bale . . .*" (*yes, yes*). This train, then that train, then a third train. When the conversation ended, she turned to look at me and asked if I had understood clearly.

"What?" I asked. "Understood what?"

"Where we are going tomorrow," she said. "Our destination."

"I didn't understand a thing," I said. "I wasn't paying attention. Where are we going?"

"To the American Embassy."

"Why?"

"Don't you want to see your Dai'e Mammad?"

"Yes," I said. "I'd like to see Dai'e Mammad, but I don't want to see Robabeh Khanoom."

Dai'e Mammad was Mom's brother, the one we had stayed with during the early rioting in Tehran. He had made it to Virginia, where he was living with his three eldest children, but his unpleasant wife, Robabeh, was still in Iran, trying to get out with their youngest son.

"Don't worry about Robabeh Khanoom," Mom said. "She's still stuck in Tehran, waiting for a visa."

"We're going to visit America?"

"Yes," she said. "And listen closely. When we're at the Embassy, I'm going to need you to translate everything I say. You must translate it exactly as I say it, word for word, and—no matter what I say—don't act surprised."

"Why? Are you going to say things that will surprise me?"

"Maybe. But you mustn't let it show."

"Tell me now," I said. "So I won't be so surprised."

"No," she said. "You'll find out tomorrow."

In the morning, Mom took Afsaneh and me to the American Embassy. Before we went inside, she reiterated what she had told me the previous day. "I'm going to speak in Farsi, and you will translate for me. And no matter what I say, you will not react. You will not be shocked or surprised. And you will not talk back or ask questions. Is that understood?"

"Yes," I said. "I guess so."

We went inside and waited for a long time, then we were ushered into a room to meet with the consul. There was a woman in the room with him, an Austrian, and she just listened without saying anything. Mom told the consul our story, in Farsi, pausing from time to time so I could translate. I told him that our father had been executed, that Afsaneh and I had just completed our first year at Sacré Coeur, and that we wanted to visit our uncle in America. We hadn't seen our uncle in a long time.

"It will be a short visit," my mother went on. "Two or three weeks. Then the girls will return to Sacré Coeur, a truly excellent school. They both love it very much."

I guess that was the "surprise" part. And I *was* surprised, unpleasantly so. I almost said something in protest, but then I remembered my mother's warning and translated for the consul. I did take a few editorial liberties, however. I left out the part about Sacré Coeur being an excellent school, and I said absolutely nothing about loving it.

After the consul heard our story, he took our passports and asked us to wait outside. Mom was a little nervous. We were still in the middle of the Iranian hostage crisis, and she didn't think the consul would be favorably inclined toward us. In fact, the waiting room was full of Iranians looking for visas, and we learned that some of them had been trying for months on end to get them, so far without success.

But a little while later the consul and the Austrian woman came out into the waiting room and handed Mom the passports. "Have a good time in America," he said. "Hope you kids enjoy your summer vacation." The Austrian woman translated his words in flawless Farsi.

"Thank you," my mother said. She was overwhelmed, and I could see she was fighting tears. "Thank you very much."

When we went outside, she sighed a big sigh of relief. She told me it was a good thing that I had translated everything per her directions, since that Austrian woman had understood every word, and clearly she'd been there to make sure we were telling the truth.

"Were we telling the truth?" I asked.

"Not entirely," she said. And now the truth came out of her. The money was gone, and she could no longer afford to keep us at Sacré Coeur. But the schools in America were free, and we could live with Dai'e Mammad until she and the boys were able to join us.

"When will that be?"

"Oh, soon—soon. Don't worry." And now she began to tell us how wonderful America was. Everyone went to these big, beautiful schools, with the best teachers in the world. And all the people were very, very nice.

"But when will you come?" Afsaneh said, only half-listening.

"In one year," Mom said. "I will go back to Tehran, sell the house, and get everything organized, and then I will come with the boys. It'll be wonderful in America, you'll see. You'll have so much fun. And the year will go by in a flash!"

She made it sound so exciting that I actually bought it. Maybe this time Mickey Mouse would actually be waiting for us at the airport. After all, Mickey was an American.

For the next few days, Mom kept hyping America. We were going to be so happy there! We were going to love it so much! Everything was going to be an adventure!

She took us shopping in Vienna. We went to Benetton, and she let us pick out a few shirts, even though she couldn't afford it. I remember I found a red shirt with thin, blue, horizontal stripes. I was crazy about it. Then we passed another store with cowboy boots in the window, and Afsaneh said she wanted a pair of cowboy boots. "Everyone in America wears cowboy boots," she insisted. So we went in and bought cowboy boots. She got a pair of brown boots, and I got a pair of white ones with red stitching, though I didn't really want them.

Then it was time to go to the airport, and Mom was still selling this whole idea of America and how much we were going to love it. And in retrospect I see that she was doing it as much for herself as for us. She needed to believe that this was the right thing to do, since she was completely out of options. She needed to believe that we were going to be happy in America. "I'm going to be there next year," she said, smiling broadly. "The year will go by in the blink of an eye!"

When we got to the airport, Mom remained calm and upbeat. She took a picture of us. I was wearing white Bermuda shorts and my new Benetton shirt, along with a white vest, and I was actually happy. Mom had completely sold me on America.

"When you land in New York, your uncle will be there, waiting, and he will drive you down to Virginia," she said. "He can't wait to see you." She then pressed an envelope in Afsaneh's hands. "Put this somewhere safe," she said. "There's three thousand dollars in there. Give it to Dai'e Mammad for safe-keeping when you arrive, okay?" Afsaneh took the envelope, nodding. "And don't forget that you're the big sister: You need to take care of Afschineh."

Afsaneh almost started crying, but Mom gave her one of her looks. "I want you to study hard," she said. "And behave yourselves. Listen to your uncle. I love you both very much, and I will see you next summer. It will be very soon. I promise."

Then she kissed and hugged us both and sent us on our way, and we marched down the ramp and onto the plane. We didn't cry. Crying was not permitted. We were the children of a soldier. We were on our way to America.

DAI'E MAMMAD AND AFSANEH

SHAMSI, ME HOLDING NASSIM,
NASSER, AND AFSANEH

MOM WITH HER SISTER MALI, OUR FAVORITE AUNT

CHAPTER NINE

America

DAI'E MAMMAD, ON THE DRIVE FROM JFK TO NORFOLK,
OUR NEW HOME

DAI'E MAMMAD AND NAHEED

ON AUGUST 24, 1982, my sister and I arrived at New York's John F. Kennedy International Airport to start a new life. We were there, ostensibly, as tourists, and Mom had warned us, repeatedly, to *act* like tourists. "You are visiting your beloved uncle and his charming family," she reminded us. "That's the story, and I expect you to stick to it." We were to say nothing about school. Nothing about Mom's plans to join us in the near future. Nothing about our little brothers. And certainly nothing about Dad.

As it turned out, we had nothing to worry about. The lady immigration officer didn't ask us a single question. She welcomed us to America, stamped our passports, and waved us through with a broad smile. "Enjoy your visit!" she said.

Afsaneh and I made our way toward the luggage carousel in a daze. "Can you believe we're actually in America?" she asked.

"No," I said. "And I can't believe we're going to be living with Robabeh Khanoom, either." Khanoom means "Mrs.," and it is a sign of respect, and as much as we disliked her, we never showed disrespect, even in private.

"We're not," she said. "You weren't listening. Robabeh Khanoom is still waiting for a visa."

"I can't believe any of this," I said.

"Neither can I," Afsaneh said. "What has Mom gotten us into now?"

Dai'e Mammad was waiting for us just outside the baggage claim, beaming. He was with Naheed, who was in her late twenties, and they both gave us a big hug and a warm welcome and fussed over how nice we looked. Mickey was nowhere to be seen.

"Well?" our uncle asked. "What do you think of America?"

"I don't know yet," I said. "I hope I like it."

We followed them out of the terminal, toward the parking structure. Dai'e Mammad somehow looked different. Back in Iran, he'd had a bit of a reputation as a womanizer and bon vivant, and I'd always been attracted to his energy. But here, in America, he seemed somehow deflated, less playful than the uncle I remembered, though maybe he was just tired. Naheed, on the other hand, looked exactly the same: short and shapely, with long, brown hair and a pretty smile. "How was your flight?" she asked.

"It was great," I said.

"Except for the food," Afsaneh said.

Before we knew it, we were barreling down a highway unlike any highway I'd ever seen in my life. It was unimaginably wide and spotlessly clean, and the cars flew along at incredible speeds.

"How come all the signs are green?" I asked.

"That's just the way it is," my uncle said. "In America, the signs are green."

"Are we near Disney World?"

"Oh no," he said, laughing. "That's in Florida. Far away. Very far away."

Naheed tried to explain that Florida was in another state, located at the southeastern extreme of the country, more than a thousand miles away. We were presently driving past New York City, she said, which was in New York State, and we were en route to Norfolk, Virginia, where they lived. It had taken them seven hours to reach the airport, so we had a long ride back.

"Can we stop at Disney World?" I asked.

Dai'e Mammad laughed. "No," he said. "It's not on the way. It's *below* Virginia. We'd have to keep driving for two days!"

We made one stop along the way to use the restrooms and to get something to eat, and Dai'e Mammad bought me one of those huge, multicolored Mickey Mouse lollipops, the size of a dinner plate. "That's as close as I can get you to Disney World," he said. "For now, anyway."

It was dawn when we arrived in Norfolk. I had been dozing on and off for most of the trip, but as we approached their house, I woke up and took stock of my surroundings. They lived on Tate Court, a dead-end street, just like our street in Saltanat Abad, but that's where the similarities ended. The houses were on the shabby side, and the lawns were poorly tended. They lived in the last house on the left. We pulled up, and Dai'e Mammad cut the engine and got out of the car. "Here we are," he said. He looked tired from the long drive.

We went inside, and they showed us around. The house had three bedrooms. Dai'e Mammad and Nader each had one of the smaller rooms, and Afsaneh and I would be sharing the master bedroom with Naheed. The rest of the house consisted of a kitchen, a dining nook, and a good-sized living room. There was a big television set in the living room, along with a horrible plaid couch and two matching chairs.

"Where's Farhad?" Afsaneh asked.

Dai'e Mammad looked suddenly glum. "He's in Los Angeles," he said. "He wants to be a musician."

"And Robabeh Khanoom?" I asked, secretly hoping for bad news.

"It's a nightmare," my uncle said. "She and Fareed are still trying to get visas."

Dai'e Mammad and the older kids had left Iran early, before the deluge. They had arrived in the United States with tourist visas, like us, but had applied for political asylum and were now permanent residents. We hoped to do the same.

Naheed showed Afsaneh and me to the master bedroom. Her bed was on one side of the room, and two single mattresses had been placed head to head at the other. She had also made a little room for us in the closet.

"So," Afsaneh asked. "Is it nice here?"

"I don't know about 'nice,'" Naheed replied. "But I'll tell you this: It's not like in the movies."

"Where's Shamsi?" I asked. Shamsi was the daughter of Khaleh Mali, our favorite aunt.

"We don't see her much," Naheed said, and she gave us a look and left the room.

I didn't understand why Naheed was being so cryptic. "Is it me," I asked Afsaneh, whispering, "or is everything a little weird around here?"

"No, it's not you," she said. "Everything is a little weird around here."

The phone rang. Dai'e Mammad told us Mom was on the line, and we hurried into the living room.

"Did you arrive safely?"

"Yes."

"Is everyone being nice to you?"

"Yes."

"Are you happy?" she asked.

"Yes."

"What's America like?"

"Mom, we just got here!"

We drifted into the kitchen. I looked through the window and saw a heavyset black girl sitting on the stoop of the house across the street, staring blankly at her cluttered lawn. She had a huge head of hair that looked as if it hadn't been washed in years.

"Who's that?" I asked.

"Watch out for her," Naheed said. "She's crazy. She's retarded, and she was raped once."

Dai'e Mammad walked in. "Don't tell them such things," he said. "You'll frighten them."

"I'm just telling them the truth," she said, turning back to face us. "There are only two white families on the block, and we're one of them."

We didn't know very much about Americans, black or white, but from her tone we knew enough to be frightened. We had no intention of leaving the house on our own, and no one invited us to go anywhere, so we drifted back into the living room and watched television. *Family Feud* was on. We didn't understand a word. Dai'e Mammad and Naheed, on the other hand, spoke very good English, and they took great delight in shouting out the answers. I understood just enough to see that they were generally wrong.

"Oh, I know this one!" Naheed exclaimed. "The answer is George Washington!"

Wrong again. The answer was Abraham Lincoln, whoever he was. Not that it really mattered, since we didn't even understand the questions.

"Why does the show keep stopping?" I asked.

"For the commercials," Naheed said.

We had commercials in Iran, but they always appeared at the end of each broadcast, never in the middle. And it was much the same in Austria: The shows played through, uninterrupted, and the commercials aired on the hour and the half-hour. In America, however, you were bombarded with commercials.

"I'm getting hungry just watching," I said.

By late morning, our cousin Shamsi came over to see us. It was very odd. She arrived at the door and rang the bell but refused to enter the house. Not that anyone invited her in. On the contrary, they barely said hello to her.

We followed her to the car and got in, and, as soon as we pulled away from the house, she became her old self again. She was smiling and laughing, and she told us how much she missed us and how nice it was to see family again. She also told us that she'd had a falling out with Dai'e Mammad, over money, apparently. They had all been living together in a nice house on a pleasant, tree-lined street, but things fell apart, and they went their separate ways.

"But what happened?" I asked.

"It's nothing," Shamsi said. "Families are complicated."

Shamsi lived in a small, two-bedroom apartment with her brother, Nasser, and we sat down in front of the TV and watched *The Price Is Right*. It seemed that television was a big part of people's lives in America. We didn't understand what was being said, but it was easy enough to follow the show, and many of the prizes were pretty wonderful.

"This show's not bad," Shamsi said. "I don't mind if you watch this one. But there are many shows that are downright immoral and disgusting."

I immediately felt like changing the channel and looking for those shows, but I restrained myself. We kept watching. "I can't believe it," I said. "People win cars on television just for guessing the price of stuff."

"That's America for you," Shamsi noted.

That weekend, Naheed and a friend took us to Busch Gardens in Williamsburg. It was a huge amusement park, and I especially remember the Lochness Monster, an endless, double-looping rollercoaster. I was screaming with happiness. The place reminded me of Luna Park in Tehran, only ten times better. I remember thinking that America was pretty cool and that I was pretty sure I was going to love it.

On Monday, we were again stuck in the house, parked in front of the television. Nader had a job in a nightclub, and Naheed worked in a store at the local mall. Dai'e Mammad stayed home with us, but he kept to himself. He had managed to get a little money out of Iran, and he had invested in a car dealership, but he was a silent partner, and he had no job to go to.

Afsaneh and I didn't mind spending the day in front of the television set. We were beginning to understand a word here and there, and it was fun to guess at what was being said.

In the evening, when Naheed returned from her job at the mall, she cooked. It was mostly Persian food and not bad, but it didn't compare to Mom's cooking.

In Robabeh's absence, Naheed was the woman of the house, and Dai'e Mammad deferred to her on everything. Nader came and went, rather independently, and we seldom heard about Farhad, the aspiring musician, struggling to make it in Los Angeles. As for Robabeh, she would call from Iran two or three times a week to report on her situation, which remained unchanged, and our uncle always seemed brought low by those conversations. He wouldn't say much, but sometimes he'd join us in the living room and watch TV with us. He introduced us to *Dynasty*, which quickly became a big favorite.

In the middle of our second week, Naheed drove us to Maury High School, in Norfolk, to help us register. We met with a very nice woman from the school, but it was still pretty overwhelming. I spoke absolutely no English, and I understood nothing of what was going on. Afsaneh had taken a few English classes at Institut Maryam, so she had a slight advantage over me, but it was clear that she only understood a fraction of what was being said.

Naheed translated. As it turned out, the woman thought Afsaneh could survive, despite her rudimentary English, but felt that I needed to take some language classes and reapply in January. I didn't like that idea at all. I didn't want to be separated from my sister, and I said so. The woman relented. "Okay," she said, smiling pleasantly. "Let's give it a whirl. Let's see how you manage."

I thought it had been settled—Afsaneh and I would be in school together—but the woman needed to determine what grade to put us in, so she herded us into an empty classroom and made us take a proficiency test in math. When we both placed higher than expected, she decided to put Afsaneh in the tenth grade and me in the ninth. At twelve, I was way too young for the ninth grade, but if they held me back I'd have to attend the junior high school, and it was clear to everyone that I had no intention of being separated from my sister.

Classes were already in session, and, on that very first Monday morning, Naheed drove us to the corner where the school bus made one of its scheduled stops. It was eight blocks from the house, through a very hostile-looking neighborhood. She parked, got out with us, and together we waited for the bus, standing at a safe distance from the knot of kids who had arrived before us. We could hear the bus coming before we saw it—it was full of rowdy, screaming kids—and when it finally pulled up, I was too terrified to get on board. Naheed and Afsaneh tried to talk me into it, but I held my ground. "I'm not getting on the bus," I said, whining. "Those kids don't like me."

"What do you mean they don't like you? They don't *know* you."

"Well, they wouldn't like me if they knew me."

The driver got tired of waiting, shut the door, and pulled away.

Naheed looked at me and shook her head. "Okay," she said, sighing loudly. "I'll drive you to school."

From the moment we walked through the school's front doors, I was lost. Afsaneh and I were in different classes, and as soon as the opening bell went off we had to go our separate ways. That first hour went by in a blur. I only understood one word in ten. When the bell rang, everyone stood and filed out, making as much noise as possible, and I followed them into the corridor, more confused than ever. I didn't understand that we were expected to move from one class to the next, and that we only had a few minutes to do so, which fed into my fear of being late—especially since I didn't know where I was going. In Iran and in Austria, the students stayed in one room, and the teachers moved between the classes. Now I was being forced to find my history room, and I didn't know my way around, and I didn't speak the language, which made it hard to ask for directions, if I'd even had the courage to do so—which I didn't. Worse still, I had to keep going back to my locker to get the right books, and I was never good with those combination locks. Left, right, left again, move past that final number and presto!—nothing happens.

By the time the day was over, I was a basket case.

"What's wrong with you?" Afsaneh said. "You look traumatized."

"I am traumatized," I said. "I'm not going back."

"Come on," Afsaneh said. "It wasn't that bad."

"Maybe for you. I don't even speak the language. And I hate the way everyone stares at me."

We went back the next day, but only because Naheed had agreed to drive us, and it didn't get any easier. It was Sacré Coeur all over again, two girls from Iran, forever destined to be freaks. We looked weird. We wore weird clothes. We spoke a weird language.

"You have to make an effort," Afsaneh said. To show me what she meant, she wore her cowboy boots to school the next day. Everyone stared at her. *Double* freak. "Maybe you're right," she said. "We're not cool. We'll never be cool. There's no point trying."

At the end of that first week, I found the situation completely hopeless. I remember standing in the middle of the hallway, clutching my books, with my schedule in my hand, listening to the late bell, and within a minute I was the only person left in the corridor, alone and clueless. I told Naheed and Dai'e Mammad that I wasn't going back. "I don't speak English, I'm always lost, and in class they treat me like an idiot," I said, fighting tears. It was true, too—especially the idiot part. Some of the students spoke to me very slowly, as if that would help. Others raised their voices to near-deafening levels. And still others tried to mimic my accent. "It's driving me crazy," I said. "We should never have come to America."

Naheed felt bad for me, and she told us she would take us to King's Dominion the following day. This was a huge amusement park in Doswell, Virginia, north of Richmond, and it was even more fun than Busch Gardens. They had a water park and live shows. I loved the water ride so much that I made everyone go back a second time, and we had to wait in line in the hot sun for almost an hour. At the end of the day, on our way out, we came across a family of caged monkeys. The sign said not to feed them, but they looked so skinny and stared at me so imploringly that I couldn't resist: I gave them a whole bag of peanuts. As I watched them chatter and chew, I realized I was wrong about America. America was a great country. I totally *loved* it here.

On Monday, Naheed came to the school with us, to talk to one of the counselors, and asked if it would be possible to put Afsaneh and me in the same class. The counselor said she didn't see how she could do this: Afsaneh was two years older than me, and I was already pushing it—I was the youngest person in my class by far. Naheed suggested that perhaps there were two or three classes where my age wouldn't be an issue, but the counselor appeared unconvinced.

"Then I'm not going to school," I said. I couldn't understand their words, but I could certainly see what was happening. "I'd rather be illiterate."

Naheed translated, and the counselor studied our schedules again. Suddenly she saw a few possibilities. It might be possible to let us take German and English together, and perhaps math would work out, too, if the teacher approved. I was so relieved I almost burst into tears.

The first class we took together was English. When the teacher asked Afsaneh a question, she was able to answer it. She could even talk to the other students. "How are you?" she would say, enunciating clearly, and to me it sounded like flawless American English. I looked at Afsaneh in awe. I thought she was Einstein.

My favorite class, for obvious reasons, was German. It was taught by Mrs. Ramsey, a thin woman with short, salt-and-pepper hair, and it was the highlight of my week. I could actually *talk* to Mrs. Ramsey. And she *understood* me. She was very sweet to both of us. She had made some inquiries about our history, and she knew we were struggling. She went out of her way to befriend us.

We also met an interesting girl in German class, Rachel Owens. If I remember correctly, she lived in Ghent, a very upscale neighborhood, with her parents and her brother, who was also a student at the school. I half-expected her to be stuck-up, but she was completely unassuming and actually smiled and said hello to me from time to time. I desperately wanted to be her friend—I wanted to have an *American* friend—but I didn't know how to approach her. I looked for an opportunity every time I went to class, but it continued to elude me.

"Can't I just take German all day long?" I asked Afsaneh one day. "Why do I need all this other stuff?"

"Now you really *are* being an idiot," she said.

I also came to like Mrs. Chang, our math teacher. She was one hundred percent American, with all-American features—short brown hair, perfect teeth, big eyes—and I was mystified by her surname. It never dawned on me that she might be married to an Asian man.

Mrs. Chang introduced us to pop quizzes, which I didn't like at all. In Iran, tests were scheduled, and you had plenty of time to go home and prepare for them. So I found this pop quiz business unpleasant in the extreme.

Mrs. Chang was very good to me, however. As she slowly made her way up and down the room between the desks, she would look at my answer and move off a little and catch my eye. If the answer was right, she would give a barely discernible little nod, suppressing a smile. But if it was wrong, she would give her head a little shake. I loved her for her generosity.

If classes were generally confusing, the breaks between classes were downright terrifying. The school was almost equally split along racial lines. Half the students were black, and many of them were bussed in from outlying neighborhoods. The other half were white, including an elite contingent from Ghent. You could always tell the Ghent kids apart from everyone else: The boys wore polo shirts and driving shoes, and the girls wore pink-and-green skirts and carried clutch purses. Afsaneh and I made fun of them—we'd heard people referring to them as *preppies*—but in our hearts we desperately wanted to be like them. We wanted to be white, rich, and American. We wanted to exude that kind of poise and confidence. And we wanted to live like they lived. The few times we had driven through Ghent, we had been struck by how beautiful it was. It was full of big townhouses, and there were always expensive cars parked out front or in the driveways.

"This must be the Saltanat Abad of Norfolk," I told Afsaneh.

"Yes," she said, "this is where we should be living."

"This is where we would be living if Baba were alive."

I remember one of the girls from Ghent, a senior, and I remember thinking that I wanted to *be* her, that I would have traded places with her in a moment. She was beautiful and hip and had the flashiest clothes I'd ever seen, and that's what I aspired to: to be that charismatic, that popular. Yet I could hardly bear to look at her. She was too intimidating. I knew I was wildly overreaching.

Between classes, in the corridors, I was scared to walk past the white kids. They all had lockers at one end, as if the school had assigned them along racial lines, and my face would flush whenever I moved past. I was afraid I would be ridiculed, and I know that they made fun of me for not speaking the language, but none of them ever addressed me directly, and I wouldn't have understood them if they had.

"It's a good thing I don't speak English," I told Afsaneh. "I know they're saying mean things about us."

"How do you know that?"

"Just by the way they look at me."

"You don't know how they look at you," she said. "You always walk hunched over with your eyes on the floor."

That wasn't entirely accurate. I sort of had a crush on one of the preppy boys. He was tall, with dark brown hair and beautiful green eyes, and he was a year ahead of me. Every Thursday, we would cross paths on the stairs, and it was the highlight of my week. That's how pathetic I was. If I was having a bad Monday, I would tell myself, "Don't even think about it. You have Thursday to look forward to." I'm not sure he ever noticed me, though there was one time when he actually smiled at me and I almost swooned. Still, when I thought about it later, I wondered if perhaps I had imagined the whole thing.

The black kids at the school were definitely much nicer to us. They were more open and sort of playful. I think they were curious about who we were. We weren't really white, not in the *Mayflower* sense of the word, anyway, but we certainly weren't black, either. Whatever we were, we were outsiders just like them, and I think they saw us as kindred spirits.

"You know," I told Afsaneh one day, "this school is divided right down the middle: the poor black kids and the rich white kids." And she said, "No. It's divided into three. The poor black kids, the rich white kids, and us." She was right.

The worst part of the school day was lunch break. The school had a cafeteria, and it was noisy and out of control. There wasn't any violence—that was the one thing the school didn't tolerate—but we found it intimidating nonetheless. Where would we sit? What if we sat at an empty table, and it belonged to someone else? What if someone tried to talk to us?

Back in Austria, and, prior to that, in Tehran, we had grown accustomed to a proper lunch break, with a proper meal, in a safe, friendly environment. But at Maury High, we were on our own. So we'd go outside and buy junk food from the vendors who showed up in their trucks. We ate Twinkies or Suzy Qs, and we drank Fanta orange soda, which was familiar to us from Tehran, and we would watch the other students from a distance. It was strange. In Austria, we had actually managed to make friends. Many of the students were curious about us, made inquiries, or had heard our story from someone on the faculty. But here, no one seemed interested enough to ask, which made us both feel very alone.

It was almost worse when school ended, and we went back to the house. The warm welcome had turned very cold very quickly. We were living with family, but they didn't feel like family. No one greeted us when we walked through the door. No one asked us how our day went. No one offered us a snack. In a matter of months, I began to feel like an unwanted guest. I had been happier in our dorm room at Sacré Coeur, without a so-called family.

The bad feelings were compounded by the ongoing drama with Shamsi. She would arrive, usually on a Saturday, ring the bell, and refuse to set foot in the house. We would then get into her car and go back to her place, and the moment we stepped through the door we would park ourselves in front of the TV. Sometimes, Nasser was there, and he would invite us to have dinner with him and Angie, his American girlfriend. Other times we'd drive to McDonald's, but by this point the novelty had worn off. A Big Mac wasn't what it used to be.

One Saturday, Shamsi took us to Military Circle Mall, in Norfolk, and it literally changed our lives. We had never seen anything like it. There had been bazaars and a couple of unimpressive department stores in Tehran, and in Austria we had seen some fancy, high-end shopping districts, but America had created and perfected the very concept of a mall. In this country, the mall was pure entertainment: noise, color, music, and humanity in its myriad shapes and sizes. The mall was a little oasis of insanity and exactly what we needed.

We weren't there to shop, however. We'd learned our lesson in Austria. Plus money had become something of an issue. The day after we arrived, Afsaneh took the cash Mom had given us and turned it over to Dai'e Mammad. Since then, we'd been forced to go to him every time we needed a few dollars—for notebooks, Twinkies, pizza, ice cream, etc.—and he doled it out grudgingly. We didn't understand this. It was Mom's money, not his, but he insisted on putting us through the third-degree every single time: "Didn't I give you five dollars on Monday? What are you spending it on this time? Do you think money grows on trees?"

We knew money didn't grow on trees, but we also knew that this was *our* money. Mom had told us so. And it kept coming in bits and starts. Whenever Mom could scrape a few extra dollars together, she would mail a small check to Dai'e Mammad.

We also knew this was a struggle for her, but it was clear we only had a vague idea of just how bad things were at home. Mom was in the process of leasing out the family house, to help settle her accounts with Mammon Bozorgeh, and she, Khaleh Mali, Mammon Kobra, and the two boys were planning to move in with Dai'e Hossein. At around this same time, Mom finally learned what Mammon Bozorgeh had meant with that cryptic, courthouse comment about the price of steel: She was using part of the settlement to add two stories to her house. It was hard to believe. Her daughter-in-law and her two grandchildren were being forced from their home, and she was busy remodeling! Shamsi was right. Families were very complicated indeed.

In late October, Dai'e Mammad told us that he'd made an appointment for us with the U.S. Department of Immigration and Naturalization. Our tourist visas were about to expire, and we were going to try to convince the authorities to give us political asylum. We were going to have to skip school.

The following morning, Afsaneh and I dressed in nice clothes, and our uncle drove us to the federal building. We were directed to the right floor and into a huge, airless waiting room, and before long we were ushered into a small office. A large, American man was seated behind the desk, and he stood to greet us, which only made him seem larger and more intimidating. Dai'e Mammad did all the talking, of course. He had brought a copy of the letter that Edwin Wasilewski had written to Cyrus Vance, in which he described our family in glowing terms, as well as a copy of the Iranian newspaper that had reported my father's execution. The newspaper was yellow with age, and I could see my father's photograph on the front page. The man glanced at the newspaper—it was clear he didn't read Farsi—then took a minute to read the letter. When he was done, he asked my uncle a few more questions, and at one point seemed to become mildly irritated. I could see Dai'e Mammad struggling to explain himself, and in a matter of moments the American man was smiling again. He stood, we stood, and he shook our hands, one at a time, and told us that we would be hearing from him soon. Then he sent us on our way.

Before we had even reached the elevator, Afsaneh was peppering Dai'e Mammad with questions. "What did he say? He seemed angry. Did we do something wrong?"

"He *was* angry," Dai'e Mammad replied. "He said you lied to the embassy in Vienna."

"But we had to," I protested. "If we hadn't lied, they wouldn't have let us come."

"Don't worry," Dai'e Mammad said. "I told them you couldn't go back. I said your lives would be in danger if you were forced to return to Iran."

"Are they going to let us stay?" Afsaneh asked.

"I imagine so," Dai'e Mammad said. "I can't think of two people who would be better candidates for political asylum."

"Are you sure?" I asked, still quite worried.

"Yes. If they were going to kick you out, they would have done so already."

On Monday, we were back in school, where I continued to make my way along the corridors with my eyes on the ground and my books pressed to my chest. Still, I was slowly coming to terms with the fact that this was my life, for the foreseeable future, anyway, and that I should try to make the best of it.

I would hear the kids greeting one another—"What's happenin'?!" "Wassup, brother?!"—and I would repeat these phrases to myself in my head. I thought they sounded cool. I thought *I* sounded cool.

There was this black kid in our math class who was very funny. I only knew he was funny because every time he opened his mouth, the entire class would burst out laughing. One time he asked Afsaneh what was happening, and she kept telling him that *nothing* was happening. Finally he pointed at Afsaneh's watch and repeated himself, enunciating slowly and clearly: "What. Time. Is. It."

He'd been asking her for the time all along, and I was suddenly struck by the complexity of the English language. "What's happening?" and "What time is it?" didn't even sound remotely alike, but we hadn't been able to tell them apart. Maybe Afsaneh wasn't the Einstein I'd taken her to be.

Back at the house, little changed. We would watch TV, do our homework, eat dinner, and go back and watch more TV until it was time for bed.

"Why don't they like us?" I asked Afsaneh one night.

"Who?"

"Everybody," I said. "Our uncle and his family and the people at school."

"They don't know us," she said.

Once a week, Mom would call, and it was the highlight of our week. But it was painful, too. Afsaneh and I had decided not to complain about our situation. We knew she was having problems of her own, and we didn't want to add to the burden by telling her about the comparatively small miseries we were being forced to endure. So we did our best to keep it light: "School was hard but fun. We were eating well and studying hard. The malls were super fun." I often found myself fighting tears, my answers reduced to monosyllables because anything beyond a word or two would have made me fall apart: "Yes. No. Good. Saturday. McDonald's. The mall."

After I got off the phone, I felt worse than ever. I was living in a house with people who seemed to grow more hostile every day, and I was going to school with kids who thought I was a freak—if they thought about me at all. I wondered if there was any place on earth for me; I knew *this* couldn't be it.

To compound matters, Naheed announced one evening that she could no longer drive us to school. "You're going to have to start taking the bus," she said.

The next morning we had to walk the eight blocks to the pickup location, and I was so terrified that I held onto Afsaneh's hand for dear life. I didn't understand what was happening to us. This wasn't the America I had pictured. This wasn't at all what I'd been expecting.

As we approached the appointed corner, we saw a knot of kids up ahead, waiting for the bus, laughing and horsing around with easy familiarity. We kept our distance, and, when the bus finally arrived, we were the last to board. It was absolutely deafening. Kids were screaming, throwing things, and shoving one another around, and Afsaneh and I negotiated our way down the narrow aisle as if we were walking the gauntlet. We finally found two seats near the back, and I held her hand until we got to school.

From then on, that was how our school day started. The long, stressful, eight-block walk at seven every morning. The noise and wildness. The endless struggle to find a pair of seats together.

By the end of that first week, Afsaneh had picked up a new phrase, and she learned to use it, *forcefully*. "Scoot over!" she'd snap, glaring, and some sullen kid would move his or her backpack and make room for us. I remember being very impressed by my sister's self-confidence. I was a timid little wallflower. If you looked at me the wrong way, I would have burst into tears. But not Afsaneh. She was a survivor. She was also all I had.

When we got to school, we were forced to go our separate ways, and I drifted from class to class, understanding almost nothing. The only class that made any sense to me was our German class, and this was truly the one bright spot in my academic day, my own little oasis.

I spoke to Mrs. Ramsey in German, and she replied in German. It was such a rare and wonderful thing to talk to an adult who actually seemed to care about me! She would smile, ask me what I'd been up to and how things were going, and tell me my dress was pretty. It was almost too much happiness. I came to depend on it.

Also, from time to time and as part of the day's lesson, Mrs. Ramsey might make a somewhat oblique reference to our situation. "What do you think it would be like for you to move to a country where you didn't speak the language, and no one understood a word you said?" She never made it obvious that she was talking about us, but the smarter students got it, and I think they understood what she was trying to do. She wanted them to be nicer and more accepting; she wanted them to try to put themselves in our shoes.

In most of my other classes, I remained lost, and I despaired of ever picking up the language. I had always felt like a fairly intelligent little girl, but nothing was clicking for me, and I was beginning to get very frustrated.

"Maybe you need to take English classes after school," Naheed suggested at one point.

"No way," I replied, "I'm not going anywhere without my sister."

So our life continued along much the same lines. We would get home at three or three-thirty, and I would rush into the living room and reach for the remote. I would sit on the plaid couch and watch all the Looney Tunes cartoons—*Road Runner, Bugs Bunny, Tom and Jerry*—with all the intensity of someone watching a political debate. I enjoyed myself, certainly, but I honestly felt I was parked in front of the tube to study and learn.

Dai'e Mammad soon became irritated with my viewing habits. "Aren't you tired of those cartoons?" he asked.

"No," I said. "Every day, I learn more."

It was true. I would watch the cartoon characters for their reactions, and the little animated faces would convey exactly what being said: "I tawt I taw a putty tat!"

When the cartoons were done, I'd watch *The Brady Bunch*. People in this country are highly critical of television's laugh tracks, but I found them quite useful. Once again, they cued me as to what the characters were saying. "Okay. I get it. This is funny." However, they also confused me. *Where were the laughing people? How come I never saw them?*

"Still watching TV?" Dai'e Mammad would ask, shaking his head disapprovingly.

"Yes," I said. "Would you care to join me?"

By November, everyone pretty much stopped paying attention to either Afsaneh or me. We kept out of their way, and they kept out of ours.

Naheed and Nader both worked, Farhad was in Los Angeles, and Robabeh was still having trouble securing a visa. Dai'e Mammad occasionally went out to see friends, and, from time to time, his friends came to the house to see him and the children. All of these people were from the local Iranian community, and Naheed made an effort to serve good Persian cuisine, as was expected of her.

There was a little laundry room at the rear of the house, which opened onto the small backyard, and they kept a small hibachi in the corner, near the door. Naheed used to open the door to keep the air circulating and make lavosh bread on the little grill. It was a very time-consuming job, and she hated it, so one day she enlisted our services. "If you help me make the bread tonight, you can skip school tomorrow," she said. It took us almost three hours to make the bread, but it was worth it. The next day, we were home all day, in front of our beloved TV, like a pair of addicts and just as insatiable. By this time I had begun to find even the commercials entertaining. I actually looked forward to them. I found them challenging.

At night, the guests would arrive, and we wouldn't know quite what to do with ourselves. Afsaneh and I never felt as if we were part of the evening festivities because no one made any effort to include us, but we greeted everyone politely and tried to make ourselves useful. We were guests in that house, like the ones who were arriving for dinner, but unlike them we were not made to feel particularly welcome. On the contrary, we felt very much in the way.

Things continued to deteriorate. On Sundays, when the phone rang, it was understood that we were not to answer it, even when we knew it was Mom calling from Tehran. Dai'e Mammad would pick up the receiver and immediately launch into his litany of complaints. "The girls don't study. They will flunk out. All they do is watch TV all day, every day."

When it was my turn, Mom would of course ask me if there was any truth to what her brother had told her, and I would explain that I couldn't study because I didn't speak the language, and that watching cartoons was a form of studying. She never reprimanded me, but she never tired of reminding me about the importance of school. "Remember what your father said. You have to study hard. I promised him I'd make sure all of you would get a good education. I told him all four of you would become doctors."

I redoubled my efforts at learning English. Before long, I was driving everyone in the family crazy with questions. "What does 'green' mean? What is 'family way'? What does 'hip' mean? How do you say *peeaz* in English?"

"Onion."

"How do you spell it?"

It was very annoying for everyone involved. Afsaneh. Naheed. Nader. Dai'e Mammad.

"Afschineh, stop being such a pest!"

"How do you expect me to learn English?"

Eventually, I changed my tactics. In Iran, I had an annoying habit of reading road signs, billboards, and all the storefront signs out loud, and I took it up again with a vengeance: *su-per-mar-ket, gas sta-tion, dis-count de-sig-ner shoes.*

I was learning a lot of new words, but I hadn't quite figured out how to access my newfound knowledge. I still loved only German, which I spoke fluently, and math, which transcended language.

One Monday, Rachel Owens showed up in German class with a new girl, Suzanna. She was an exchange student from Germany, and she was staying with the Owens family. I was crushed. Now I didn't stand a chance of befriending Rachel! But right after class, Suzanna hurried to catch up with me. She was delighted to find someone with whom she could speak German. "I was worried," she said. "I thought I was going to be completely isolated here." I knew exactly what she meant.

Before long, Suzanna was hanging out with me and my sister. And when Christmas rolled around, she asked Mrs. Owens to invite us to the house for dinner. It was the Friday before Christmas, and I expected Rachel to be home, but she was too cool to be home with her parents and an exchange student on a Friday night, and she'd gone out with her friends. Despite her absence, it turned out to be a lot of fun. We spent the evening making Christmas cookies with Suzanna and Mrs. Owens. Christmas music played on the stereo, and Mr. Owens was sitting in a comfortable chair in the den, reading the newspaper in front of the roaring fireplace. It was very homey and toasty warm.

When it was time for dinner, Mr. Owens joined us at the table. He asked us a lot of questions with genuine interest about our lives, and we shared some of our history. We even told him about Baba Joon. Then we asked Mr. Owens a few questions. He told us he was a lawyer, and he explained what he did for a living. I enjoyed listening to him. I kept looking at him and thinking, *This is what it means to have a family.*

Back at the house on Tate Court, in contrast, things were increasingly strained. As the weather grew colder, so, too, it seemed, did our relationship with our hosts. And as if to drive home the point, Dai'e Mammad refused to let us turn on the heat.

"It's too expensive," he said. "We can't afford it."

We were always padding around the house in sweaters and two pairs of socks or wrapped in blankets. Then one chilly night, while Naheed and Nader were at work, Dai'e Mammad went out to see friends, and Afsaneh said she'd had enough. "I'm turning on the damn heat," she said. "We'll listen for the car, and, when we hear it pulling up, we'll shut it off."

Several hours later, we heard Dai'e Mammad returning, and we turned off the heat as planned. Unfortunately, it was an electric heater, and it was rumbling like thunder when he walked into the house. My uncle was livid. "I thought I told you not to turn on the heat!" he shouted. "Things are very expensive in this country. This isn't like the old days. We don't live the way we used to, so you better start getting used to it!"

A few days later, he snapped at me for taking a long shower and told me I was only going to be permitted to shower every other day. "The water isn't free in this country!" This was even more upsetting to us than the business with the heat. Both of us had always been sticklers about cleanliness, and we didn't see how we could possibly go two days without a shower.

I didn't understand what was happening. Dai'e Mammad had always been such a carefree, fun-loving person. But here, in America, he was dour and stingy. Even if his investments hadn't paid off, his kids worked. Didn't they help out? However, maybe that's just the way it was in America. Everything was outrageously expensive. This was only the land of plenty if you could afford it, if you lived in Ghent.

I began to worry in earnest about the future. Maybe this is what lay in store for our family, too. How in God's name were we going to make ends meet in America, especially without a father?

In January, my birthday came and went, unnoticed and unacknowledged by anyone in the house except Afsaneh, of course, but the following Saturday Shamsi surprised me with a small cake. She, Afsaneh, and Angie sang to me, and I blew out the candles. We each had a slice of cake and a glass of milk. I remember sitting at the table in Shamsi's apartment, in a long, frilly dress, eating my cake, with a doll in my left hand, and wishing my mother were there. Just thinking back to that day makes me overwhelmingly sad, and I was sad

then, too. Back in Tehran, everyone always made a huge fuss over me on my
birthday, especially Baba Joon. On my last birthday, he had actually taken us
out to the balcony and set off fireworks. I looked at that lonely candle and
remembered the fireworks, and it was all I could do not to burst into tears.

ME

ME

"Do you think we should go live with Shamsi?" I asked Afsaneh later, back
at Dai'e Mammad's house.

"No," she said. "She doesn't have any room."

It was true. Shamsi's brother, Nasser, was about to marry Angie, and he
was at her place almost every night, but the second bedroom was still his
bedroom, and we didn't think we could in good conscience ask him to give it
up. And it's not as if Shamsi was a day at the beach. She was such a Puritan
about TV that she was constantly switching it off in the middle of the good
parts. "This is immoral! You can't watch this. I don't understand the kinds of
people who put such things on television!" Shamsi was quite bossy, too. And
she was always right about everything, even when she was wrong. The two
shows she tolerated, despite a small measure of immorality, were *Love Boat*
and *Fantasy Island*. I was crazy about *Love Boat*. I loved the way Isaac pointed
his index fingers at people, gun-style, when he was making a point. There
was a period when I walked around the house doing the same thing, much to
everyone's chagrin.

✿ ❀ ✿

On Sundays, whenever Mom called, I was
desperate to complain. I wanted to tell her
about the electric heat, about the hot water,
and about my really sad birthday celebration, but Afsaneh asked me not to. Mom
had enough to contend with, she said.
Lack of money. War. Her ailing mother.
An increasingly militant regime that was
recruiting boys as young as thirteen. This
was 1982, and Ali was only eight, but at
school they had already forcibly shaved
his head, despite Mom's protestations, and
both he and Amir were being subjected to
all sorts of pro-Khomeini propaganda.

Then, too, this whole situation was partly our fault. If we hadn't been so irre-
sponsible with Mom's money, we probably wouldn't be in this unhappy place.

So we told her that things were great, that life was wonderful. We painted
a very rosy picture of America, and Mom bought it. Sometimes I could hear
her voice cracking with emotion: At least there was one thing she didn't have
to worry about; at least the girls were happy.

"I had a wonderful birthday," I lied. "Everyone was super nice to me."

We kept the charade going, Sunday after Sunday, for months on end. We
were trying to be considerate, but—as with so many acts of kindness—we
were looking out for ourselves, too: We felt that if we gave her less to worry
about, it would help her get through the difficulties at home, and we would all
be reunited by summer, as promised.

✿ ❀ ✿

By March 1983 barely seven months after we'd arrived, all the TV watching
was beginning to pay off. I now understood almost seventy percent of what
I read and heard, and I was proud of myself. I was still getting straight F's in
everything except German and math, but I knew I was improving by leaps and
bounds, even if no one else was aware of it or even cared.

One afternoon, I got a D+ on an English test, and I could barely contain myself. When I got on the bus at the end of the day, I pulled out my test and sashayed down the aisle, waving it aloft. "Look at me! I got a D+! I got a D+!" Everyone knew I'd been getting F's pretty much across the board, and they were all very happy for me. They hooted, cheered, and erupted into loud applause, and I was grinning so hard my jaw ached. A D+ may not seem like much to most people, but to me it was a giant, forward step.

The school thought I was making progress, too, which ended up working against me. They decided to separate me from Afsaneh, and they put me back in the classes where I actually belonged. It was very odd. In some ways, I felt as if I was being punished for doing well, and I didn't know how I would manage. But that first day I kept telling myself that I could handle it—*If I can handle missing Mom, I can handle this*—and by the end of the week it was clear, even to me, that I would survive.

Before long, I began to feel more optimistic about the future. I knew Mom and the boys would be in Virginia that summer. We would move into a nice house of our own, maybe not in Ghent, not at first, anyway, but somewhere where we didn't feel unsafe. And it would be just us again, the immediate family, and we would all be immensely happy. I began to study harder than ever.

By the end of the school year, both Afsaneh and I had just missed making the Dean's List, which astounded a good many people.

"You see?!" I told my mom. "I studied hard like you asked me to. I'm doing better every day. When are you coming?" Afsaneh and I had rushed home from school to call her; this was big news, and we didn't want to wait until Sunday. I had held up my end of the bargain, and I was now pressing her to hold up hers.

"I'm working on it," she said tentatively. "I still don't have visas for the boys."

I heard the doubt in her voice, and it worried me. For days afterward I forced myself not to think about it. I kept telling myself that Mom was coming. Absolutely. Definitely. Positively. She would get visas for the boys and be on her way before school let out.

But every time we spoke on the phone, she said the same thing. "I'm working on it. Mammon Kobra is very sick. Money is tight."

I tried to be positive, but things at Tate Court were becoming increasingly unpleasant. Robabeh would call from Tehran every week, and every week we could hear Dai'e Mammad responding to her questions in a loud voice, clearly for our benefit. "Yes, they're still here. No, I don't know when they're leaving. Yes, I agree, but what can I do? I'm stuck with them."

When he got off the phone, he and Naheed would sit around discussing us as if we weren't there, their voices loud and plaintive: "What are we going to do about them? Family is family, but enough is enough. We have our own lives. Do these girls expect to stay here forever? Are we expected to feed them forever?"

Feed us? We weren't even allowed to serve ourselves at the dinner table. Naheed was in charge. If one of us so much as reached for a platter, she would stop us with a look.

A black Doberman had joined the family by this time. They called him Siah, which is Farsi for "black," and everyone absolutely doted on him. "They are nicer to Siah than they are to us," I told Afsaneh one night.

"Don't worry," she said. "Mom's coming for sure. It'll end."

The following week, when Robabeh called, it was more of the same. "Maybe they can move in with Shamsi. Haven't we done enough for them already?"

Looking back on it, I actually think my uncle felt badly about treating us so shabbily, but it was clear he was being pressured by Robabeh, who had never liked us. And we were *his* family, not hers. Plus she probably resented us. We were in the United States, in her home, and she was back in Tehran with her young son, trying without success to get a visa.

Still, it was hard to fathom. We were just two little girls, and we were being deliberately tormented by our own relatives. I had never in my life felt so unloved and unwanted. If there had been a hole under the house, I would have crawled inside. Afsaneh and I would have been better off in the home of complete strangers.

"When is their mother coming to get them?"

"This is getting ridiculous."

"It'll be nice when we have a little privacy again."

"Before they were around, I used to look forward to coming home."

That summer, Mom took the boys to Turkey to try to get visas to the United States. The U.S. Embassy in Tehran had long since closed, and the one in Istanbul was literally deluged with desperate Iranians. After spending an entire day in the crowded waiting room, Mom was actually issued a tourist visa, but the boys weren't so lucky. The Americans knew that she and the boys would remain in the United States forever if they were permitted to enter together, and they weren't about to let this happen.

"I'm sorry," she said when we spoke again. "I couldn't get visas for the boys."

"Then come alone," I said.

"I can't," she said. "I'm sorry."

I started bawling. I wanted to tell her all about Dai'e Mammad and Robabeh, about all the ugly things that were happening to us, and about the way the other kids treated us in school, but I was crying so hard I couldn't speak.

"I'm very sorry, *azizam*," she said. "Next year for sure. I promise."

Next year?! I didn't think I could make it through another *week*. The only thing that had kept me going was the knowledge that Mom would be there that summer, and now she wasn't coming. I thought I would die.

I was still crying when I crawled into bed that night. "What are we going to do?" I asked my sister. "How are we going to survive another year?"

Afsaneh didn't answer. She was wondering the same thing.

ONE OF AFSANEH'S "GLAMOUR SHOTS"
FOR HER MODELING PORTFOLIO.
IT NEVER TOOK OFF.

AFSANEH AND ME IN THE ISLAMIC SECTION OF THE
METROPOLITAN MUSEUM OF ART

CHAPTER TEN
Waiting

SHAMSI, ME, AND AFSANEH. I FELL IN LOVE
WITH NEW YORK THE MOMENT I ARRIVED.

THE SUMMER OF 1983 got off to a slow, painful start. We were trapped in the house at Tate Court with no one to talk to but each other, and nothing to do but watch TV. Two weeks into our dull vacation, I found myself longing for school to start. It wasn't exactly fun, but it was better than this.

"Let's go to the mall," Afsaneh suggested one morning.

"How?"

"We'll take the bus."

"With what money?"

Afsaneh found Dai'e Mammad in the kitchen, lingering over his coffee. "Can we have twenty dollars?" she asked.

"What for?"

"We want to go to the mall."

"No," he said. "You'll only get into trouble at the mall. That's where the bad kids go."

"We're not that stupid," Afsaneh said. "We won't get in any trouble. Please let us have twenty dollars. It's ours, anyway."

"What did you just say to me?" he asked, his voice rising.

"I spoke to Mom," Afsaneh said. "She's been sending you money regularly."

"Show a little respect," he snapped. "You are living in my house. I will not allow you to speak to me in that manner."

She apologized, but she stood her ground. After a few moments, Dai'e Mammad reached for his wallet, none too happily, and gave her twenty dollars.

We went to the mall and walked around for hours, and at the end of the day we came home with fourteen dollars in our pockets. We had learned our lesson in Vienna.

The following weekend, we went over to Shamsi's, and the three of us had dinner with Nasser and Angie. Angie was a lovely girl, and she became a real savior over the course of the summer. She had us over to her apartment almost every weekend, for meat loaf and lasagna, two of her specialties, and from time to time, she and Nasser took us to the movies. Dai'e Mammad still looked upon Shamsi and Nasser as the enemy, but he no longer complained when she came to pick us up since it got us out of his hair.

Weekdays were a little harder to get through. We watched TV to polish our language skills, and made occasional trips to the mall, and one day out of sheer boredom we stopped by the high school to talk to the counselors about the summer jobs program for kids. As it turned out, they had something for me at a branch of the Virginia Beach Public Library, and a few days later I found myself lost among the stacks, shelving books. I spent more time reading than shelving, however, until one of the librarians suggested I take a few books home.

"I don't have any money," I said.

"Money? You don't need money. It's free."

"Free?"

She looked at me as if I were an alien, which in fact I was. "Yes," she said. "You get a library card, and you can borrow as many books as you want."

"And it doesn't cost a thing?" I asked.

"Not a penny," the woman said. "Unless you bring the books back late. Then we charge you a late fee."

This was news to me. There were libraries in Tehran to be sure, but we had never frequented them. Mom would come home every two or three weeks with armfuls of new books, and we would devour them hungrily. We were much too spoiled to share books with anyone.

The librarian processed my card on the spot. I couldn't believe it. It felt like the biggest gift of my life. I went to the shelves and picked out a book by Judi Blume. I didn't know anything about Judi Blume, but her books were always flying off the shelves, so I figured they must be pretty good.

By the end of that summer, I discovered a whole new world. Books. Words. Stories. I got in touch with my inner geek. Reading was not only exciting, it offered escape. When I was reading, my other life didn't exist. There were days when I didn't even think of Mom.

❀ ❀ ❀

In September, we were back in school. I was glad to be back, but roll call killed me: "Afschineh Latifi Moghadam Tehrani."

"Here!"

Afsaneh hated it, too. "Let's change our names," she said. And we did. She became Janey. I was Julie. A few weeks into it, however, we decided we didn't like our new names, so we tried again. This time she was Amy, and I was Ashley.

"Hey, girl!" one of our classmates remarked. "You changed your names *again?!*"

Yes. We did. And we just kept changing them. We wanted to be anyone other than who we were. We thought that if we changed our names, we'd become different people, with different lives. But it never happened. We were still a couple of geeks from Tehran, fated to remain forever on the outside looking in.

We felt this most intently in gym class. All the girls, except us, shaved their legs. We had *never* shaved our legs. We looked like gorillas in shorts. Every time we walked into class, the girls would check out our legs, smirk, and roll their eyes. It was very embarrassing, to understate the case.

"Mom, we have to talk," Afsaneh said the next time they spoke on the phone.

"What is it?"

"We need permission to shave our legs."

"Absolutely not!"

"But Mom, you have no idea how humiliating this is!"

At long last, she relented. We went out to McCrory's, where Naheed worked, and bought a jar of Nair, the magical depilatory we'd seen advertised on TV: *Shave, lady? Don't do it. Cream hair away in a beautiful way with Nair.* We went home and spread the cream on our legs, per the instructions, and after a few minutes we ran wet sponges up and down our legs. It burned a little, but who cared? The hair was gone! I still remember looking in the mirror and seeing my bare legs. I thought they looked wonderful. I was sure my life would change overnight. But of course my life didn't change. I was still that weird girl from Iran, albeit with hairless legs. Afsaneh was weird, too, but she didn't let it faze her. She even tried out for the cheerleading team, jumping up and down and spouting slogans she didn't even understand. Poor thing. She'd gained a little weight from all the junk food, so she wasn't exactly the picture of grace. I sat in the bleachers watching her, and I couldn't help but laugh. But before long the laughter turned to tears. She was trying too hard, and it wasn't working.

In a way, it's a pity people weren't more accepting of us. Afsaneh had always been a terrific athlete, but no one seemed particularly keen on exploring that side of her, and she lost her enthusiasm for sports. In Tehran, she had spent her free hours running from one athletic event to another, but here in America her talents were going to waste. She was bored, and she needed something to fill the hours. We were wandering around Military Circle Mall one day when she found the answer on the far side of the parking lot, at McDonald's. We had just ordered Big Macs and chocolate shakes when she saw the "Help Wanted" sign in the window. She filled out an application, not thinking much of it, and spoke briefly to the manager, who had a few questions for her. A few days later, the manager called and told her she had the job. We were amazed. This country was unbelievable. The fact that you could be sixteen years old, have a job, and make money was almost beyond our comprehension. Afsaneh rushed back to the house to share the good news with Dai'e Mammad and Naheed, but they were underwhelmed. "How do you think you're going to get to work?" Dai'e Mammad asked.

"I can drive with Naheed," Afsaneh said. "She's working at McCrory's from five to nine. I'll ask for that shift."

"You think they're going to give you any shift you ask for?" Naheed said.

"Let me try," Afsaneh said. "If the man at McDonald's says yes, will you take me to work?"

Naheed shrugged. She couldn't think of any reason not to.

A week later, Afsaneh had the job: five to nine, three days a week. I went to see her on her first day behind the counter, standing there at attention behind the cash register, like a little soldier. She had changed her name again, back to Amy. She liked the way it looked on the name tag. Three little letters, perfectly centered. She was wearing her little McDonald's outfit with its burgundy accents. She looked good, and she was very happy.

The next day, at school, she was telling everyone about the job, bragging. She said she would give extra fries to anyone who stopped in to see her. It was kind of sad, really. She was trying so hard to make friends.

The job was demanding, but she liked it, and she was proud of herself. The day she got her first paycheck, she walked across to McCrory's and bought herself a pair of plastic shoes for $7.99. When Naheed drove her home that night, she showed me the shoes. I thought they were totally hot.

By the second week, things had begun to deteriorate. The manager was making her clean the bathrooms, and she didn't enjoy it, but she did it without complaining. She complained to *me*. "The bathrooms stink, I can't breathe in there, and they give me this old, gray mop that's falling apart. And I have to keep running outside for fresh air, or I'll faint." She was back to her old self,

Princess Afsaneh, from Saltanat Abad. I didn't blame her. I wouldn't have been caught dead cleaning a toilet.

Still, Afsaneh wasn't a quitter, so she kept at it. By the fourth week, they asked her if she could come in on a Saturday, for another shift, and she agreed. She asked Dai'e Mammad if he could take her to work, but he refused. "I told you not to take that job," he said.

On Saturday morning, she got up early and asked again, but Dai'e Mammad was even more blunt: "This is your problem, not mine." She asked Nader, who was also home, lounging around with nothing to do, but he refused. It was as if they wanted to break her spirit. Still, Afsaneh wouldn't let them. It was almost nine miles from Tate Court to the mall, and she put on her uniform and left early. It was an unseasonably hot day, and it was especially hot in that nylon uniform and those new, plastic shoes, but Afsaneh pressed on. She just kept walking. Men in passing cars honked and hollered, but Afsaneh wouldn't even look at them. She thought they were trying to pick her up, until she remembered that she was wearing her little McDonald's cap. She realized it must look ridiculous, and she removed it, and the honking stopped. Maybe there were a lot of McDonald's fans in the area, and that had been their way of showing support.

By the time Afsaneh got to work, her plastic shoes had practically melted into her feet. "The first thing I did was go into the bathroom and try to bathe in the sink," she told me that night. "The soles of my feet were burning the whole day."

Before she left, she asked the manager if he would change her schedule. She didn't want to depend on Dai'e Mammad and Naheed, so she asked for straight shifts on the weekend. Shamsi's place was close to the mall, and she could walk from there, and she knew Shamsi would let us stay over on Saturday nights. From then on, we spent every weekend at Shamsi's, and, when Afsaneh was at work, I was either reading, or watching TV, or hanging out with Nasser and Angie, who had married and were expecting their first child. It wasn't a bad life.

Before long, however, the people at McDonald's began to take advantage of Afsaneh. They would make her come in at 5:00 A.M., open up the place, clean it, and have her out of there by seven, before the customers even arrived. That was her shift: two lousy hours at three dollars and sixty-five cents an hour.

Not even enough for a new pair of plastic shoes. So she quit. "This is bullshit," she said. "This isn't fair."

"So tell them to change it," I suggested.

"No," she replied. "I've worked hard, I'm good-natured, I always do what they ask without complaining—and this is how they treat me? No way. Screw McDonald's. I quit."

Shamsi came home and listened to the story. When it was over, she said, "How would you like to go to New York City with me next week?"

"Who?" Afsaneh asked.

"Both of you," she said. "I have an Afghani friend in Queens. I've never been. She wants me to come. She says I should think about moving there."

We were delighted. We had a family friend of our own in New York City: Mahsheed, the sister of Maryam, the neighbor from across the street in Tehran who had moved to Vienna with her husband, Forood.

We arrived in New York at dusk on a Friday, and I will never forget my first glimpse of the city. All those gleaming buildings! I had never seen anything like it. I thought the island would sink under their weight.

We stayed with Shamsi's friend in Queens that first night and didn't see much of New York. But the next day we got a ride to Mahsheed's place, on Seventy-fifth Street and Second Avenue, on the Upper East Side, and the adventure began. When we arrived at her building, a doorman announced us, which was of course very exciting, and, when we entered the apartment, I was struck mute by the view. They were on a very high floor, with floor-to-ceiling windows that looked south, toward Midtown. It was early evening, and the city was ablaze with lights. I stood at the window, openmouthed.

"Beautiful, isn't it?" Mahsheed said, coming to stand next to me. I couldn't answer. "Come. Eat something. I have a big day planned for you girls tomorrow!"

In the morning, we walked to Bloomingdale's. I loved just making my way along the sidewalks. The streets were teeming with people in all shapes, sizes, and colors. We were part of it. We looked like we belonged.

We walked into Bloomingdale's, and I thought I was dreaming. It was the most fantastic store I'd ever seen. (And yes, I know: I'm speaking in superlatives, but everything about New York City overwhelmed me, in the best possible sense of the word.) Pretty girls spritzed us with perfume as we entered.

Most of the shoppers ran away, but not me and Afsaneh. "More, please! Yes, I'd *love* to try that one, too."

Mahsheed bought me a pair of expensive red leather shoes, and Afsaneh picked out a gorgeous, sky blue dress, then we went off to visit the Empire State Building. In the elevator, on the way up to the observation deck, we must have heard seven different languages. And when we reached the top, Mahsheed pointed out the sights: Central Park, the South Street Seaport, the Statue of Liberty.

"Where's the Statue of Liberty?" I asked. "I can't see it."

"Don't worry," she said. "The day is young. You'll get a closer look."

She was right. In the afternoon, we took a helicopter tour of Manhattan. It was one of the most magical days of my life. I was in love with New York. I didn't want to leave.

The trip back was a total bummer.

"What's wrong with you two?" Shamsi asked.

"Nothing," Afsaneh said. "We don't want to go back to Dai'e Mammad's house. We hate it there."

"Why don't you come live with me?" she said. "Nasser and Angie are moving to Florida soon."

It was a nice offer, and we thought about it, briefly, but finally decided against it. The fact is, between Shamsi's puritanical streak, her penchant for giving orders, and her need to be right about absolutely everything—well, we didn't think it would be much of an improvement over life at Dai'e Mammad's. And in some ways it had the potential to be worse. At our uncle's place, nobody paid attention to us. Shamsi would have watched us like a hawk. ("No kissing on TV! Change the channel!") So we decided to muddle through at Tate Court, for the time being, anyway.

⁕ ⁕ ⁕

Academically, our second year went well: By December, we were on the Dean's List. Socially, we were at about the same place: nowhere.

The weekly phone calls with Mom continued, but they now seemed to carry less weight. I think we had forced ourselves to expect less from her and from life. We figured nothing was going to change in the foreseeable future and that we would simply have to make the best of a bad situation. We also knew that Mom had it much worse than we did and that we really had no right to complain or wallow in self-pity.

Still, in many ways, I feel as if I missed a huge part of my childhood. I feel, in fact, as if I never really had the freedom to be a kid. There were exceptions here and there, to be sure—Busch Gardens, the mall, that trip to New York City—but they were few and far between. And I missed the most critical part of being a kid: having a mother.

As a result, Afsaneh became my surrogate mother. In the morning, before school, she would try to fix my hair, which was long, straight, and didn't lend itself to anything terribly creative. When we got on the bus, Afsaneh always stood up for me: "Scoot over!" We always had lunch together—Twinkies and Fanta—and she was always waiting for me by the entrance when school let out in the middle of the afternoon.

By this time, Afsaneh's hormones had begun to rage, and she became increasingly maternal. She made it easy for me to fall into the role of the daughter, and she kept struggling to be a better mother. She wanted to rescue me and give me the life I deserved. She always seemed to be looking for a way out of our unhappy situation.

I remember a Saturday at the mall. We stopped to watch one of those low-rent fashion shows, staged as entertainment for the shoppers, and Afsaneh was decidedly unimpressed by the models. "Those girls are nothing special," she said. "I can do that."

When we got home that evening, she found the little camera Mom had given us before we left Vienna, and she put on a little fashion show, which I dutifully photographed. As she changed in and out of her uninspired, mismatched outfits, she told me that this time she really was going to change our lives. "I'll become a famous model. I'll make lots of money. We'll bring Mom and the boys to America and move into a nice house in Ghent." She looked ridiculous, with that permed hair and those silly costumes, and that crazy, full-lipped pout she directed at the camera, but deep down I was in awe of her. I wished I had that kind of self-confidence. I envied my sister her guts.

When we got the pictures back, we laughed as hard as we had ever laughed in our lives. Afsaneh looked as if she had just escaped from an asylum, and she knew it. We found ourselves rolling on the floor in hysterics. It was probably

163

the most fun we'd had in a year. It was better than Busch Gardens. Better than King's Dominion. It was *almost* as good as that trip to New York.

By this time, I was doing very well in school, and my love affair with literature continued. I had discovered Jane Austen, and I read her books slowly, savoring the words, not wanting the stories to end. There was always a lost, lonely girl in her novels, struggling mightily against an indifferent universe, and I felt that Jane Austen understood me. Reading her books filled me with hope.

That winter, just before Christmas, Afsaneh got a job at Merry-Go-Round, a clothing store at Military Circle Mall. The place catered to both men and women, and it was a little on the racy side. They sold leather jackets, miniskirts, and spandex tank tops in a variety of wild colors.

My uncle was very upset. "You can't work there!" he barked at Afsaneh. "I'll tell your mother."

"It's just a store," Afsaneh shot back. "What's going to happen?"

"It's *trash*. If I ever catch you in any of those outfits, I'm not letting you into my house."

Afsaneh didn't care. She went to work and fell in love with the job that very first day. Her manager was a black woman called Wanda, and she wanted to know absolutely everything about Afsaneh's life. So Afsaneh told her about Tehran, about Baba, and about Austria. Wanda was both moved and amazed by these stories, and she did everything she could to be accommodating. She let Afsaneh choose her own hours, and she even taught her how to work the customers.

Before long, Afsaneh discovered that she had a gift for sales. If someone tried on a pair of boots that were too tight, she had an answer: "They'll stretch. They're just right. You wouldn't even want the next size up." If they were too loose, she also had an answer: "Wear thick socks. It's like extra cushioning—like walking on air."

She got an hourly wage, plus commission, and, at the end of that second week, she got a check for seventy-three dollars. I was at the mall that day, reading in the food court, and she came running over after work, waving her check. "We're rich!" she shouted. The people at nearby tables probably assumed we had won the lottery.

Wanda cashed the check for her, and we wandered around the mall spending her money. We bought two skirts, a few pairs of socks, and T-shirts for each of us. Afsaneh wouldn't have dreamed of buying anything for herself without buying something for me first. Unfortunately, she thought—wrongly —that she had real fashion sense, and I often found myself stymied by her choices. But I deferred to her. In those days, I thought she knew better, too.

Still, I kept working on myself. From time to time, back at the house, I would ask Naheed if I could borrow one of her things. A sweater, say, or a pair of shoes. She would look at me with disgust, as if to suggest that only a low-class *dahati* would ask to borrow clothes, then grant permission as if she were cursing me: "Fine! Take what you want!" I couldn't help myself. I wanted to look good for school. Fashion was a big part of school, and I didn't want to be left out. I usually went for that preppy look, like the kids from Ghent. The polo shirts. The plaid skirts. That whole rich-but-conservative thing. Afsaneh, however, wanted to be hipper, and sometimes it misfired. One day she went to school in a hat she'd picked up on sale. It was black with a broad rim—the kind of hat older women with thick ankles wear to church. Needless to say, it was nowhere near as cool as Afsaneh had imagined. She never wore it again; the poor hat went the way of the cowboy boots.

Christmas came and went, and I found myself practically living at the mall. Afsaneh was working four or five days a week by now, and I always went with her. I would take books and schoolwork, hang out at the food court, and take breaks now and then to check out the stores. When Afsaneh broke for dinner, she'd come get me, and we'd grab a bite together.

In the spring, I finished reading *Emma*, which I found as deeply inspiring as the rest of Jane Austen's books, and I went back to the library for the next one. It was a very bleak day for me.

"What do you mean there aren't any other books by Jane Austen?" I asked the librarian. "What has she been doing?"

"Nothing," she said. "She's dead."

I was crushed. I had simply assumed that Jane Austen would be writing books for as long as I was around to read them. I had no idea she had lived and written in the previous century.

At the end of the school year, we were on the Dean's List again. I know it's hard to believe—especially when you consider my Jane Austen moment—but you can go back and check the records. As they say in America, the Latifi girls were kicking butt.

Afsaneh kept working at Merry-Go-Round, and Wanda increased her hours. She never worked on Tuesday mornings, however, because that was Dollar Day at the movies, and we had fallen in love with movies. We saw *Watcher in the Woods*, which starred Bette Davis. It was about a family with young girls who move to a country home where very strange things start happening. That's about all I remember, except that it was super scary. Nasser took us to see *Raiders of the Lost Ark*, which we all thought was fantastic. And one night Mrs. Ramsey invited us out to see *E.T.* She paid full price and took us for ice cream afterward.

At this point, with half the summer still ahead of us, I was desperate to get a job of my own. I thought this whole notion of young people making money was pretty wonderful. It was unheard of in Iran, at least in our circles. But I was only fourteen, and there weren't many jobs out there for kids my age, and most of those were taken. Then Shamsi told me about some Afghani friends who owned a little pizza parlor in Norfolk, and she took me out to meet them. They were very nice people, and all of them spoke Farsi. We chatted over a slice of pizza, and they offered me a job.

I had to take the bus from Dai'e Mammad's house to get to work. It wasn't that complicated—I didn't even have to transfer—but Dai'e Mammad didn't like the fact that I had a job, and he put the fear of God in me.

"Do you know how many girls get raped in this city every day?" he asked me.

"How many?" I asked, shaking.

"I don't know exactly, but *many, very many.*"

I didn't care. I desperately wanted that job. I got on the bus that first morning, put exact change in the coin box, and walked all the way to the back without making eye contact with any of the other passengers. I looked at my feet the whole way, listening for my stop as the driver called out the street names. When we arrived, I stood and waited at the doors. They opened with a pneumatic hiss, and I stepped out onto the sidewalk, looked up, and saw the pizza parlor in the middle of the block. I was so relieved! I had actually managed the trip on my own, and nothing bad had happened.

The Afghanis showed me how to make submarine sandwiches. Lettuce, tomatoes, onions, cold cuts, topped with a generous sprinkling of olive oil. I was their subway sandwich person. They also made gyros and pizza, so the place was part Italian, part Greek, and part American—which is probably as American as it gets.

The owners liked me. They were very supportive and always complimentary. "This is a perfect submarine sandwich, Afschineh! No one makes a better submarine sandwich!" At the end of my second week, I got my first paycheck and took the bus all the way to Military Circle Mall. I marched into Merry-Go-Round with the check in my hand. "Look at this!" I shouted at my sister, beaming. "Sixty dollars!"

Afsaneh took her break, and we went shopping. That was the day she told me all about this amazing thing called a layaway plan. I had never heard of anything so fantastic. If I wanted to buy a sixty-dollar dress, I only had to put twenty dollars down, and the store would let me pay off the balance over the next few weeks. That way, I could really stretch my paycheck. I was on the moon. Was there anything these fabulous Americans hadn't thought of?

In the weeks ahead, I started building an actual wardrobe. Afsaneh always went with me, still convinced of her superior sense of style, but I had begun to rebel by this time and made many of my own choices. In retrospect, I realize I didn't have much sense of style, either, but I didn't realize it at the time, which was a good thing. We were turning into a couple of American teenagers, a pair of genuine fashion plates.

Interestingly enough, Naheed didn't seem to enjoy our transformation, and before long she began to get competitive. She was now the night manager at McCrory's, making good money, and every so often she'd rush off to buy things that we couldn't afford. She would then show us what she'd purchased, and she'd always make a point of telling us exactly how much she'd paid: "One hundred and nineteen dollars and twenty-seven cents!" If the intention was to make us feel small, she succeeded.

"I hate it here," I told Afsaneh.

"You're right," she said. "Maybe we should move in with Shamsi."

"Not maybe. We're moving."

A few days later, she told Dai'e Mammad that we were moving out. "I don't understand," he said. "Why?"

"We just think we'd be happier at Shamsi's place," Afsaneh said, a tad too politely. "We feel we're underfoot here."

167

"But not at all!" our uncle protested. He looked genuinely pained, and it struck me that he wasn't a bad man and that perhaps he was being heavily influenced by his wife, Robabeh. Of course, this was only one possibility. There was also a chance he felt shame for having failed his sister. And still another possibility: Mom continued to send money from Tehran; it wasn't much, and it wasn't regular, but perhaps he had come to depend on it. "You have to stay here," he insisted.

It was very confusing. For two years he and his family had behaved as if they couldn't wait to get rid of us, and now he was begging us to stay.

"Shamsi has an extra room for us," Afsaneh noted.

"An extra room? That's nothing. I wasn't going to tell you this, but I'm in the process of buying a new house in Virginia Beach. It's a townhouse, much bigger than this place. And brand-new. It has three bedrooms upstairs and a fireplace in the living room."

He made it sound very convincing, so we waited it out. Two months later, we were living on Blackpoole Lane, in a section of Virginia Beach known as Bayside. We were still sharing a room with Naheed, but it was much larger than the last one. The townhouse was new and clean, and the fireplace worked, and, for some odd reason, this gave me hope.

In September, going into our third year in the United States, we transferred to Bayside High School. Afsaneh was a senior; I was a junior. The school was a step up from Maury High, with a larger number of middle-class kids, but I still felt like an outsider, and I still depended on Afsaneh for everything. We were taking the bus to school, and she was often late, and, if we missed the bus, I wouldn't go to school without her. I was too tied to her, and I knew it. It wasn't healthy. My dependence on her kept me from reaching out to other people, and as a result I remained reclusive and socially awkward. However, she was out there trying. Early in the year, she met and befriended a pudgy girl with braids named Dawn. She had her own car and invited us to a football game. We had never been to a football game, and Dai'e Mammad was reluctant to let us go. But Dawn came over and made a good impression, and he allowed it. We found ourselves sitting in the stands, watching the game, eating hot dogs.

We were way high up in the stadium, and it was hard to see, but it didn't really matter. I didn't understand the game. I saw these big boys chasing the ball up and down the field, and when our side cheered, I cheered. I had no idea what had happened on the field or why I was cheering, but it felt good, and I kept it up all night. I felt like part of something larger than myself; I felt like a real American.

On the way back home, we stopped at a 7-Eleven. I had a Big Gulp and a Hostess blueberry pie. Mom would never have allowed us to eat such food, but she wasn't there, and we were in America and trying to be as American as possible. If it took Big Gulps and Hostess pies and Twinkies, we were willing to make the necessary sacrifices, even if it showed on our hips.

Afsaneh still thought she was going to become a model, and I did nothing to disabuse her of the notion. I didn't know exactly what I wanted for myself, but I often lost myself in books and fantasized about being rescued by a handsome, sexless prince who was just nice to me. That's all: *nice*. Sex was not part of our vocabulary. If it existed at all, it existed in another part of our minds. We had compartmentalized sex. I wasn't even ready to try to figure out what it might mean. We talked about boys, sure, but it never went beyond some remark about their looks: "He's cute. He has nice eyes." We were über-virgins. Meanwhile, the rest of the girls were coming to school in tight sweaters and short skirts that left nothing to the imagination. If that's what it took to fit in, it didn't look like we were ever going to.

I remember buying a tube of inexpensive lip gloss at the mall, going into the restroom, and trying it on. I studied my reflection in the mirror and smacked my lips together, the way I'd seen my mother do years ago. I thought I looked pretty good. But when we got home Dai'e Mammad took one look at me and barked: "What are you? A cheap girl? A loose girl?" It would be a year before I had the courage to try again, and by then my life had taken a number of dizzying turns.

That fall, Farhad, the wayward son, returned from Los Angeles without a music contract. He was in his late twenties and definitely a little strange. He wandered around the house playing air guitar and laughing out of context, but he ended up being the nicest member of that entire clan. "Don't trust my family!" he would say, whispering furtively. "They're complete psychos. Stay away from them." In the end, we decided he had a point. He was the only sane member of his family.

On January 16, 1984, I celebrated my fifteenth birthday, though "celebrated" is probably the wrong word. I woke up in the morning, Afsaneh wished me a happy birthday, and we got ready for school. She was on time that day, which was a present in and of itself.

On the way to school, I remember thinking about our lives. We had been in the United States for two and a half years, without our mother, and we were making do. But we seldom talked about our situation: The things we felt most deeply remained largely unsaid and unexplored. We probably knew we couldn't handle it.

Afsaneh continued to work, and I lost myself in books. And sometimes at night we'd study together or plop down in front of the television. We tried to catch every episode of *The Brady Bunch*. It was on every night. We were in love with the entire family: Marsha, Jan, Cindy, Greg, Peter, and Bobby.

Florence Henderson was a perfect mother, and every night, for a little while, she was *our* mother. I thought it would be lovely to someday have a family just like that, where everyone was happy and all of their problems were neatly resolved at the end of the half hour. How wonderful! Even when the kids fought, they always made up at the end, wisely acknowledging their respective roles in the misunderstanding. We were so naive that for a time we almost believed the Bradys were a real family. I guess that's a measure of how much we wanted to believe. We didn't even realize we were watching reruns.

Looking back on those years, I'm still sort of amazed that we got through them. We knew very little about America. Our exposure to the country had been limited and superficial, and it remained so for many years. Everything seemed unreal, as if we weren't a part of it. Even the school seemed somehow fictional because we relied largely on each other and communicated almost exclusively with each other. We felt shut out. There were no doors opening, no one reaching out to befriend us.

And the house on Blackpoole Lane was even worse. We had gone there with great hope, but the neglect was really getting to us. If I got good grades, nobody cared. And if our uncle expressed concern about our going to a football game or riding a bus to work, it didn't come from his heart. Everything seemed designed to keep us from having a good time or from evolving.

I could talk only to my sister, and with her, as I've said, only about certain subjects. We could not talk about the past, and we could not talk about the future. We were here, now. It was about living in the present. In that sense, by default, we were very Zen.

"Everything is great, Mom. The new house is really nice."

"I can't wait to see it."

I wouldn't even acknowledge that last remark. Why bother? She'd tell us she was coming and cancel at the last moment. Then one day she called with good news: Her best friend, Sabi, was on her way to Virginia, and she was really looking forward to seeing us. Sabi, as you may recall, had been a neighbor in Saltanat Abad, with her husband and two young children. She had been in California, visiting a niece, and she was on her way to Virginia to see Shamsi, with whom she would be staying. "She's going to call you the minute her plane lands," my mother promised.

Sure enough, two days later Shamsi phoned to tell us she was on her way to the airport to fetch Sabi, and we went over as soon as they returned to the apartment. We really loved this woman—she had been like a sister to Mom—and she treated us as if we were her own family. She was full of life and energy, and the first thing she did was take us to the mall. She bought us tons of stuff—dresses, shoes, blouses—then took us to Piccadilly's, a cafeteria-style chain. "Okay," she said, plunging in before we'd even sat down with our food. "I want to know exactly what's going on." She didn't beat around the bush. It wasn't her style. She had always been very direct. "I'm on a fact-finding mission. I need to know how they're treating you."

Clearly, despite our best efforts to keep things to ourselves, Mom had sensed something during the weekly phone calls, and she had sent Sabi as an emissary to get the truth. So we told her the truth. We told her everything. We told her that we had gone to Busch Gardens and King's Dominion during our first month and that we'd had the time of our lives. And we told her that things had quickly gone downhill from there. Now, three years later, we'd become the ugly stepsisters. We lived in a house where we were unloved and unwelcome and where we were reminded of it on a regular basis.

Sabi was stunned. Neither she nor my mother had had any idea of just how bad things were. They knew it had to be difficult for us, two young girls from Iran, thousands of miles from home, but they had never imagined anything like this.

"Why didn't you say anything?" Sabi asked.

"Because we didn't want to upset Mom," Afsaneh said. "We knew she was struggling, and we didn't want her to worry. We wanted her to be strong and do what she needed to do so that she and the boys could come and join us."

Sabi sat there for a few moments, trying to process the information. "I have to tell your mother," she said finally.

"No," Afsaneh said, "we'll manage."

"But this isn't right," she said.

I almost wept. For the first time in years, an adult was listening to us, acknowledging what we had gone through and were still going through.

"What is it, Afschineh?" she asked me.

"Nothing," I said, fighting tears, "I'm just glad we told you."

"I *have* to tell your mother," she repeated. "She's under the impression that her brother is taking very good care of you."

Two nights later, Dai'e Mammad had a small dinner party to welcome Sabi to Virginia. It was truly pathetic. He kept telling her what a pleasure it was to have us in his home, two wonderful girls, so bright and helpful and such good students. "We have a lot of fun together," he said, and he repeated it over and over again. But Sabi knew better. She kept exchanging little looks with me and Afsaneh, as if to say, *Don't worry. I know what he's up to. He doesn't fool me.*

For the next few days, we spent as much time as possible with Sabi. It was almost painful. She acted like a mother and asked us the types of questions one expects from a mother: "How are you doing in school? Is that the new fashion? Who are your friends? What are your favorite classes? What are you reading? Are you doing sports?" We had been living without love or support for such a long time that we really didn't know how to handle it. *So this is what it's like!* I remember thinking. *This is what it means to be loved.*

And then of course it ended. Abruptly. Sabi got on a plane and went home, and we were alone again—more alone than ever.

ME AND AFSANEH WITH SABI, DURING HER VISIT

AFSANEH AND THAT INFAMOUS PROM DRESS

OUR TRIP TO WASHINGTON

CHAPTER ELEVEN

The Visit

MOM AND SHAMSI

Shortly before we moved to Blackpoole Lane, in the winter of 1984, I left my job at the pizza place—it was too hard to get there from Bayside—and began looking around for something else. Afsaneh was still working at Merry-Go-Round, and she always shared every last penny with me, but it wasn't the same as having a job of my own. I missed the feeling of independence that came from making a little money.

In March, I got lucky. Nader was working at a local steakhouse, and one of the women who ran the place, Eva, was looking for a babysitter. I went over to the restaurant to meet her, and we liked each other right away. I admitted that I didn't have much experience—my only professional babysitting job had been for a local Persian woman who lived near Dai'e Mammad's new home in Bayside—but she smiled and said she didn't mind. She asked if I could start that weekend.

On Saturday night, Eva picked me up at my uncle's, and we went over to her place to meet Elena, her seven-year-old daughter. The minute I arrived, Elena took me by the hand and showed me around the lovely condo. She had a modest doll collection, and for a moment I remembered my own room in Saltanat Abad.

When we returned to the living room, Eva told me to help myself to anything I wanted and suggested I order dinner from a fancy restaurant down the street. She had an account there, and they delivered.

Then her boyfriend, Dennis, showed up in his brown Mercedes, and she kissed Elena good night and hurried off. Elena and I played cards, watched television, and ordered a terrific dinner, and, shortly after eight o'clock, I put her to bed. When Eva got back, I told her that everything had gone well and that Elena was a perfect angel, and she thanked me, paid me, and told me that Dennis was waiting outside to drive me home.

The next time I went over, a few nights later, Eva said I could either order from the same place or take Elena out to dinner. There were several restaurants within walking distance of the condo. She left money on the kitchen counter, then hurried off. It was pretty wonderful. I always looked forward to seeing Eva and Elena. Plus Eva was paying me seven dollars an hour, which was almost twice the minimum wage. It was incredibly generous of her. She could have hired someone in the building or a girl from the neighborhood, but she had heard a few details about my life from Nader, and it was clear that she was doing this from her heart.

Eva didn't need me the following weekend, and on Sunday, when Afsaneh wasn't working, we went over to Shamsi's place and hung out with Nasser, Angie, and their baby girl, Nassim. Angie didn't feel like cooking, so we went out to Chuck E. Cheese for dinner. There was a guy at that branch who used to come out and sing to the kids, and I would always sing along, often with more fervor than the other children. It was a little odd, admittedly; here I was, fifteen years old, going on sixteen, and I was belting out tunes as if my life depended on it. I'm sure a therapist would have had something to say about that.

After dinner we went to Flipper McCoy's, an arcade—Pac-Man was a big favorite—and late in the evening Afsaneh and I got dropped back at the house on Blackpoole Lane. I remember that night very clearly. It was maybe a few minutes after eleven, lights were burning inside, and we made our way to the front door and rang the bell. We didn't have a key to the house: We'd been living with Dai'e Mammad for three years, but he still didn't trust us with a key. There was no answer. We rang again, and there was still no answer. So I walked around to the side of the house, and I could see Naheed and Dai'e Mammad in the kitchen, playing cards. It was really strange. Why weren't they answering? For a moment I was almost sure that Naheed had looked up and seen me.

"Maybe the bell isn't working," I told Afsaneh, and we knocked loudly. Still nothing. We knocked again. There was no way they couldn't have heard us. "Afsaneh," I said, stating the obvious, "they're not opening the door."

Afsaneh looked angry. "Screw them," she said. "Let's go."

"Where?"

"To Maryam's," she said.

Maryam was the Persian woman for whom I'd done a little babysitting. She had two kids and lived only a few blocks away. Her husband was still trapped in Iran, trying to get out.

"Why didn't he open the door?" I asked.

"I don't know," Afsaneh said. "Maybe he's punishing us because he doesn't like Shamsi, Nasser, and Angie."

"That's not our fault."

"No," she said, "but maybe he thinks we're showing disrespect by spending so much time with them."

We stopped talking about it, both of us suddenly spooked by the dark streets and the long shadows, and made the rest of the trip in nervous silence. When we got to Maryam's, we rang the bell, and a moment later a light went on inside, and she opened the door in her bathrobe, clearly roused from sleep and visibly startled. "What happened?" she said. "What's wrong? Is someone hurt?"

It was an awkward moment for us. In Persian society, you do not air your dirty laundry. Even under the most trying circumstances, you do everything you can to save face. It was hard to know what to tell Maryam or how much to share with her, especially since we really didn't know her very well. But what choice did we have? And Afsaneh was angry. Dai'e Mammad was always playing the martyr in front of his Persian friends: "Look at me. Look what a great guy I am. I take such good care of my sister's daughters, and I do it without complaining." She wanted Maryam to know the truth. "Our uncle locked us out of the house," she said.

"What do you mean?" Maryam said. "What did you do? Did you do something bad?"

"No."

"Tell me the truth, girls."

"No," Afsaneh repeated, "not at all. We've *never* done anything bad. Maybe we came home a little later than usual, but that was all. And he was still awake. He and Naheed knew we were at the front door. They could see us through the window. He just did it to be mean."

I started crying. I don't know why, exactly. I think I was overwhelmed because my sister was standing up for me.

Maryam was suddenly livid. "Well, I'm going to call him right now," she said. "I'm going to get to the bottom of this."

"No," Afsaneh said. "I'd rather spend the night here. Let him think about what he's done."

At seven the following morning, Maryam made us a nice breakfast and drove us back to our uncle's house. She rang the doorbell, and Dai'e Mammad opened the door very matter-of-factly. "Where the hell have you been?" he asked.

Maryam interceded before Afsaneh could say anything. "Why don't you girls get your books and get ready for school?" We did as we were told, but we stopped at the top of the stairs to listen, and their voices reached us from the kitchen. Maryam was respectful but firm. "What kind of man are you to turn away two young girls that you're supposed to be caring for?" she asked.

"Turn them away? I don't know what you're talking about. I didn't hear the bell."

At this point, Afsaneh couldn't contain herself, and she ran downstairs to confront him. "That's a lie!" she shouted. "We rang the bell three times, and then we banged on the door."

"I didn't hear anything," Dai'e Mammad insisted.

And Maryam said, "If you feel you can't take care of these two girls, call their mother and tell her so. But don't pretend you're taking care of them when you're not doing so."

That was the beginning of the cold war. For the next week, we didn't even talk to one another, and Afsaneh and I fended for ourselves in the kitchen, after they were done with dinner. On Saturday, we went over to Shamsi's and told her what had happened, and she picked up the phone and insisted that we call Mom right away. We didn't argue. We called her and told her exactly what had happened, and she was very upset. "I'll be there this summer," she said. "I promise. I'll straighten everything out the moment I get there."

I didn't want to believe that she was really coming, so I tried not to think about it. But a few weeks later we found out that someone else was coming: Robabeh. She and Fareed, the youngest son, had made it out of Iran and into Germany, and more recently had landed in Toronto. They had been waiting in Toronto for the American consulate to approve their visa applications, and at long last the American consulate had come through. For Robabeh, anyway;

Fareed would have to wait. This was terrible news. Even Afsaneh refused to soft-pedal this one. "If you think things have been bad until now, wait till she gets here," she said. I couldn't believe she would be so blunt. This was my big sister, the one person I could look to for support, and she was basically telling me to brace myself for the days and weeks ahead.

She was right. From the moment Robabeh arrived, the family meetings started. They would take place in the master bedroom, and they were always about us. Robabeh had a tight, pinched voice, but she could make it carry if she wanted to, and during these family powwows she certainly wanted to: "Well, Mammad, you need to talk to their mother. This is ridiculous. This has gone on long enough. We have lives and a family of our own. These girls need to be gone."

On some level, young as I was, I knew she had a point. We had overstayed our welcome long ago, and, now that she had finally made it to America, the house felt very crowded. Their family was one member shy of being reunited. They wanted to get on with their lives. But we were family, too. And it's not as if we had any options. Without them, we were truly on our own. This was the part she was unable to acknowledge: that we had nowhere to go, that we were without recourse. And if she was aware of it, she certainly didn't care. She would look at us with such hatred that we dreaded coming home from school. It was asphyxiating. We lived in a house where we weren't wanted, and, at least two or three times a week, at Robabeh's insistence, the family would congregate to discuss the problem, loudly and at length: "You really must do something, Mammad! I can't take another day with them in the house."

Afsaneh found relief at work, and I looked forward to the nights when Eva needed me to care for Elena. But at the end of the day, this was our home, and it was the only home we had. Every time I returned from school, my stomach would act up before I had even set foot in the house. And the moment I stepped through the door, I had to brace myself for the night ahead. There was no escape. Robabeh went out of her way to make things as unbearable as possible, and she succeeded. She told us what to eat and what not to eat. What time to go to bed. How much water to use. And whenever mail arrived from Mom, Robabeh always got to it first and took it upon herself to review it.

At around this time, as if that wasn't enough, Afsaneh found herself with a problem on her hands at school. She was a senior, only a matter of months from graduation, and she had heard the other kids talking about the various colleges they would be attending or hoping to attend. Afsaneh hadn't applied to college because she didn't understand the system, and no one had bothered to tell her about it, not even at home. When she turned to Naheed for advice, Naheed told her she shouldn't even bother, since she had almost certainly missed the deadline.

The previous year, she had taken her SAT along with the rest of her class, but she hadn't really understood the implications. I, too, had taken a version of the same test—the PSAT—and I had been equally clueless about what it meant. I was too embarrassed to ask anyone, of course, until the morning of the test, when I was ushered into the cafeteria with hundreds of other kids. "What are we doing here?" I asked a girl next to me. She looked at me like I was a moron. "We're taking the PSATs," she said. "You blow this, you don't get into college."

I still didn't have a clue, and my understanding of English remained pretty basic. But I sat down, and I read the questions and darkened the little circles in pencil, as I'd been told to do, and, not surprisingly, I scored very badly indeed. Afsaneh hadn't done much better, and her test carried serious weight. If she'd been expecting NASA to send for her, it wasn't going to happen. Still, she wasn't going to let this stop her. There were two local universities: Norfolk State University and Old Dominion University (ODU). She decided to apply to ODU since she had heard it was the better school, but they told her she had missed the deadline and suggested she apply for the following term. She filled out her application on the spot, then went over to Norfolk State and begged them to let her start in September. They bent the rules a little, and she was in. She figured she could transfer into ODU after one semester and that this would keep her from falling behind. Now she told them that she didn't have any money, and they explained that she could apply for student aid. They pointed her in the direction of the financial aid office. "Can you believe this?!" she said later. "The day classes start, they're going to cut me a check. They're actually giving me money to go to college. Me, a little nobody! This country is amazing." It would be just enough to cover tuition and books, along with a minimal allotment for living expenses, but there was something wonderful and miraculous about it. If you wanted an education in America, all you had to do was ask.

The biggest problem now was going to be transportation. Between college and work, Afsaneh couldn't depend on public transportation, so she went off and got her driver's license without telling anyone but me. She then called Mom and told her to ask Dai'e Mammad to use his contacts to help her find a cheap used car. She had saved seven hundred dollars, and she was sure it would be enough. Dai'e Mammad hemmed and hawed. He played the role of the concerned uncle, noting how dangerous it was to drive in America, but he finally caved in. One of his associates found a boxy little thing called Le Car made by Renault, and I went to the lot with Afsaneh to pick it up. It was bright yellow and looked like something out of an amusement park, but it worked. We were both grinning like idiots as she pulled into the street.

A few weeks later, with the academic year drawing to a close, a handsome black guy asked Afsaneh to the prom. She accepted immediately—she was thrilled; she knew how much the prom meant to her fellow seniors—and she decided she was going to do it right. She went to Thalheimer's, a hot local department store that has since gone out of business, and spent a hundred and twenty dollars on a dress. It was incredibly ugly. It was this frilly little taffeta number, worn off the shoulder, with colored, horizontal stripes. When Afsaneh tried it on for me, she did that little pouty thing with her lips, like she used to do for the camera in the days when she thought she was going to become a famous fashion model.

"What do you think?" she asked.

"I'd rather not say," I replied.

"Good," she said. "Very smart."

That night, when our aunt and uncle heard about the prom, they tried to disallow it on moral grounds. "What kind of girl goes to the prom?" Dai'e Mammad asked. Then he answered his own question: "Loose girls go to the prom, that's what kind."

"You're wrong," Afsaneh said. "The prom is an American tradition, and we're in America. I'm going."

Robabeh was about to add her two cents, but Afsaneh wouldn't let her. "Why don't we stop this charade?" she said. "You don't care about me, and I don't really think you care about me going to the prom." And that, as they say, was that.

In the weeks leading up to the prom, Afsaneh and I would watch *Soul Train* and *American Bandstand* on TV and practice the steps. We were such geeks! When the big day finally arrived, her date showed up, and I opened the door and invited him into the house. Then Afsaneh came down the stairs in her horrible taffeta dress, and he was either too polite to say anything, or he didn't think the dress was all that horrible. She said hello, and he said hello, then he put a corsage on her wrist, and they went on their merry way. Dai'e Mammad and Robabeh were home, but they didn't even bother seeing them off. I thought that was kind of sad.

I stayed awake, waiting for her to return from the party, and she arrived a little before midnight. She came upstairs, changed, and told me all about it. She said the guy had been a really good dancer, and she told me what everyone was wearing. "It was fun," she said. "Next year, when you go, I'll show you the ropes."

"I'm not going," I said. "Nobody's going to ask me."

"Don't be silly," she said. "You're beautiful."

I didn't know how to respond. It had been a long time since anyone had told me I was beautiful. And I certainly didn't *feel* beautiful. I knew my sister was trying to be kind, but I felt awkward and self-conscious. I wasn't used to kindness. "You're just saying that," I said, and I left the room. I didn't know how to deal with my feelings. Everything was jumbled and confused.

❋ ❋ ❋

Suddenly it was the summer of 1984. Michael Jackson's *Thriller* album was the big album of the year. I couldn't get "Beat It" out of my head. I used to sing it in the shower, with my Iranian accent, an accent I knew I was never going to get rid of.

On the political front, which I was only marginally aware of and which I found boring in the extreme, President Reagan and Vice President Bush were again running for office, and Walter Mondale surprised everyone by picking Geraldine Ferraro as his running mate.

I was still babysitting two or three nights a week, and Afsaneh still had her job at Merry-Go-Round. But that July she took a second job working the coat check at Big Apple, a rowdy nightclub, because she knew she was going to have to cut back on her hours as soon as college started, and she needed every penny she could scrape together.

Sometimes, on the weekends, we'd get up early in the morning, Nair our legs, drive down to Virginia Beach, and spend the day on the sand. I had my learner's permit by that time, and occasionally Afsaneh would let me drive Le Car, though never on the freeway. If we stayed into the evening, the beach streets became like a scene out of *American Graffiti*. Kids would cruise along the strip, checking one another out, and we cruised right along with them, giggling. I don't know what we thought we were doing. Neither of us had ever kissed a boy, and I know I didn't even want to. The last time I'd been kissed by a strange boy had been back in Iran, at the Jewish school, when I was six, and I'd been mildly traumatized by the experience. I wasn't ready to get over it yet, nor would I be for a number of years.

In early July, Mom called to announce that she was coming to see us the following week. She said she hadn't said anything earlier because she wanted to make sure it was really going to happen, and she could tell us now, unequivocally, that it was really going to happen. She was leaving the boys with Khaleh Mali, and we would have her all to ourselves. "I can't wait to see you," she said. "I have been dreaming of this day for three years."

We had been dreaming of it, too, but neither of us fully believed it. I was very pessimistic where my mother was concerned. I was convinced that something would go wrong at the last minute. I remembered leaving Tehran, four years earlier; remembered her words when the plane finally lifted off. "Now we are on our way," she had said. Now we are on our way.

But nothing went wrong. She called us from John F. Kennedy Airport in New York to tell us she had arrived and was about to board the connecting flight to Norfolk. Even then I found it hard to believe. We had just spoken to Mom. It had been a domestic call. We heard American voices in the background. She was on her way to Virginia. But it *still* wasn't real.

An hour later, Afsaneh and I were on our way to the airport, wearing our nicest dresses. Dai'e Mammad, Robabeh, and Naheed insisted on tagging along, as did Shamsi. We were trying not to get excited, but at this point we had both turned into true believers. By the time we reached the airport, I was walking on air. Then the plane landed, and I had a moment of doubt and pain. I thought for sure she wouldn't be on it, that she had somehow managed to miss her flight. I looked over at Afsaneh, and I saw the horror and doubt in her face, too. "She's not coming," Afsaneh said.

I turned to look at the gate as the passengers began to emerge from the plane. They kept coming, one after another, but there was no sign of Mom. I felt as if I would crack from the tension, then suddenly there she was. I let out a huge sob, ran to her, hugged her, and practically knocked her down. Afsaneh joined us. The three of us sobbed, hugged, and jumped up and down with such fervor that I was having trouble catching my breath.

"My God," my mother said, tears streaming down her cheeks. "Look how big you've gotten! You've turned into young ladies! And look: You've both cut your hair. Look how grown up you've become. I can't believe it! My two little girls. Where has the time gone!"

Dai'e Mammad drove us back to the house, with Mom squeezed between me and Afsaneh. We were making small talk—"How was your trip? How are the boys? Any progress on the visa front?"—and I found myself immensely irritated by the meaningless chatter. Didn't these people understand? This was my *mother*! I had been dreaming of being held by my mother for three years, and they were ruining it!

When we arrived at the house, the charade kicked into high gear. Dai'e Mammad played the role of the wonderful brother with such conviction that Laurence Olivier himself would have been impressed. "These girls are wonderful girls. And good students, too. I must admit that I had some doubts at first, what with all the television watching, but they proved me wrong. Didn't you?" On and on it went, until he was running out of adjectives to describe our wonderfulness, and finally Mom begged off, saying she was tired. She, Afsaneh, and I took refuge in the bedroom. Now the crying began in earnest. I wouldn't let go of her and neither would Afsaneh. The three of us squeezed into one twin bed, with our mother in the middle. I was seven years old all over again.

In the morning, the charade continued. We had breakfast with Dai'e Mammad and his family, and some of their Persian friends began dropping by to meet Mom, whom they'd been hearing about for years. We didn't have her to ourselves for a moment.

That night, they had a big dinner in her honor. More Persians arrived, including Maryam, whose house we had fled to when our uncle locked us out, and Shamsi, the archenemy. Mom was served first, of course, as the guest of honor, and Afsaneh and I were next, the little princesses. "Such smart, good girls, these two!" Dai'e Mammad repeated. Smart? How would he know? He had never once asked to look at a report card.

For the next two days, we couldn't get away from these people, so we had to steal a minute here and there. We told her about our teachers. We showed her our report cards. Afsaneh described the prom, her date, and the dancing. We showed Mom our bare legs and the bottle of Nair.

"Look," I said. "Feel my leg. Isn't it smooth?"

"Very nice," she said. "But what about school? I want to hear more about school."

So Afsaneh told her all about college, the premed courses she would be taking, and the loans that had been promised to her.

It wasn't until that weekend that we were finally able to get away from the others. We piled into Le Car and drove to Shamsi's house, just Mom, me, and Afsaneh, and the moment we got there she said, "Okay, I need to know what's going on."

As it turned out, Sabi had gone to see Mom as soon as she got back to Tehran, and she had told her that she was going to have to go to Virginia to deal with certain things. She hadn't wanted to scare her, of course, so she was very low-key about it, but she stressed that it was important for her to make the trip. And here was Mom now. She had seen the falseness at her brother's house and the tension, and she could see that the situation was even worse than Sabi had let on.

So we told her everything. It all came pouring out of us. The way we were being mistreated. The family conferences. The discussions about how to get rid of us. The total lack of support. The night we were locked out. We were completely honest with her, and it was painful because we could see we were upsetting her, and at long last we decided she'd heard enough. She was at a loss. Usually, when Mom was troubled by anything, she adopted a serious tone and—in a flat, emotionless voice—never failed to remind us that things could be worse. *Zendegi meetoone badtar bashe.* But this time she said nothing; she was rendered speechless. She was our mother, and she desperately wanted to fix this problem, but she didn't know where to begin. Our lives were complicated. We were not people with many options.

186

Then Nasser showed up, smiling broadly, unaware of what we had been discussing, and made an announcement. "I just rented a big car," he said. "We're going on a road trip. I want you guys to see Washington, D.C. It's an amazing city."

The next morning, we were on our way. Mom and Afsaneh, Nasser and Angie and their young daughter, and Shamsi and me. And Nasser was right about Washington. He took us to see all the important sites. The Washington Monument. The White House. The Lincoln Memorial. Arlington National Cemetery. We had lunch and walked along the Mall and, for some strange reason I couldn't understand, I felt immensely proud.

Then Nasser decided we should go to Long Island. He had a friend there who said we could stay with him. And we went. And we walked around and ate pizza, and at one point I found myself strolling along the beach with my mother, holding her hand, and I felt almost unhinged with happiness.

On the ride back, there was talk of visiting New York City, but Mom decided that this was too much. She wanted to get back to Virginia. And on the drive home I literally crawled onto my mother's lap and held her tight. She wouldn't be leaving for several days, but already I had begun to miss her. At one point Shamsi turned in her seat and looked at me disapprovingly. "Afschineh, this is ridiculous! You are a grown woman, and you weigh a lot. Stop suffocating your mother."

"No, no," my mother said "It's okay. We're fine." And she held me all the way from Williamsburg to Virginia Beach.

We returned to the "House of Horrors," but in the morning and in the days that followed, we spent most of our time away from it, with Mom, driving her around the city. She wanted to get a feel for our lives, so we drove her past the high school and the two universities and then to Military Circle Mall to show her where Afsaneh worked. We told her about the job at McDonald's and about the long walk in the hot sun, the honking horns, and the way Afsaneh's plastic shoes had practically melted into her feet. But we were able to laugh about it this time.

We went shopping. She needed presents for the boys, and she ended up buying four of those wild, Michael Jackson, *Thriller*-style jackets with zippers everywhere. Two for Ali and Amir, and two for Sabi's kids. Then we stopped by Merry-Go-Round, and she met Wanda, the manager, who told her that

188

THE "THRILLER CRAZE" HAD SPREAD WORLDWIDE. ALI AND AMIR LOVED THE
MICHAEL JACKSON JACKETS AND T-SHIRTS MOM BROUGHT HOME—SO MUCH
SO THAT THEY TRIED TO DANCE LIKE HIM, TOO.

Afsaneh was the greatest saleswoman ever and a wonderful person, too. And
when we left the mall, we drove to the steakhouse, so she could meet Eva and
hear some nice things about me, too.

At the end of the day, she appeared somewhat relieved. "I'm glad to see
that there are some good things in your lives," she said. "Not everything is
good, and I understand that, but there is *some* good. And I promise you that
there are more good things to come. I am working very hard to get the boys
out of Iran. I want us to be a family again."

As the time for her to leave drew closer, the speeches started. "You have to
study hard. Don't forget what your father said: 'Studying is the most important thing.' No one can ever take that away from you. You are smart kids. All
four of my kids are very smart. You will all become doctors, I know it. You will
open a clinic. The Latifi Clinic. And it will be so wonderful that people will
come from all over the world just to be treated by a Latifi."

I began to cry. I couldn't help myself. "Be like a nail!" she said. "That's the way of the Latifis. Every blow makes us stronger."

The night before Mom left, we were in the garage, helping her pack. In the course of her visit, she had listened carefully to everything we said, and she had asked us many questions, but she hadn't uttered a single bad word about Dai'e Mammad or Robabeh. That's just the way she was. Mom never said anything bad about anyone. She was old-school: If you don't have anything nice to say, say nothing at all. But on this night, she just couldn't help herself. She began to mimic Robabeh's pinched voice and the way she nodded her head, like a little puppet. "What on earth will we do?! One can't find a decent tomato in this country! And the spices are simply unacceptable! How can these people live like this?" Afsaneh and I were doubled over with laughter. We were rolling around on the garage floor.

But an hour later we were all in bed, and I was dreading her departure. "Don't worry," she said, kissing me good night. "I'm selling the house. I'm selling everything. The boys and I will be here next year."

Mom crawled into bed, and she was crying quietly, hoping we wouldn't hear. But how could we not hear? She was a few feet away. After a while, she fell silent, and I could hear her faint, rhythmic breathing. I couldn't sleep. I looked across the room and saw that Afsaneh was awake, too. "Why did she have to come?" I whispered. "I wish she hadn't come at all. Now she's leaving, and I feel worse than ever. I don't think I'll survive." I didn't realize Mom was still awake, didn't realize she had heard every word.

The next morning, we drove to the airport in silence, all three of us numb. I held Mom's hand the whole way. I really didn't know how I would go on without her. Shamsi, Nasser, Naheed, and Dai'e Mammad also came to see her off.

We arrived, parked, got to the terminal, and checked in. And then it was time for her to go. The plane was boarding, but we sat there with Mom between us, holding her hands, refusing to let go. Finally she stood and gathered her things. It was just heart-wrenching. I didn't want her to leave, and she could see I was on the verge of falling apart. She looked at me hard. "Don't cry," she said. "You are the daughter of a soldier." By this time, all the passengers had boarded, and the ticket agent, a young man, was looking in our direction.

"Ma'am?" he called out. "We're waiting on you."

Afsaneh burst into tears. "Please don't go," she said. She was crying so hard that she swooned, lost her balance, fell to the carpet, and refused to get up. Mom tried to help her to her feet and lost it. Then I lost it. Then even Dai'e Mammad fell apart. We were crying so hard that people en route to neighboring gates felt compelled to stop and stare. The young ticket agent came out from behind the counter, trying to be helpful. "Now, now," he said, gently. "It's not that bad. She's only going to New York."

"That's not true!" Afsaneh said, bawling. "You don't understand!"

I was bawling, too. "We haven't seen her in three years, and now she's going back to Tehran, and she says she's coming back, but what if she never comes back?!"

Suddenly the ticket agent was crying, too. It was bedlam. At long last, two flight attendants came out and led Mom down the ramp, onto the waiting plane. She was still bawling.

I don't remember how Afsaneh and I made it to the parking lot. I just remember sitting in the car, sobbing, with Afsaneh next to me, sobbing even more loudly. I felt I would never recover. I felt I had lost a piece of my heart forever.

We went back to the House of Horrors, crushed. Afsaneh had to work that afternoon, and she went to the mall, alone. I had nothing. I didn't want to see anyone. So I lay in bed, staring at the ceiling.

The next day I went to the Bayside Public Library and asked if they had any work for me. I was an experienced book-shelver. I needed to keep busy. They didn't have anything just then, so I checked out a handful of books, went back to Blackpoole Lane, and hid in my room for a week. Then one morning the phone rang. It was the Bayside Public Library. One of the girls had quit, and they wanted to know if I was still available.

I went back to shelving books three afternoons a week, and I distracted myself by leafing through the more interesting ones. There was a company called Chilton that had a series of books on car repair, with crazy titles like *Your Pinto from A to Z.* I don't know why I was so fascinated by these books. They were filled with photos of car engines, and with drawings of pistons, carburetors, and whatnot, and with long passages about how everything worked. I didn't understand a word, but I still remember telling Afsaneh to let me know if Le Car started acting up. "You have nothing to worry about. We can check out one of those books and fix it ourselves."

In September, I went back for my senior year at Bayside High, and Afsaneh started classes at Norfolk State. She didn't like Norfolk State, and she was looking forward to the following semester when she'd be transferring to Old Dominion. She wanted me at Old Dominion with her, so right away she began to fill out my college applications for admission and student aid. It never occurred to us that there were other universities to choose from. No one had ever told us that we could apply to schools in different states. We thought it was like high school: You went to the school that corresponded to your neighborhood. We actually thought it was a step up from high school, in that we had *two* choices. So we opted for ODU, the better choice.

While Afsaneh busied herself with my paperwork, Robabeh told me I should forget about college. She suggested I take a six-month technical course. "You could become a dental assistant or something, get out in the world, and start earning your keep." That wasn't what I wanted, and it went against everything we had been told to do by our parents, but I was tempted. I knew Robabeh just wanted us out of her hair, and she thought this might expedite matters. But I also wanted to help Afsaneh, as she had been helping me these many years, and I told her about it.

"Are you crazy?!" she snapped at me. "I never want to hear that from you again."

So we gimped along. I told myself that it would be just one more year. Mom had promised she'd be back with the boys. I chose to believe her this time. But at school I missed Afsaneh. When lunch came, I had to eat my Twinkies by myself. I was very shy, and nobody went out of their way to befriend me, so I was always alone.

I was doing a little better in school, but I was having trouble with my eyes. I couldn't see the blackboard very well, and I was too terrified to say anything. Whenever there was a pop quiz, I couldn't make out the questions on the board, so I just sat there, doing nothing, collecting C's and D's. I didn't understand how this had happened. Either the classes had gotten a lot harder, or I'd gotten dumber. Or maybe it was my eyes. But who was I going to tell about my eyes? Dai'e Mammad? He probably would have told me it was my own fault. I was being punished for wearing lip gloss that one time. "This is what happens to loose girls."

Afsaneh was working at the mall four days a week, and she had arranged her schedule so that she'd be done with classes by two. On those days, she would swing by Bayside High to pick me up, and I'd go to the mall with her. I'd hang out at the food court and do my homework, and then I'd wander around like a homeless person. I didn't mind, though. It was better than going back to the House of Horrors. And Afsaneh and I always had dinner together. Wendy's. Or Chick-fil-A. Or maybe just a slice or two of pizza.

Then she'd go back and finish her shift, and at the end of the evening we'd climb into Le Car, return to Blackpoole Lane, wash up, and crawl into bed. The house was basically a place to sleep, nothing more. We were respectful because that's part of the Persian culture: Even if an adult is mean or treats you shabbily, you are not permitted to raise your voice to them. But it was very cold: "Hello. Good night. Thank you. Yes, please." There was nothing there for us. We lived with a minimum of human contact. Once again, all we had was each other.

We told ourselves it was all right, that life was good, but the truth is, it was crushing, both spiritually and emotionally, and we both knew it.

"Do you remember Mr. Owens?" Afsaneh asked me one night as I was drifting off to sleep.

"Rachel's dad? From school? The night we baked Christmas cookies with that exchange student from Germany?"

"I'm going to call him," Afsaneh said.

"What for?"

"He's a lawyer. He can help us."

"He won't even remember us," I said. We hadn't seen him in almost four years, since Christmas 1981, and even then we'd only met him that one time.

I was wrong. Afsaneh called him, and he remembered us immediately. "We are not doing well in our situation," she said. "Can we meet with you?" He was completely accommodating. He asked us to come see him in his office, and he checked his schedule and made an appointment.

A few days later we drove down together in Le Car. It was the first time I'd ever been inside a law firm, and I was truly impressed. The serene corridors, the thick carpeting, the heavy tomes that filled the wall-to-wall, ceiling-high bookshelves.

A nice lady ushered us into Mr. Owens's office, and he stood, smiled broadly, told us how nice it was to see us after all this time, and how he wouldn't have recognized either of us. "You've turned into young ladies!"

We sat down, and Afsaneh tried to tell him a little about our situation. She said it was not a healthy environment for either of us and that we wanted to go out on our own. "I would like to become my sister's legal guardian," she said. "I've heard that it's possible to do this."

Mr. Owens asked Afsaneh how old she was, and she told him she was seventeen. But when she saw the look on his face, she backtracked a bit. She said that it was different in Iran, that the Persian calendar is based on the lunar calendar, so that in America she was really eighteen and of legal age. "Technically I was born in 1966, not 1967, which in America would make me eighteen and of legal age," she said, choosing her words carefully.

Mr. Owens looked at her. I'm not sure he believed her, but I could see he wanted to. He was also quite impressed. The girl was thinking on her feet, and she was clearly determined to take care of me, her little sister. He also sensed that we were pretty desperate.

"Okay," he said. "It's a process, but let's see what we can do."

He explained that we would have to go before a judge in family court. We would have to describe our situation and explain how and why it had become untenable. He asked us a few questions about things at Blackpoole Lane and a few more questions about our family, back in Tehran. He made notes on everything, and when he was done he said he would get things rolling and contact us the moment he had news.

"Please don't call us at the house," Afsaneh said.

"Okay," he said. "Then I want you to call me in two weeks."

When we left the office, I was in quite a state. Mr. Owens had made a huge impression on me. It wasn't only the fact that he was going to try to help us, but that he had the power to do so.

"What a cool profession," I told Afsaneh.

"What?" she said.

"Being a lawyer. To be able to help people like that; what a cool thing. Two little girls just walk into his office, and he helps them."

"He hasn't helped us yet," Afsaneh said.

The next time we spoke to Mom, we told her what we had done. She was very shaken up. She knew we were unhappy at her brother's home, but this was the first time she was made aware of the true extent of our unhappiness.

"Is it really that bad?" she asked.

In an odd way, the fact that we hadn't said anything for so long worked against us. Mom couldn't believe that we had endured so much unhappiness without a word of complaint. And she didn't want to believe it, probably because it was too painful to bear. But part of her knew we were telling her the truth: We needed to get out, and we needed to get out *now*.

"Mom," Afsaneh said bluntly. "It's torture. You just didn't see it clearly because they were on their best behavior. You have no idea. Robabeh Khanoom was actually trying to talk Afschineh into going to technical school!"

Now *this* was bad. *This* she understood. It bordered on criminal.

Two weeks later, we called Mr. Owens. "Good news," he said. "We have a court date." It was only a few weeks away, but it felt like an eternity. Afsaneh made a note of the day in her calendar, though neither of us was likely to forget it. "Come by my office in the morning," Mr. Owens said, "and we'll go to court together."

On the appointed day, we were very nervous. We woke up, got dressed in our nicest outfits, had breakfast, and pretended we were going off to school. Not that Dai'e Mammad or Robabeh asked. They had no interest in our lives, and they didn't even notice our nice dresses or the way we'd fixed each other's hair. For once, their indifference worked in our favor: There was nothing to say, nothing to explain.

When we arrived at Mr. Owens's office, he said, "I'll do most of the talking, but if the judge asks you something, always use the words 'Your Honor' when you respond."

When we walked into the courthouse, I was deeply impressed by the majesty of the place. The flag, the statues, the state seals, the symbols of freedom. The way our footfalls echoed off the vaulted ceiling. I found myself thinking, *This is where they hand out justice. This is where people come to right wrongs.*

We were taken into the courtroom, and I'm sure it was a modest room, but to me it felt as spacious and as overwhelming as a cathedral. Everything in the room—the wooden benches, the judge's upraised desk, the American flag—seemed fraught with meaning. My entire future hinged on what would transpire in the course of that morning in that room, but strangely enough I wasn't even anxious. I was excited. I knew in my heart that things would go well, and I had faith that from that day forth my sister and I would be free. To me, young as I was, that courtroom represented a first, giant step toward a better future.

There were about two dozen people in the room, whispering quietly here and there. Mr. Owens had picked a bench in the second row, and, from where I was sitting, I could actually see the gavel on the judge's desk. I had to squint to see it—my eyes were pretty bad—but there it was: a real gavel.

Presently, the bailiff entered. "All rise," he called out, and we stood in unison. Then the judge, a middle-aged man in a gray robe and shiny black shoes, walked in and took his seat. As he turned his attention to the papers in front of him, Mr. Owens nodded, and we sat down.

"In the matter of the guardianship of the minor Afschineh Latifi Moghadam Tehrani . . ." I was stunned. We were the very first case of the day. There would be no waiting.

Mr. Owens stood and smiled supportively. "Okay, girls," he said, "come on."

We approached the bench. "Your Honor," Mr. Owens said. "I'm here today because the minor's sister is making an application to become her guardian."

"For what reason?" the judge asked.

Mr. Owens explained that our father was deceased, that our mother was back in Iran with our two young brothers, and that we were living in less than ideal conditions with relatives who were neglecting their responsibilities.

When he was done, the judge turned to look at me, indicating Afsaneh. "Is this your sister?" he asked.

"Yes," I said. And then I remembered: "Your Honor."

"Do you want your sister to be your guardian?"

"Yes, Your Honor."

Then he turned to look at Afsaneh. "Young lady," he said. "Do you think you can take care of your sister?"

And Afsaneh said, "Yes, Your Honor. I think I can do a very good job."

And the judge said, "Okay. Application granted."

And that was it.

We left the court, and we thanked and hugged Mr. Owens, both of us fighting tears. And Afsaneh asked how much we owed him. And he said, "Don't worry about it. I'm just happy I could help. Please call me if you need anything. And take good care of your sister."

We said good-bye—he shook hands with both of us—and Afsaneh took me to a little restaurant to celebrate. It was nothing fancy, but it was definitely a notch or two above the usual food court stuff.

"I'm the boss now," she joked. "And don't you forget it."

"I can't believe that after all these years you still had Mr. Owens's number," I said.

She just shrugged. "I thought we might need a lawyer someday, and he was the only lawyer I knew, so I wrote his number down and kept it."

"He was so wonderful," I said.

"There are angels in all of our lives, sprinkled here and there," she replied. "Mr. Owens is one of ours."

Afsaneh was my angel. I idolized her. I idolized her the way a child idolizes a parent. I didn't tell her that, of course, since at the time I didn't know it myself. Instead, I said, "Well, it's a good thing. I was a little worried about how this was going to work out, but not *too* worried. I knew that even if it didn't happen, Mom was coming in six months, and all we had to do was hold on."

"Maybe," Afsaneh said.

"What do you mean?" I said. "You think Mom's not coming?"

"It doesn't matter now. I want her to come, of course. And I miss her as much as you do. But I'm not going to think about it. If she doesn't come, we'll be all right. No one can tell us what to do anymore. I'm an adult, and I don't have to answer to anyone."

When we got back to the house, all hell broke loose. Someone at Bayside High had called to report me absent, and from the way Dai'e Mammad and Robabeh carried on when we walked through the door, you'd almost think they cared. "Where were you? What is the meaning of this behavior? We need an answer at once!"

I was nervous, and I half-hid behind Afsaneh, but she seemed drunk with power. "We were in court," she said, taunting them.

"Court? What court?"

"Family court. I'm in charge of Afschineh now. I'm her legal guardian."

"What are you talking about?" Robabeh said in her pinched voice.

"Exactly what I said," Afsaneh answered. "I'm my sister's legal guardian. You no longer have any jurisdiction over her. So if the school calls again, let me know because it's not your problem anymore. I'll deal with it."

By this point, I didn't know whether to be impressed or terrified, and two words popped into my head: *Oh shit!*

Robabeh was seething. Her head was jerking one way and another, and she looked more puppetlike than ever. "I can't believe this: to be so young and so sneaky!"

And our uncle got into it, too. "I can't wait to see what your mother is going to say about this! We need to call her right away."

"Please do," Afsaneh said. "She already knows. Please call and let her know that everything went as planned."

That pretty much shut them up. Dai'e Mammad looked at his wife, she looked at him, and they seemed literally struck dumb.

"We're moving out," Afsaneh said. "I'm sure this will be better for everyone. I know you've been looking forward to it for a long, long time. You certainly made no secret of it."

It was strange. We had won, but what had we won, really? When I looked at my uncle's face, I saw how badly he felt. I saw the guilt in his eyes. He knew he had wronged us, and I think that for a moment he was overwhelmed by his failure. It made me feel sad. I was almost tempted to reach up and hug him, to tell him it was all right, that we all make mistakes, but the moment passed.

A few days later, on Saturday, we packed up our suitcases and went to stay with Shamsi. This was just before Christmas, and it was temporary. We assured her we would begin looking for a place of our own as soon as we could manage it. Meanwhile, we had a rather daunting problem to deal with. I was no longer in the Bayside district, and I would have to spend the final semester of my senior year at Booker T. Washington, which had the worst reputation in the city. "I'm not going to Booker T.," I told Afsaneh. "Kids get knifed there every day." I was exaggerating, but not by much.

"You don't have a choice," she said.

"Then I'll drop out. My education is over. I'll become a dental technician."

"Stop being so melodramatic," Afsaneh said. "It's just one semester."

"Just one semester? Fine. Sure. I'll go. I'll end up in a pool of blood in a quiet corner of the cafeteria."

Before we had managed to resolve this issue, Le Car started having problems. The problems were too expensive to fix, and—despite my claims that we could fix anything using those Chilton books I'd found in the library—we decided to sell it. Afsaneh called Nasser, who had opened a used car lot with a friend, and asked if he had something we could borrow. All he had was an old, red Pinto, he said, and it was in terrible shape. We told him we didn't mind and went to the lot to get it, but it was even worse than we'd imagined. The driver's-side door didn't open and had in fact been roped shut. You had to get in from the passenger side or crawl through the window.

"Great," I said. "We're the *Dukes of Hazzard*."

A few days later, Afsaneh went to the school district to see what she could do about my final semester. They tried to be accommodating, but they couldn't let me return to Bayside. The best they could do was to let me finish the year at Lake Taylor High School, which was only marginally better than Booker T. But they would only bend the rules for me if I had a parent or guardian who was willing to drive me to school, since there was no other way for me to get there.

"I'm her guardian," Afsaneh said. I think she was very proud of herself. It was the first time she was able to say this in an official capacity. "I'll drive her."

In January 1985, I transferred to Lake Taylor. It wasn't great, but at least I wasn't scared for my life. Afsaneh, meanwhile, had transferred to Old Dominion, and she was already much happier than she'd been at Norfolk State. She would drop me at school on her way to the campus every morning, but I made her leave me around back. I was too embarrassed to be seen in that red Pinto. She understood. When she got to campus, she always parked in the most remote lot and walked a quarter-mile to class. "If anyone saw me in this thing," she said, "I would die."

By February, Afsaneh began to suspect that Mom wouldn't be coming that summer, as promised, and she tried to prepare me for it. "Look how long it took Robabeh Khanoom to get her visa, and most of her family was already living in the U.S."

"So you don't think she's going to make it?"

"I didn't say that," Afsaneh said. "I think she might make it. But if she doesn't, we should be ready for it, and I have a plan."

"What's the plan?"

"Don't worry about it," she said. "But save money. Save as much money as you can."

In those days, I was still babysitting for Eva and Dennis, and I was also putting in a few hours at the public library, at minimum wage. I was making fifty or sixty dollars a week total and spending most of it on junk, but I changed my ways and began to horde my pennies. As for Afsaneh, she was still at Merry-Go-Round. She hadn't lost her knack for sales—okay, the truth is that she was pushy: a shopper's worst nightmare—and Wanda had given her a couple of raises.

As the academic year drew to a close, I received my official acceptance from Old Dominion, and Afsaneh—an old pro by now—made sure my financial aid package went through. Everything was going swimmingly, but there was one bit of business weighing on her mind. "What are you going to do about the prom?" she asked me.

"Prom?! I'm not going to a silly prom. It's not even my school. I don't know anyone there. I'm just glad it's over."

But Nasser found out I wasn't going to the prom, and he had a friend whose younger brother couldn't find a date for *his* prom, so Nasser volunteered me: "She's great. You'll really like her." I couldn't back out.

I wore Afsaneh's dress—that horrible, frilly, off-the-shoulder taffeta number—and off we went, a geek and her geek date. We stood in a corner for an hour and a half, then he dropped me back at Shamsi's and left.

"How'd it go?" Afsaneh asked.

"It was the most magical night of my life," I said, deadpan.

Afsaneh laughed.

The next day, we called Mom. I didn't want to pressure her, but I couldn't help myself. "You're coming, right? You said this summer for sure."

There was a long pause, and I knew what was next. After all, my legal guardian had prepared me for it. "No," my mother said. "I can't make it this year. I'm sorry."

I was devastated. I couldn't even talk to her anymore, so I gave the phone to Afsaneh and left the room. Afsaneh was disappointed, too, but she had prepared herself, and in some ways she saw it as a challenge. She was simply going to make the best of a bad situation.

In June, the Pinto fell apart, and we gave it back to Nasser, glad to be rid of it. We scraped a few dollars together and bought a green Dodge Omni at auction. It wasn't much of an improvement over the Pinto, but both doors worked.

"We're coming up in the world," Afsaneh said. That was one thing about my sister: She never lost her sense of humor.

The most pressing issue was finding a new home. We had been in Shamsi's place for six months. We had contributed our fair share, but we really wanted to be in a place of our own before classes started. That gave us only a couple of months to arrange it. Then two things happened in quick succession. First, Eva asked me if I was available that summer. She was very busy, and Elena wasn't interested in summer camp, and she wondered if I'd be interested in moving in. Second, Afsaneh had met a woman in her English class whose husband was always out of town on business. She lived in a great house in Virginia Beach, and she was looking to rent out a room. Afsaneh had turned her down, not wanting to leave me alone at Shamsi's, but when she heard about Eva's offer, we decided to try it. "I'll still see you every day," she said. "And it'll be good for our plan. You'll save money, and, at the end of the summer, we'll find a place of our own." It was the first time in our lives we would be separated, but it made sense. And I took comfort in knowing that Afsaneh would only be a ten-minute drive away.

I saw my sister every night, as promised. She always made sure she stopped by to see how I was doing. During the day, I hung out with Elena. We'd go swimming or walk to the park, play games, and then come home and watch TV. It was a fairly undemanding existence. I only had a learner's permit, but by midsummer Eva decided I was responsible enough to drive Elena to the mall and an occasional movie. I know it was illegal—I was supposed to have an adult with me in the car at all times—but the statute of limitations has expired, so I feel it's all right to confess.

In August, Eva asked me to move in permanently. I could be her au pair. I'd get room and board and a small salary to boot. I was tempted, but it didn't make any sense. Afsaneh was living fairly close, but we only had one car, and we were going to attend college together. I didn't see how we could manage it. A few weeks before classes started, I moved in with Afsaneh and her friend. I found her friend a little weird. She was tall, extremely thin, and very erratic. She could be a real sweetheart one minute, then storm around the house muttering and cursing under her breath. And she had an obsessive-compulsive disorder. She washed her hands thirty or forty times a day. Still, I'm sure she found me a little weird, too. I was in my Madonna phase in those days. I never went anywhere without a pink scarf tied in a big bow on top of my head.

"Your roommate's a freak," I told Afsaneh one night. "How can you take it?"

"I guess I hadn't noticed," she said. "I've been busy. Or maybe I just didn't want to notice."

I saw her point. School was only two weeks away, and we still didn't have a home of our own. We began looking for a place in earnest. Old Dominion was in a marginal neighborhood in the heart of Norfolk, but we wanted to be near school. And the rents there actually seemed manageable.

That Sunday afternoon, as we were combing through the real estate section, circling likely prospects, the phone rang. It was Naheed, calling in tears to tell us that Dai'e Mammad had just passed away of a heart attack. We were shocked and upset. He wasn't old, and he always seemed the picture of good health. We also wondered why she had turned to us of all people, since things had come to such a bad end between our families. But I guess that's what families are all about. We knew Dai'e Mammad had not been the best guy in the world, but, at the end of the day, he had taken us in, and without his help, we would have been completely lost.

So we rushed over to comfort the family and help with the funeral arrangements, and on the appointed day, when the mourners began filing in, we were there to serve tea and dates stuffed with walnuts and little cakes.

For several days, we didn't know how to break the news to Mom. This was her brother, after all, and he had been Mammon Kobra's favorite. When we finally called, she didn't take it well at all. It wasn't only his untimely death, but the fact that there was so much unfinished business between them. He had failed her, and they both knew it.

"Make sure you pay your respects properly," she said, pulling herself together at the end of the conversation.

"Don't worry, Mom," Afsaneh said. "We're good kids. We know what to do."

We had done it already. And I thought, *My sister's right. We are good kids.*

After the funeral, we went home and continued searching for an apartment. Strangely enough, Shamsi was very upset. She was lonely and had asked us, repeatedly, to move back in. But we really wanted to be on our own.

"I don't get it," she said. "Why?"

"We just do," Afsaneh replied. "We're both in college now. We're not kids anymore."

A few days later, we went to look at a furnished, one-bedroom place on the second floor of a three-story building, not far from the campus. It was on Forty-fourth Street, just around the corner from the rowdy, infamous 4400 Club, but the rent seemed almost manageable at $240 a month.

The apartment wasn't exactly palatial. The first thing you saw as you walked through the door was an ugly plaid couch, and it reminded us of Dai'e Mammad's couch. We wondered if everyone in Virginia was wild about plaid. There was a tiny living room, and a really tiny kitchen, with just enough room for a battered stove, an old fridge, and a small, Formica table. The bedroom had two single beds, and off to one side there was a small bathroom with a shower. In short, the place was dark, dingy, and claustrophobic.

"It's perfect," Afsaneh said.

She was right. It *was* perfect. It was *ours*. It was *home*.

We had enough money for a deposit, and we took it and moved in the following weekend. There wasn't much to it—we didn't own much—and as soon as we'd unpacked we hurried to the mall, where Afsaneh still had her job at Merry-Go-Round. We told Wanda about the apartment and asked if she knew of any jobs for me. She said they might be looking for a salesperson at DJs, a men's store that was about to open in the same mall. It was owned by the Merry-Go-Round people. I went over with Wanda and filled out an application, and she put in a good word for me. Within a few days they called to ask me when I could start.

"Right away," I said.

They did their best to make my schedule work with Afsaneh's schedule, so that we could drive to and from the mall together, and, by the end of the week, I was working. I got paid minimum wage and a three percent commission. It wasn't bad. I discovered that the knack for selling ran in the family, and that I could be as pushy as my sister: "The jacket just *looks* big, but that's the style. And just think, when it gets cold, you'll be able to wear two or three sweaters under it."

When classes started, I realized that college wasn't really that much different from high school. But it was less confusing because I spoke the language now and understood what was going on. I also had the good sense to sit near the front of the class, where I could see the blackboard.

And my fellow students turned out to be far more open and friendly than those I'd met in high school. They'd stop to chat in class or fall into step beside me as I made my way down the corridor. They were curious about my background and about my age: I was sixteen, a little young for college. There were a number of Persians at ODU, and of course we were curious about one another. Afsaneh and I told them a little about our life in Tehran, and about the years since, but we avoided politics, and we never said a word about Baba Joon.

Academically, I only had one problem, and it concerned Mom. She kept pushing science—"You're going to be doctors. All of you"—but it soon became apparent that science wasn't my cup of tea. I was taking biology, physics, and all sorts of classes that were supposed to help me get into a premed program, and I found all of them incredibly dull.

"I hate this," I told Afsaneh.

"Well, don't tell Mom," she said. "She wants us to be doctors."

Our days were pretty full. We had arranged our class schedules so that we both started at nine and finished at two. At two sharp, we'd rush home, change, then race to the mall for work. A few weeks into it, one of the girls at DJs quit, and Afsaneh left Merry-Go-Round and joined me. We worked the same shift, 3:30 to 9:30, with a break for dinner, then we'd drive home and study until we collapsed.

Thursdays we didn't eat at the mall. Thursday was Pizza Night at the 4400 Club, the place around the corner. We would get a large pizza for $3.99, take it home, and eat in front of the television set, rushing to get there before *Knots Landing* started. We loved that show. All those elegant people in their elegant homes living as neighbors and friends on their lovely street reminded us of our old life in Tehran.

We checked in with Mom once a week. She was a little worried about us, especially now that we were out on our own, but she had faith. "I know you are good girls," she kept repeating, as if trying to reassure herself. "I know you will work hard, study hard, and become doctors."

Money was tight, so we also worked Saturdays. At the end of our shift, we would stop at Giant, the twenty-four-hour grocery store, and stock up for the week. Milk, sodas, cookies, cereal, plenty of cold cuts, and bread. Five mornings a week, I made submarine sandwiches—a talent I'd picked up at the Afghani-run pizza place—to get us through the long hours in class.

On Sundays we pretty much stayed home. We did our laundry, cleaned the house, and studied. And every Sunday we called Mom. That was our entire week, and our week always ended with that call to Mom.

We never went anywhere, and no one ever came to visit us. And after we were done with the groceries, the phone bill, and the gas money, we always had just enough money to pay the rent. There would be no luxuries for us, but we weren't even thinking about luxuries. We were just happy to be making it. We were happy to have a home of our own.

It may have sounded lonely, but it really wasn't bad. We seldom talked about the old days in Iran, which seemed long ago and unreal, as if that life belonged to two other girls. This was our life now. We had a home, and we were free. And we had each other.

Who could ask for anything more?

AT HIGH SCHOOL GRADUATION. ON THE RIGHT IS MRS. RAMSEY, THE
GERMAN TEACHER WHO WAS ALWAYS SO KIND TO US.

ALI (WITH TROPHY) AND AMIR FINALLY CAME
INTO THEIR OWN ON THE TENNIS COURTS.

AMIR (LEFT) AND ALI IN VIRGINIA BEACH

CHAPTER TWELVE
Reunion

IN VIRGINIA BEACH

NASSER AND ANGIE WITH THEIR DAUGHTER, NASSIM

IN JANUARY, shortly after I turned seventeen, I decided I wasn't going to become a doctor after all. It was probably the first adult decision of my life. Afsaneh was already on the med school track, and I figured Mom could live vicariously through her.

I took my first political science class that semester, and I was instantly hooked. One of my professors reminded me of Gene Hackman. He was gruff, impatient, and walked with a limp—I heard he'd been injured in Vietnam— and he had a genuine gift for making history come alive. When he spoke about George Washington, Benjamin Franklin, and Abraham Lincoln, I felt as if the Founding Fathers were right there in the classroom with us. He also taught a First Amendment course, where I learned all about the *Declaration of Independence*, and about the *Constitution*, and I found myself, once again, seduced by the American legal system. It took me back to that day in court with Mr. Owens: The fact that he had had the power to change the course of our lives isn't something one easily forgets.

I took German classes, too. There was a very good German department at ODU, and the more advanced classes were taught by Regula Meier. She was a Swiss-German, with that German side to her—rigorous, a bit of a disciplinarian, and clearly intent on molding her young charges. Given my German-language background, both in Iran and at Sacré Coeur, I had a distinct advantage over the other students, and it wasn't long before I became the teacher's pet. Under Professor Meier's direction, I began to read German literature in the original language, and I would get my international news from German papers. In short, this wasn't just a simple language class, designed to fulfill a requirement. It was as tough as any of my other courses, and I loved it.

With the decision made, all I had to do was break the bad news to Mom, but she had enough problems to deal with back home, so I decided it could wait. It waited a very long time indeed.

The fact is, things in Iran continued to deteriorate at an alarming rate. Over the course of the next two years—while Afsaneh and I worked and focused on our studies—Mom was struggling to survive. At one point she was so broke that there was nothing of value left to sell. She sold Ali and Amir's toys, their bicycles, the clothes they'd outgrown. One day, a doll collector bought my entire doll collection. Paid good money for it, too. Mom even sold the last of the Persian carpets, the ones she had hoped to bring with her to America.

But it went well beyond money. In March 1986, Ali turned twelve, which put him one year away from mandatory recruitment into the military. Mom had lost her husband, her daughters were thousands of miles away, and suddenly she was at risk of losing her eldest son. She was not going to let this happen.

She had already gone to Turkey once to try to get visas, and the U.S. Embassy there had given her a visitor's visa, but it had not done the same for the boys, knowing that if she took them along she was unlikely to return. In April, she tried again, and this time the trip turned into a real nightmare. They met a Persian man outside the American Embassy. He said he was a lawyer and claimed he could help them get their visas. My mother didn't trust him, she refused to give up the passports, and the man was very understanding. "I commend you on your caution," he said. He then explained that his contacts were at the American Embassy in Izmir, on the coast, not at the one in Istanbul, and suggested that they could meet there the next day, where he would proceed to take care of everything in the space of the afternoon. He asked for a modest advance, of course, which my mother had been expecting, and she agreed to it.

"Tomorrow at noon," the man said, hurrying off, "in front of the Embassy in Izmir."

In her heart, my mother knew she shouldn't have trusted him, but desperation makes people do strange things, and she desperately wanted to believe that he could help her.

She took the boys to a cheap hotel and found the place so scary that she propped a chair against the door, just in case anyone tried to break in. In the morning, they found their way to the central station and boarded the bus to Izmir. At noon, the bus stopped for lunch, and, when the driver went to park the vehicle, he struck Ali and knocked him down. Ali's face was bloodied, and he would remain bruised for several weeks, but he was otherwise all right.

At long last they arrived in Izmir, but the Persian was nowhere to be seen. Mom was told that the man was a swindler, as she had suspected, and that he had been scamming women for many months. Heartbroken, she took the bus back to Istanbul, but by the time they reached the airport their flight had already left. She decided to take the bus to Tehran. It wasn't scheduled to leave for a few hours, so she took the boys to a park to pass the time. At one point,

Ali and Amir disappeared into a public restroom, and they never came out. Mom went into a panic. She asked a passing Turk if he would be kind enough to look for them, but he came back a few moments later and reported that the bathroom was empty.

For half an hour, Mom ran around the park, beside herself, screaming for help in Farsi, like a crazy woman, and finally found the boys in another section of the park, playing ball, oblivious. They had left the restroom through a rear door and had completely forgotten about her. Mom slapped both of them hard across their faces, then she hugged them and started crying.

The Turkish bus took them to the border, where they crossed on foot and made their way toward the Iranian bus, which would take them on the final leg of their journey into Tehran. Mom was exhausted and not thinking clearly, and back in Istanbul she had purchased a few small bottles of liquor for her brother Dai'e Hossein. He had been so helpful to her and such a source of emotional support that she wanted to do something nice for him. But liquor was not permitted in Iran, and it was now hidden in her pantyhose. She didn't think this would be a problem, since she was wearing a long skirt and a head scarf and looked like a proper, God-fearing woman.

As they reached the border, however, she began to worry. The moment the bus stopped, she could see the checkpoint up ahead, crowded with Iranian guards, and she wondered if this had been a good idea.

"Excuse me?"

Startled, she turned to find a young Persian man leaning toward her from the seat across the aisle. "I'm carrying some music tapes," he whispered. "I wonder if you'd be good enough to hide them for me?" Music, like liquor, was illegal. Mom looked through the window and saw the Iranian guards approaching the bus. Almost without thinking and unable to resist a plea for help, she took the cassette tapes and hid them in her bra.

The guards boarded the bus and began selecting people at random. My mother was one of the first to be singled out. "Why are you traveling without your husband?" one of the guards asked her.

"He's fighting the war," she lied.

"We need you to get off the bus."

As Ali, Amir, and the young man watched through the grimy window, the guards took her outside and handed her over to a female colleague to be searched. My mother was seized with terror. What if the young man had lied to her? What if the tapes had nothing to do with music? What if they were political, or worse? Almost immediately, the guard found the tapes. They were, indeed, musical recordings, as the young man had told her, and they were confiscated and destroyed on the spot, whereupon my mother was loudly and publicly berated and hustled back to the bus. "You are lucky we don't throw you in jail!" she was told. "If it wasn't for the two boys, we would." For the remainder of the long trip home, she could think only one thing: *I have to get out of Iran.*

When she arrived back at the house, she told the family the story, and she gave Dai'e Hossein the liquor bottles that she had hidden in her stockings.

"Imagine if they had found those!" he exclaimed.

"You see?" she told him. "I've always said that you can never do enough for other people, and I'm right. I was trying to help that young man, and I ended up saving myself."

A few weeks later, she went to the French Embassy in Tehran, which remained open, and found a large crowd outside. Her most recent plan, not entirely original, was to try to get into the United State in increments, as Robabeh had done. Mom hoped to take the boys to France, where her best friend, Sabi, was living and try her luck from there, but the place was so crowded she never even made it to the embassy door.

Then she heard about one of the embassy employees. He was half-French and half-Iranian, and he would help anyone—for the right price. My mother was wary—she'd already tried that in Istanbul—but several people assured her that this fellow was legitimate. There was a trick to approaching him, though. You had to hold your passport high above your head with an envelope tucked inside. The man would scan the crowd, looking for the telltale envelope, and when he spotted it, he would signal for the person. He would take the passport and the envelope and disappear for a few moments, and, if the bribe was sufficiently impressive, he would put the process in motion. Clearly, my mother impressed him. Within days, she and the boys received tourist visas from the French embassy.

In October 1986, after selling her few remaining possessions, Mom took the boys and flew to Paris. Sabi was waiting for them at the airport, and, after several rounds of tearful hugs and kisses, she drove them out to Antony, a nearby suburb. Even after they arrived, the crying didn't stop. Sabi had been my mother's neighbor and best friend for many years. She had stood by her when my father was arrested and continued to stand by her after he was executed, when lesser friends were too terrified to associate with the family. She had even come to see Afsaneh and me in Virginia, when Mom had been unable to do so, to find out how we were getting on and to report back to Mom. Sabi's husband was also an angel. He had been an engineer for the water authority—he was the one whose tie was snipped in two by the irate security, as you may recall—and he was still in Iran, trying to liquidate the family's dwindling assets.

While she waited for her husband, Sabi was living in a high-rise with their two children. Mahsa, her daughter, was almost two years older than Ali, and Mahyar, her son, was two months younger. The kids were shy at first, but happy to see one another again, and Sabi did everything she could to make all of them feel comfortable. In a matter of days, they had fallen into a working routine. The children entertained one another in and around the apartment, and the mothers took turns cooking and cleaning.

A week and a half later, having had a little time to adjust, Ali and Amir were enrolled at the local public school. They sat through one class after another, understanding nothing. They were outsiders and they felt it. Some of the other kids went out of their way to make sure they felt it. Amir finally lost his temper one day and pinned one of the more unpleasant boys to the wall, cursing him loudly in Farsi. When Mom heard about this, she asked him why he would attack a boy when he didn't even understand what he was saying. And Amir replied, "I didn't have to understand the words. I could tell from his voice that he was being mean."

Life in France, like life in America, was devoid of luxury. There was no money, and the future looked very uncertain. From time to time, Mom took the boys to Paris, but they never saw Notre Dame, and they never visited the Louvre. They were there to try to get visas from the American Embassy, and they were relentless about it. Yes, my mother said, they had entered France on a tourist visa, but they didn't want to stay in France. She had two daughters living in Virginia, both of whom had been granted political asylum, and she wanted the same for herself and the two boys.

Christmas came and went, and there was no progress. Mom finally turned for help to a cousin of Sabi's. He had just begun practicing immigration law in Paris, and he worked tirelessly on her behalf, never charging her a penny.

By this time, Afsaneh and I had our green cards—they had arrived in the mail, with no fanfare whatsoever—and we would have been free to go to Paris to visit, but we simply didn't have the money and hadn't even entertained the possibility.

In the early spring, when the weather in Paris warmed up, the children played at a park near the high-rise. Mom and Sabi stayed indoors, cooking, talking, and knitting. After the children went to bed, they sometimes turned to the TV for entertainment. One night, as Mom was switching channels, a pornographic movie appeared on the screen. The women were so shocked they couldn't stop staring, but eventually Mom snapped out of it and tried to change the channel. She hit the volume button by mistake, and sounds of wild passion reverberated throughout the apartment. For a moment she was sure it would wake the kids, but then she found the right button, killed the picture, and slumped against the couch with a big sigh of relief. She and Sabi looked at each other and burst out laughing, and before long—as a result of what they'd just seen—found themselves talking about weighty, moral issues.

"I don't know how I'm going to handle those girls when I finally get to America," Mom said.

"I don't think you have anything to worry about," Sabi told her. "They have turned out very well. They are good girls."

"But what about dating? If they want to date, am I supposed to let them date?"

"Well," Sabi said. "It *is* America. We can't be too conservative."

"Maybe you're right," Mom said. "If I'm not free with them, they'll rebel. But if I trust them, they will be open and honest with me."

By the following morning, Mom had changed her tune. "You know, I thought about what we discussed last night, and I don't think freedom is such a good idea after all." It was very trying. Mom was forty-one years old, a widow with four children, two of whom had turned into young women in her absence. She had no idea what Afsaneh and I were up to, let alone how she was going to go about raising us, and it worried her to no end.

I thought we were pretty sensible girls, and that she really didn't have much to worry about, but one night I began to wonder about Afsaneh. She had taken an extra shift, and I was home, studying, and, when I looked up at the clock, I noticed that it was after ten. I called DJs, but they told me she'd already left. An hour went by and she still wasn't home, and now I began to worry in earnest.

As it turned out, she was making her way back to the house, on the freeway, when she got a flat tire. She went to fetch the spare, thinking she could change it herself, but that one was also flat. A moment later, a pickup truck rolled to a stop just ahead of her. A boy got out of the truck, a teenager, and he offered to drive her to the nearest gas station. Afsaneh accepted, and he picked up the spare and threw it into the back of the truck. When she went to climb into the truck, she saw another boy behind the wheel. The first boy got in next to her, and she found herself squeezed between two strangers. Suddenly, for good reason, she was terrified. She was sure they were going to rape her or *worse*. She knew she had just made the biggest mistake of her life.

They pulled off the highway at the next exit. Afsaneh knew there was a gas station to the south, and she pointed them in that direction, but they went the opposite way. Now she knew for certain she was dead!

But they didn't kill her. There was a dumpy gas station just ahead, and they pulled in. When the boy on the passenger side got out, Afsaneh jumped out, grabbed her flat tire, and ran as fast as she could toward the small building. The door was locked—it was that kind of neighborhood—but someone buzzed her through. A large black woman was standing behind the counter.

"Please," Afsaneh said, breathless with panic. "Those two boys want to rape me!"

Before the door swung shut, the boy caught it and stepped through. Afsaneh hurried around the counter, uninvited, still clutching her flat tire.

"Got any rolling papers?" the boy asked the woman.

She reached for some rolling papers, very slowly, her eyes on the boy, and set the papers on the counter. Afsaneh was cowering in the shadows, thinking how narrowly she had escaped death. These boys were not only rapists, but also drug addicts! The drug addict paid for his rolling papers and took his change, then he turned his attention to Afsaneh.

"What's wrong?" he said. "Ain't you coming with us?"

The woman reached behind her and picked up a baseball bat. "If you know what's good for you," she said in a calm voice, "you and your friend will get in that pickup and get the hell out of here."

The boy looked at Afsaneh like she was nuts, then turned on his heels and left. Afsaneh thanked the woman, tears of gratitude spilling down her cheeks, then borrowed the phone and called Nader. When she finally got home that night, still shaken, she turned to me and said, "Afschineh, whatever you do, never ever get into a pickup truck with drug addicts."

I looked at her and said, "Duh!"

By this time, the Dodge Omni was acting up, so we got in touch with Nasser and went to buy another car at auction. There was a red Audi on the lot, and it looked hot, but several people, including Nasser, told Afsaneh repeatedly that she shouldn't bid on it. She bid on it anyway, and we got it. It gave us nothing but trouble, so a few weeks later we sold it and went back to another auction. We went through a lot of cars over the years, and we always bought them at auction because they were all we could afford. In retrospect, I wonder if we wouldn't have been better off going to a lot and buying a shiny new car on credit, like our fellow Americans. It certainly seemed like the thing to do, and, at the end of the day, it may have actually been the less expensive option.

At the end of March, with Mom still stuck in Paris, we found out that ODU was sending a bus to Florida for spring break. It was incredibly cheap—some twenty bucks per student—and impossible to pass up.

"We need a break," Afsaneh said.

"I agree," I said. This was my sophomore year in college. Afsaneh was a junior. The last time we'd taken time off had been almost two years ago, in 1984, when Mom had come to visit. We were tired. No, come to think of it, we were *fried*. We *deserved* a vacation.

We decided to visit Nasser and Angie, in Tampa. They had recently moved there with their little girl, Nassim, and were trying their luck in the restaurant business. At the last minute, however, after we'd made all the arrangements, ODU canceled the bus. I was crushed. Not only had I been looking forward to a break, but we had also told everyone we knew that we were going, and we had been very proud of ourselves. We were unstoppable. We were living on our own, paying our bills in a timely manner, getting good grades, and had even managed to arrange an actual *vacation*. I imagined Robabeh at the house on Blackpoole Lane, gloating, and it just killed me. We were Persians, after all: We needed to save face. So we went out and rented a car, knowing that our own car couldn't possibly make the twelve-hour trip, and off we went.

The plan had been to leave early Friday morning, but on Thursday night at ten, when we got home from DJs, Afsaneh suggested we take a little nap and drive through the night to avoid traffic. So we took our nap and when we woke up, I made two of my famous subway sandwiches, soaked in olive oil, and we climbed into our rented car. As we were pulling out, I noticed Afsaneh setting something in the glove compartment. I picked it up. It was a butter knife.

"What's this for?" I asked.

"Protection."

"A butter knife? You brought a butter knife for protection?"

"It's not a butter knife," she said. "Look at it. It has a serrated edge. It's pretty sharp."

"Well," I said. "I guess if we're attacked by a stick of butter, we'll be safe."

Early the following morning, somewhere in the middle of Georgia, we had to stop for gas. We found a station and pulled up, and there was a young couple standing next to their car, near the pumps, arguing loudly. It was the first time in my life I'd heard a genuine Georgia accent, down to the twang.

"Me! You done cheated on me first, you filthy bastid!"

"That's a got-damn lie! I ain't done nothin' but love you, you ugly bitch, and this is the thanks I get!"

I finally understood what country-and-western music was all about.

We filled up the tank, used the bathroom, and got something to drink to go with our subway sandwiches. An hour later I had to pee again. "I'm not stopping until we get out of Georgia," Afsaneh said. "Did you hear those people back there? They're all crazy."

By that point, she was too exhausted to drive, so she asked me to take over—as long as I promised not to stop. I had my license by this time, but I wasn't a very good driver, and I really didn't enjoy driving. Afsaneh insisted, however. She pulled over, climbed into the backseat, and began mumbling to herself. It struck me that she was praying; it was the Islamic death prayer. She fell asleep before she finished her prayer.

I was a very tense driver. I would hold the wheel so tightly that my knuckles went white, and when I changed lanes, I didn't believe in doing it gradually: I jerked the wheel to my left or right and screeched into the adjacent lane as quickly as I possibly could. Afsaneh kept getting tossed around in the backseat, but she was dead to the world.

At one point, already bleary-eyed myself, I looked up and saw a big bridge, and I realized we were entering Florida. I hollered at Afsaneh to wake up. I pulled over, and she took the wheel again and drove the rest of the way to Nasser and Angie's.

It was a modest place, not far from the beach, and they were thrilled to have us there, not to mention surprised to see us so far ahead of schedule. We went to the beach, which was crowded with rowdy kids on spring break, and I had my very first wine cooler. I got buzzed, as they say, and couldn't stop grinning. Later, we went for pizza, and then we visited an amusement park. I loved every minute of it. I know it sounds juvenile—I was seventeen years old and finishing my sophomore year in college—but I never had much of a chance to be a kid, and I liked the feeling. To this day, I'm still crazy about roller coasters. I can't help myself. There should probably be a picture of me in psychiatric textbooks, under "Arrested Development."

When we got back to Virginia, I got involved with something at ODU called the Model United Nations. It was a university-level simulation of the inner workings of the UN, and it dealt with all sorts of contemporary international issues. Border wars. Famine. Flood relief. Once again, I was enthralled by the practice of law, and I was more convinced than ever that I had made the right decision. I still hadn't told Mom, of course.

One day, a student in my class passed me a note. "Do you like to play Twister?" it said. I looked over at the guy. He was at least twenty-two or twenty-three. All I could think was, Twister? *I'll show you Twister, pal!* I thought he was a total pervert. The truth is, I was very immature, emotionally speaking. From time to time, I'd notice a cute guy, but dating wasn't even in the realm of possibility. I had never had a boyfriend in my life, and I had managed to convince myself that I never wanted one. I was a nerd, after all. Who would want me?

Afsaneh was two years older and far more interested in men. But she wasn't exactly experienced, either. She had met this cute Persian guy at ODU, and they had lunch once, but she shared nothing with him. When he asked about Mom, she told him she was in Paris, waiting for her visa. And when he asked about Dad, she told him he had passed away, volunteering no details whatsoever. She liked him as a friend, and he had other Persian friends. Before long we'd formed this unofficial little clique. Nothing too deep, though. My sister and I trusted only each other. We were insular to an unhealthy degree.

There was a Greek boy in one of her classes, however, who she was genuinely interested in. He was totally gorgeous. He had dark brown hair, green eyes, and a solid build. Unfortunately, he wouldn't even look at her, so she decided on extreme measures. "I'm going to write him a note," she said, "and the next time I see him I'm going to press it into his hand."

"Yeah?" I said. "What's the note going to say?"

"I don't know," she replied. "I hadn't thought that far ahead."

She never wrote the note: She was as big a nerd as me. But here's the thing: We never let ourselves become discouraged. On some level, we were outsiders, and we had begun to accept this as the norm. Every day presented new challenges, and we were determined to meet them head-on. We had been through much worse in Iran. We could survive anything.

In May 1987, almost a year after Mom and the boys arrived in Paris, the American Embassy came through for them. We could barely contain ourselves. Mom was coming to live with us! We were going to be a real family again!

At this point, we realized we were going to need a bigger place. The apartment had been fine for us, and we'd even come to like the plaid couch, but it wasn't a home. We wanted to welcome them into a real home. From that day on, we became more frugal than ever, counting and saving every penny, and on Sundays we drove around the various neighborhoods, looking for a place we could afford.

We didn't have much time—Mom was looking around for the cheapest possible fares, and she planned to come as soon as the boys were done with classes—but luck was on our side. On the third Sunday, we found a place in Virginia Beach, at 127 Sac Lane, in a complex named Independence Square. It was a town house, one of several dozen, tall, narrow, and a bit cramped, but the complex had tennis courts and a community swimming pool. It was a huge step up for us, and we fell in love with the place as soon as we walked through the door. There was a little foyer as you entered, a kitchen on the right, a living/dining area with a sliding glass door that looked out over the complex, and a bathroom. Upstairs, there were two bedrooms and a full bathroom.

The rental application asked how many people would be living there, and Afsaneh didn't want to jeopardize our chances of getting the place, so she put down "3."

Two days later, we were approved. We were ecstatic. We got in the car and drove over to the Haynes Furniture Store. They had a whole section of damaged and discounted furniture, and we found a wicker couch with two matching chairs that seemed pretty reasonable. We thought they would look good in the living room. Then we went to a mattress store and bought three single mattresses and one double mattress. I'm not sure why we bought the double. I think Afsaneh and I just assumed we would share a bed. We had become a little too close, perhaps, but we didn't see the harm in it.

Now the phone calls from Paris became more frequent. Mom had found three inexpensive, one-way tickets. The boys were about to finish school. Everything was packed and ready to go. Then the delays began. One of the forms hadn't been properly filled out. The boys needed new photographs. Mom's reservations had expired.

Meanwhile, we moved into Sac Lane. It felt like a palace, and we worked on making it as homey as possible. We arranged and rearranged the furniture. We kept moving the battered little TV. We dragged mattresses between the two bedrooms, looking for the best possible fit. One evening, in the midst of all this moving, we plopped down on our discounted wicker couch, exhausted, and I said to Afsaneh, "Do you realize that no one ever came to see us in our other apartment? Two years, and we never once had a visitor."

"That's just the way it is," she replied.

Mom called that night. It was the end of May 1987. She and the boys would be on their way in a few days. They would be flying into Kennedy Airport and connecting to Norfolk. When I got off the phone, I was shaking. We were about to be reunited. Ali was thirteen at the time; Amir was about to turn eleven. With the exception of that short visit in Austria, we hadn't seen them in six years—half their lives.

The following day, Afsaneh and I went to the mall and shopped. We knew every inch of the place, and we knew where to get the best deals. We bought some polo shirts for the boys, already planning on turning them into preppies. We picked up a pair of matching warm-up suits, powder blue, and two inexpensive tennis rackets. We got each of them a *Miami Vice*–style jacket because that was the hot show at the time and a half-dozen colored T-shirts to complete the look.

For Mom, we shopped at Loehman's. We bought her a few nice dresses. Nothing too flashy, but nothing too conservative, either. This was all designed to spare our family any sartorial ridicule. We were going to give them the benefit of our vast experience and turn them into Americans right from the very first day so that they wouldn't embarrass themselves with cowboy boots and broad-brimmed, church-lady hats.

"It's a good thing we have great taste," Afsaneh said.

I thought that was pushing it. We had come a long way over the years, style-wise, but I didn't think we were exactly hip.

The day of their scheduled arrival, we went out and stocked up on food. I even bought a box of Betty Crocker mix and made some mint chocolate chip brownies. Then we stopped to pick up fresh flowers and drove to the airport.

We were waiting at the gate when their plane arrived, and we had promised each other not to make a scene, but it didn't work. We went completely crazy. Afsaneh, Mom, and I were jumping around, squealing and crying, totally out of control, and, when I paused to catch my breath, I saw my two brothers staring at us in shock. I wouldn't have blamed them if they'd run away. I went over and hugged them, too, and it was clear they were a little uncomfortable. I didn't really recognize them. Mom had sent us photographs over the years, but they didn't look anything like they had in the photographs. These were not the brothers I remembered. They were practically strangers.

Years later, Amir told me that from time to time Mom had also shown him and Ali pictures of the two of us, but that he had never made the connection. "The notion that I had two sisters living in America didn't really compute," he explained.

When we calmed down, we took the family back to Sac Lane and gave them a tour of the town house. Mom couldn't believe it. She loved everything about the place. She couldn't find enough adjectives to describe it. After the tour, everyone sat down on the wicker furniture, and I served my brownies.

The two boys were as quiet as a pair of mice, but Mom was bubbling over with questions. The first one was, "How are you doing in school?" I didn't think this was the time to tell her that I had no intention of becoming a doctor, so I didn't mention it. "Great," I said.

"And you?" she asked Afsaneh.

"Couldn't be better!"

The questions kept coming: "How is Shamsi? How's Naheed? How is Robabeh Khanoom getting along on her own?"

"Robabeh Khanoom!" I said. "Why do you even ask about her?"

"Because you know it's wrong to hold grudges!" my mother said.

At one point, in the middle of all the noisy, breathless talking, Amir turned and whispered something in Mom's ear.

"What does he need?" Afsaneh asked.

And Mom said, "He needs a glass of milk."

That's when it struck me: These boys really didn't get it. They didn't understand that we were their family. They thought they were in the home of two strange women.

I fetched a glass of milk for Amir, and, when he was done, we took everyone back upstairs to show them their presents. Afsaneh insisted on making them try everything on, and we started with our brothers. But nothing fit them. We had pictured them as we remembered them, as mere boys, with no regard whatsoever for the passage of time. We never imagined that they might have grown up without us there to witness it.

We had a little more luck with Mom's things. Once again she ran out of adjectives to describe them, but I think she was just being polite. She wasn't ready to be that American.

Then we went back downstairs to see what Mom had brought. There were traditional Kurdish dresses for each of us, with matching scarves. The dresses were richly layered and very colorful, not something we could have worn on the streets—except, perhaps, on Halloween. Still, they were from Iran, and I loved them. She had also brought a number of spices all the way from Iran, suspecting they would be unavailable in America. These included *zereshk*, which I can only describe as sour, red currants; *kashk*, a dry, ball-shaped yogurt used in many eggplant dishes; and *leemo amani*, the dried lemons that are a key ingredient in *ghormeh sabzi*, one of my favorite meals.

She had also brought a beautiful *gheyloon*, or hookah, a type of water pipe, to remind us of our heritage. It had a particularly striking base made of blue glass, and, when she set it in a corner of the living room, it brightened up the whole place.

As night fell, we put the exhausted boys to bed. Mom was tired, too, but, before she went to bed, she took us aside and said, "Please don't say anything to the boys about how your father died."

I was stunned. "They don't know?" I asked.

"No," she said. "They don't know."

✿ ✿ ✿

We had taken two days off to spend with Mom and the boys, and we managed to fill every minute of our time together. We went to see Shamsi. We paid a call on Robabeh and Naheed, and Robabeh smiled, nodded, and pretended to like us. She was a little upset with us, however, since we had declined to tell her about Mom's arrival.

"It's all about respect," my mother said after that challenging little visit. "No matter how you feel, the family took you in at a time when you had nowhere to go. You must never forget that act of kindness."

"Act of kindness?! Right!"

Then we went back to Sac Lane and started becoming a real family again, and almost immediately Afsaneh began slipping into the role of the father. Mom relied on her as I had been relying on her for years, and, when the boys had questions, they usually went to her first. I didn't know where she found the strength. After all, she hadn't had much of a childhood, either.

But Mom was working on making up for lost time. By the third day, she was very much at home in the kitchen, being a mom, whipping together some of our favorite dishes. *Gheymeh. Ghormeh sabzi. Kashke bademjan.* She refused to rest. Everything was boom boom boom! She had hit the ground running: "Where is the grocery store? Where are the cleaning supplies? What can I do to help?"

"Mom, *relax.*"

"I can't relax. I need a job. What kind of job do you think I could get?"

That's one of the things I've inherited from my mother: the inability to relax.

"Come on. Let's watch TV. *Dynasty* is on."

She watched for a few minutes, but when I looked up she was staring at me. "What?" I said.

"Afschineh, you squint."

"No I don't."

"I've been watching you for several days. You definitely squint."

The following day, she took me to have my eyes checked, and of course I needed glasses. In my heart I knew I needed glasses, but I didn't want to be a total geek. Now there was no escaping it.

The boys spent a lot of time in the house, watching TV, and it felt as if history was repeating itself. One Sunday, Afsaneh urged them to go outside and play tennis, and they went upstairs and put on their matching outfits. The pants were so tight they looked like hot pants, but the boys didn't complain, and they took their matching rackets and marched off. An hour later they were back, and Ali was bleeding from the mouth and nose. They had run into three bigger kids on the tennis court and had been mercilessly taunted. It wasn't every day one found such an easy target: two little Iranian boys in hot pants.

At one point, Ali explained, one of the boys had taken Amir's tennis racket, and Amir had turned to him and said in a very docile voice, "Puh-leez . . . Puh-leez give." That was the extent of his English, and it went unheeded. To compound matters, the boys started laughing, at which point Ali lost his temper. Punches were thrown, and he got Amir's racket back, but the hot pants were history.

In June, we went to Washington, D.C. for a night, to visit the Kareemzadeh family. Mr. Kareemzadeh had been a military officer, like Baba Joon, and his wife had been a teacher, like Mom. They had known one another in Iran. Their three sons were a few years older than us, and I didn't really remember any of them. That visit was the first of many, and the Kareemzadehs became like a second family to us. They would invite us to Persian concerts, and they'd take the boys to play soccer. When we returned to their house, they made us feel that it was our home, too. I will never forget something my mother said during that first visit. It was dusk, and she and I had stepped out into the backyard, which was broad, nicely manicured, and ablaze with flowers and fruit trees. "Maybe someday I'll have a garden again." I had never heard her say anything so wistfully, and the phrase never left me. "Maybe someday I'll have a garden again."

That was the summer of 1987. The summer Klaus Barbie was sentenced to life in prison by the French. The summer of Iran-Contra. The summer a four-year-old girl was the sole survivor of a Northwest Airlines crash at the Detroit Metropolitan Airport, a crash that claimed one hundred and fifty-six lives. People talked about that little girl for days, and my mother saw the lesson in it. "There is tragedy everywhere," she said. "We are very fortunate. You should never feel you've been singled out for bad things."

She was right. We were struggling financially, and the future looked uncertain. But we were together again, and we had one another. Each of us had been shaped by the death of Baba Joon, to one degree or another, but life wasn't about the past; life was about forward movement. And no one was more committed to forward movement than my mother.

"Shamsi, can you find me a job?" she said. "I need a job where I don't have to speak English."

Shamsi, who came frequently for dinner, said she would ask around. The only thing that came immediately to mind was a local newspaper plant, where she had been briefly employed years earlier, but it was heavy, monotonous work.

"Nothing is too heavy or too monotonous," my mother said.

The next day, as we were leaving the house to go to the grocery store, we discovered that the car had a flat tire. There was a young family in a neighboring town house, and the mother offered us a ride to the station to get the tire fixed. She brought her little boy with her. En route, she told us that her husband was in the navy, that she worked, too, and that she was on her way to drop her son off at the babysitter's—a half-hour away. When I translated for my mother, she said, "Ask the lady if she would like me to babysit her handsome boy."

"No," Afsaneh said in Farsi. "That's too embarrassing."

But my mother insisted, and we asked. The woman seemed to think it was a good idea. "Let me discuss it with my husband," she said.

Early the next morning, she, her little boy, and her husband came by the house. They were very friendly until they saw the *gheyloon*, at which point they concluded that these foreigners smoked drugs, and they then tried to beat a hasty retreat. Luckily, Afsaneh saw what was happening, and she explained, much to their amusement, that the pipe was strictly *decorative*. The next thing we knew, Mom had a full-time job taking care of their three-year-old boy.

As for Ali and Amir, they had plenty to do. In good weather, they swam or played tennis, though not in hot pants. In bad weather, they watched TV, which was unlike anything they'd seen in either Tehran or Paris.

"They remind me of us when we first arrived," Afsaneh remarked.

Amir was an avid cartoon watcher, and he especially liked those robotlike *Transformers*. He used to walk around the house transforming himself, complete with metallic sound effects, but his showbiz aspirations weren't limited to television. Sometimes he and Ali would disappear upstairs, only to reappear a few minutes later, with Ali trumpeting their return like a master of ceremonies. "Elvis is in the building!" he would say in broken, accented English, and Amir would burst into the room with one of Mom's coats draped over his shoulders like a cape, his hair slicked back into a half-baked pompadour, and with a pair of badly drawn eyeliner sideburns. His favorite song was "Tutti Frutti," and we often had to suffer through every last stanza.

One Sunday we took the family to Busch Gardens, which was the highlight of their summer. They charged a hefty fee at the door, but all the rides were free. Since we wanted our money's worth, it turned into a very long day indeed.

From time to time, to break things up, we would invite people to the house for dinner. Most of them were Iranian families we had met through Daï'e Mammad, people of Mom's generation, and she was glad for the company. She would cook, and everyone would have a good time, and a few weeks later they would invite us to their homes and do the same for us. The women often took Mom aside to say nice things about me and Afsaneh. "You are very lucky," they would tell her. "You have two such nice, traditional girls, not wild like some of these other creatures. You should be very proud."

And Mom *was* proud. For a number of years, she had been hearing less than favorable reports from Daï'e Mammad, and, later, from Robabeh: that we didn't study; that we watched cartoons all day; that we worked at a terrible place in the mall frequented by a "bad element." Now she could see that she had had nothing to worry about. We were perfect geeks; we were geeks to the core.

Afsaneh was twenty by now; I was eighteen. Neither of us had made much progress since that big breakthrough day when we shaved our legs. Neither of us had even considered plucking our eyebrows. In Iran, back when we were little, a girl was not supposed to pluck her eyebrows until she was a woman, and she only became a woman when she got married.

Mom was proud of us, yes, but her pride was mixed in with lots of other feelings. I suspect she felt badly about all the years we had missed together. She had not been there to watch us turn into young women, and I could see it pained her. She was curious, too, about our history—What had we lived through in the course of those six long years? What did we know about life, love, and men?—but she didn't know how to broach it. We were her daughters, certainly, but not fully her daughters. Not yet, anyway.

"Why don't you have high heels?" she would ask, looking through our closets, as if she could find some answers there. "Why only flats? You can't go to a dinner party in flats. That's not done. It's unacceptable."

It amused us. She took comfort in the fact that we were traditional, but she seemed eager to help us catch up. On the outside we were young women; on the inside we were still lost little girls, the girls we'd been in Tehran.

"Why do you dress like this? Long skirts? Long sleeves? It is one thing to respect tradition, but, really, this is too much!" my mother would say.

There were many things she would have probably liked to ask us outright, all the things a normal mother would want to know, and there were many things we probably longed to tell her, but we didn't know where to begin. And the fact is, to this day, none of the Latifi women are quick to open up or express emotion (except at airports, where we seem to lose all self-control). I would have to say that this is directly connected to the death of Baba Joon. When he died, it was almost more than we could bear, and I know that I closed off a part of myself to survive. Still, I believe I'm getting better at it. So is Mom. She used to say nothing at all. She wouldn't allow herself to show any emotion whatsoever, no matter how upset she was. "Oh, everything's fine!" she would say. "Don't worry about me!" She was the wife of a soldier—as tough as the hardest nail. Emotion was a luxury she couldn't afford. And in those early years, she didn't even allow herself to think about it. There were practical matters to attend to. She wanted to be a mother, but she also wanted to be useful. I could see how much it frustrated her to be trapped in the house, dependent on her two daughters, the two daughters she was still trying to get to know.

"I need you to take me to get a driver's license," she said one night over dinner.

"What do you need a driver's license for?" Afsaneh asked. "We only have one car, and it's not a very good car at that."

"We're not always going to have one car," she replied. "This is America."

So Afsaneh took her to the Department of Motor Vehicles. She had a valid Iranian license, so she didn't have to take a road test, but the written test was a requirement. Afsaneh asked the clerk if she could translate for her, since Mom spoke only Farsi, and he allowed it. Mom passed with flying colors. I believe Afsaneh did a little more than translate.

As they were leaving, with Mom's provisional permit, they ran into an Iranian friend of Nasser's. "This is Fatemeh," Afsaneh said, indicating Mom as she made the introductions. They made a little small talk, then went on their way, and, when they got into the car, Afsaneh could see that Mom was upset.

"What's wrong?" she asked.

"What is this 'Fatemeh' business?" Mom said. "Nobody calls me Fatemeh. Why didn't you introduce me as your mother? Am I not your mother?"

Afsaneh was struck by the realization that she was having a genuinely hard time coming to terms with the fact that this was *really* her mother and that she even *had* a mother. She had usurped that role for so many years that she wasn't ready to relinquish it. And in fact if she eventually learned to give it up, it was only because she had begun taking on the role of the father.

❀ ❀ ❀

Later that same summer, I left DJs and went to work for Benetton, the colorful, international clothing emporium. They had opened a store at Military Circle Mall, and it reminded me of their store in Vienna. This wasn't an entirely pleasant memory—we had blown a lot of money in that store and in many other stores, and had managed to seal our own fate. But I was ready for a change, and I filled out an application. They hired me on the spot, to work part-time. After a few days they told me they liked my style and that I could name my own hours. Before long, I was an assistant manager, and, when they opened another store, at the Lynnhaven Mall, they asked me to help manage it. I talked to Afsaneh about it and arranged to have her drop me there three nights a week, on her way to her own job at DJs. Within a few weeks, the Benetton people asked me to go to Washington with them to help them decide on next year's lines.

It was pretty amazing. I was only eighteen, but I felt like an adult. They kept giving me raises. They had me take care of the banking. If anyone came in with a complaint, I would handle it. Best of all, I got 40 percent off on the merchandise, and I kept buying beautiful things for myself, Afsaneh, and Mom. We didn't feel like such geeks anymore. We felt pretty damn fashionable.

The people at Benetton had faith in me and that nourished me. It made me feel normal, accepted. My sister and I had been in the country for many years, but we had always been very isolated. Now we had our family back. We felt more complete, healthier.

We began to entertain more, and from time to time invited some of the Persian students to the house. Mom made a great impression on everyone who met her. She was charming, a good cook, and had a great sense of humor, and one would never have guessed what she'd endured in Iran. This was not something she shared readily, by the way: She preferred to keep most details of her life to herself.

"Don't tell anyone about the babysitting," she would caution us before the guests arrived, and we never did, though she reminded us of it every time. It's not that she was ashamed of what she did or that she thought it was beneath her, but that other, less enlightened people might think less of her if they found out. Once again, it was connected to this notion of saving face. There's a popular Farsi expression: *Sooratesho ba sili sorkh meekoneh* (She reddens her face with slaps). Simply put, it's about bringing color to your face by slapping your cheeks. This makes you look healthy and happy, and this is the face you should show other people. They don't need to know that your red cheeks have nothing to do with happiness.

❀ ❀ ❀

In late August, Afsaneh finally left DJs. She went to work for Dollar-Rent-a-Car at the airport. She enjoyed the work, but for months on end she found herself stymied by a section of the rental contract. The form said, "Initial here if there is no discrepancy." Afsaneh did not know what this meant, and—to compound matters—she had misread it. Every time she rented a car, she told the customer, "Initial here if there is no conspiracy." She got a lot of strange looks, especially from the military men. They must have thought she was trying to pass code.

We would laugh about these things over dinner. We were becoming a family again. We were getting to know one

AFSANEH

another. Mom was becoming more of a mother every day, and every day she seemed more determined to transform us. She made us get rid of the long sleeves and the long skirts. She bought us heels. She bought us our first pantyhose. She even took pity on me and had me fitted for contacts, despite the expense, to make me more presentable.

Suddenly, Afsaneh and I were looking pretty hot, if I may say so myself. And now that Mom was in town, we were easier to approach. "Do you know what Pezeschgi Khanoom told me last night?" my mother would say, looking at Afsaneh. "She said, 'This is just the type of girl I would want for my son.'"

Suddenly, Afsaneh was getting proposals. People would come over for tea, as if this was a regular *khastegari*, but of course Afsaneh had no interest in showing off her nonexistent tea-serving skills, and Mom didn't really want her to. "My daughters are not interested in marriage," she would tell the prospective mothers-in-law with as much tact as she could muster. "They are much too young to marry. They are going to have careers. All my children are going to be doctors."

When the guests left, she would tell us that marriage would come in due course. "With kids! Lots of kids! But don't think about marriage now. Your careers are more important. You will be doctors, and you will always be able to take care of yourselves, no matter what happens."

In September, Afsaneh drove the boys to Bayside Junior High. As our self-appointed paterfamilias, she had gone to the school several weeks ahead

229

of time to sign them up, and she now wanted to make sure that their first day of school went smoothly. She even went to their first class with them, which I'm not sure they appreciated, and showed them how to put their hands over their hearts during the *Pledge of Allegiance*. At night, she and I would help them with their homework, and we began to talk to them in English.

"What's for dinner?" Ali asked Mom one night.

"Speak to me in Farsi," she said. "I don't understand English."

Don't get me wrong: Mom was thrilled that the boys were learning English, and she was already in love with her new life and her new home in America, but she felt very strongly about their mother tongue. "Every language you learn makes you a stronger person," she used to say. "But to forget your mother tongue is to forget your roots, and a tree without roots will not stand."

In some ways, I understood what she meant. For many immigrants, English is the language of success, and they push their children to learn it at the expense of their mother tongue. Often, these children become lost between two cultures.

In October, with the four of us in school, Mom found two more kids to baby-sit. She tended to her little menagerie from eight in the morning till seven at night. Also that September, Shamsi moved in with us. She had been struggling to make ends meet ever since Nasser and his family had left for Florida, and she asked if we'd make room for her. There was nothing to it. We put another mattress on the floor. The upstairs was littered with so many single beds that we began to refer to it as the emergency room.

The one other thing I remember clearly from this period was the day I came clean with Mom about my academic aspirations. I was a junior in college, and I couldn't keep it from her any longer.

"I've decided I want to be a lawyer," I told her.

"A lawyer? What do you mean a lawyer? You've been studying medicine for two years."

"Not really."

She was very upset. It was as if the Latifi Clinic were going up in smoke. "What about *royay'e man*, my dream?" she asked. "And a lawyer? What kind of person becomes a lawyer?" I might as well have told her I wanted to be a pole dancer.

"Mom, it's different here," I said. "In Iran, you're either a doctor or an engineer. But in America, being a lawyer is an honorable profession."

She didn't believe me, so she asked around, and her new friends set her mind at ease. "It's a good thing, being a lawyer. Very handy—having a lawyer in the family. And having both a lawyer and a doctor, well—that's a real blessing!"

Then I told her I wasn't going to be *just* a lawyer. I had been working on a double-major. I would study law, yes, but I'd also been studying German. This made her very happy. She gave me a big smile, and I smiled right back.

"Afschineh," she said abruptly, no longer smiling. "We have to do something about that overbite."

The following month we found an orthodontist, and I got braces—on the installment plan.

"What a great country!" my mother said.

"Yes," I said. "Isn't it?"

With the new braces, it took me a long time to smile again. But I was smiling on the inside.

VIRGINIA BEACH AT ONE OF MANY PERSIAN GATHERINGS

CHAPTER THIRTEEN

The American Dream ↷

ON GRADUATION DAY AT OLD DOMINION UNIVERSITY

OUR TABLE, ALL SET FOR NOROUZ

As winter approached, the family settled into a steady routine. Mom had her babysitting job, Ali and Amir were in school, Afsaneh and I remained focused on our studies, and Shamsi was working erratic hours as a home-care nurse.

By this time, too, we had a second car, a sputtering green Omni, also purchased at auction. Afsaneh and I let Mom have the Nissan and relied on the Omni for our own needs. One snowy afternoon, Afsaneh had an evening class, so I took the car, went to work, and arranged to have Mom fetch Afsaneh at school. When the time came, Shamsi happened to be home, so she got in the car with Mom and off they went together. Later that night, when I returned from work, I found the boys alone in the house, parked in front of the TV.

"Where's Mom and everybody?" I asked.

"She and Shamsi went to get Afsi," Ali told me.

Just then, the phone rang. It was Afsaneh, calling to say that she had been waiting for Mom for more than an hour. I looked out the window. It was still snowing, and it worried me. "I'll come get you myself," I said.

Not fifteen minutes later, as I was making my way along the freeway, I saw dozens of flashing emergency lights up ahead, on my side of the roadway. A split second later, I recognized our Nissan Maxima, wedged under the hood of a truck, then spotted Mom and Shamsi off to one side, talking to a police officer. I hit the brakes and went into a skid, but I somehow managed to regain control of the car and eased myself onto the shoulder. I got out, breathless, and ran back toward the scene.

"What happened?!" I asked my mother. It was a silly question. I could see what had happened: They'd almost been killed. But neither of them had a single scratch. A few minutes later, the officer wrapped up his paperwork, a tow truck came for the Nissan, and we all piled into the Omni and went to fetch Afsaneh. The snowstorm continued unabated. "Well," I said, trying to make light of the situation. "It's going to be a white Christmas."

Of course we didn't celebrate Christmas, but we bought a few things for the boys and took a few days off to spend time together, like a regular family. Right after the holiday, however, the property manager came to see us with some bad news. "You told me that only three people would be living on the property, but I see all sorts of people coming and going all day long," she said. "I'm afraid I'm going to have to ask you to move out."

Afsaneh pleaded with her—after all, she was the head of the household—but the woman said her hands were tied. "I know you are good, quiet people, but you lied on your lease, and my job is in jeopardy. I'm afraid I have no choice."

The following weekend, we began looking for a new home. As expected, all the applications asked us to specify how many people would be living on the premises, and we were afraid to lie. "It's just a harmless little lie," Mom remarked. "Put down 'four' if you must."

"Oh really?" Afsaneh said. "You don't remember what you used to tell us when we were children? *Dooroogh goo doshman'e khoda'st.*"

Technically, the phrase translates as "a liar is God's enemy." But in spirit it is much less harsh than it sounds; it is probably closer to "liar, liar, pants on fire."

"You're making too much of this," Mom said. "If you don't lie, we'll never find a home."

But Afsaneh refused to lie this time, and we were invariably turned away. There were six of us, including Shamsi, and six people in a two-bedroom apartment was unacceptable, if not downright un-American. If we could have afforded a three-bedroom place, we would have jumped at it, but an extra bedroom was simply not in the budget.

Finally, in desperation, Mom began to take the car out in the early mornings, while we were still asleep, to cruise the various neighborhoods. She returned home after one such mission to report that she had seen a notice nailed to a town house in nearby Kempsville Lakes—a nice, solid, middle-class neighborhood—and she needed one of us to come along to translate. I went with her. The town house was the last one on the street, right up against the dense woods. It was one of several neighborhood properties in foreclosure.

"Are the schools good here?" Mom asked.

They were. When Afsaneh and I had been looking for a new home, just before the family arrived, we were told that Kempsville High was one of the better public schools in the area. This was important, since both boys would be ready for high school in no time at all.

At her insistence, I called a broker, and he came over and gave us a tour of the place. I knew right away we didn't stand a chance. It seemed palatial. The downstairs consisted of a nice-size kitchen with a living room and a dining area, a family room that had the potential to become a fourth bedroom, and a half-bathroom. Upstairs, there were three bedrooms and two full baths. The complex also featured a community swimming pool and two tennis courts, and the grounds were very nicely maintained.

"There's no yard," I said, looking for something to make the place seem less appealing.

"It doesn't matter," Mom said. "My garden can wait."

The broker was kind enough to explain the process. We would be asked to make a bid on the house, he said. This particular house was on the market for a very reasonable $68,000, and the minimum bid, which would constitute a down payment, could be no less than a thousand dollars.

"There will probably be several bids on the house, and in my experience, everyone invariably bids the absolute minimum," the broker said. "So, if you want my advice, you'll throw in an extra hundred dollars. You'd think an extra hundred dollars wouldn't make much difference to the bank, but it does."

The following week we submitted our bid, per his directions, and twenty-four hours later he called to tell us that the house was ours. We were over the moon. We asked if we could take the boys to see it, and he met us there that very afternoon. The boys loved the house. They couldn't wait to move in.

When we finally signed the last of the paperwork, the broker turned the keys over to Mom, and she thanked him in halting English. "Very nice. Very much to be happy." We watched from the empty house as he returned to his car, and, when he got in and pulled away, he smiled and waved at us. We waved back in unison. The moment he was out of sight, we turned our attention to our new home. The boys ran from room to room, whooping and hollering.

"I can't believe this," I said. "I never thought it would happen."

"Well, it happened," my mother said. "And now we have to get serious." She was worried. The mortgage alone was six hundred and forty dollars a month. "I need a real job," she said. "I can't keep relying on you two for everything."

"Let's do one thing at a time," Afsaneh replied.

The first thing we had to do was make the place livable. The house needed painting, *badly*, so we talked to some of the Persian students we'd met at ODU and asked if they'd help. On the appointed weekend, they all came over and pitched in. It was a marathon painting session. There was music and plenty of cold drinks, and Mom just kept the food coming and coming. It turned into one of the most fun weekends we could remember: two crazy days of laughter, plaster, and paint—the beginning of a whole new chapter in our lives.

We moved in a week later, the boys in one room, Mom and Shamsi in another, and me and Afsaneh in a third. We invested in some mirrored vertical blinds, which at the time we thought were very happening, but which were in fact absolutely horrendous. Afsaneh bought a small desk and set it up in a corner of the family room, where she intended to take care of our finances. I had always given her my paycheck, and she'd always been in charge of all of our bills. This is how it continued. She was meticulous about money, but it continued to be a major concern.

"I need a job," Mom kept repeating. "We can't go on like this."

She was no longer babysitting for our neighbors, since they were no longer our neighbors. A few days after we moved in, she met an Iranian man who lived in the neighborhood. He and his American wife were looking for someone to take care of their child, preferably someone who spoke Farsi, and Mom told them she was available. A week after that, we met a second couple, from a town house just down the street, and they were looking for someone to care for their two children. Mom took that job as well. Suddenly she was running her own day care center, albeit an illegal one, from eight in the morning until six at night.

But money remained tight. Our mortgage was almost twice what our rent had been, and we had been so desperate to find a new home that we had convinced ourselves, erroneously, that we could manage. Now reality set in. I was at Benetton, Afsaneh was at Dollar-Rent-a-Car, Shamsi had her nursing job, and Mom was putting in more than ten hours a day, five days a week, with the three neighborhood kids—and we were *still* coming up short.

One evening, Afsaneh returned from her job at the airport with an American girl who worked for a competing car rental agency. She was looking for a place to rent, and Afsaneh had told her she could stay with us until she found one. We put her up in the family room, which had its own bathroom, and she seemed very happy there. At the end of the week, she asked if she could stay and pay rent, and she ended up living with us—and helping with the bills—for the next four months.

Mom kept pushing us to find her a real job, though we didn't see how this would be possible, considering that she was busy babysitting all day and she didn't have any marketable skills—not in America, anyway. "I can do some-thing at night or on the weekends," she insisted, and she was relentless. "Find me a job. You're not looking. I'd look if I could read the newspapers."

Finally, Shamsi made inquiries at the old printing plant where she had once worked, and they asked her to have Mom come in and fill out an appli-cation. She went in, with Afsaneh, and they asked her when she could start. "Now," she said. "Thank you." That was almost the extent of her English, but it was enough.

The following Monday, she was hard at work. It was a horrible job and an even more horrible shift. She started at midnight and worked till four in the morning, and her duties consisted of assembling the newspapers as they came off the presses. The comics, the inserts, the advertising pages—they had to be packed in a certain order. It was heavy, manual labor—real backbreaking work—but Mom returned from her first day on the job and professed to like it. "It was great," she said.

We felt awful. Here was our mother, a forty-two-year-old woman, lifting heavy stacks of newspapers for four straight hours, with only two small breaks in between, then returning home to try to get a little sleep before putting in a full day of babysitting. She had no intention of giving up the babysitting job. At night, when the three children went home to their parents, she would clean up and get dinner ready for us, her own family, and after dinner she would try to sleep for a couple of hours before heading back to the newspaper plant. To compound matters, her schedule changed from week to week. She never knew which nights she would be working, and she was often expected to show up on at least one weekend night.

Afsaneh and I were working pretty hard ourselves, but it didn't bother us because that was the only life we knew. I would have class till about two, then race home, grab a bite to eat, and arrive at Benetton by four. Whenever the store was quiet, I'd try to do a little homework, and, when ten o'clock rolled around, I locked the doors. I'd usually be home by eleven, at which point Mom was just getting up, preparing to leave for work, and I wouldn't see her until the next morning at breakfast. She would light up when I walked in, and sometimes she'd do a little dance in the kitchen, holding her arms out to her sides and swinging her hips like a hula dancer. It was very funny, especially since Mom had never once in her life danced in public, not even at her own wedding.

"What is that crazy little dance you do?" Afsaneh asked her one morning. "I'm just happy," she said, laughing. "Why don't you join me?"

On weekends, if she wasn't working at the plant, she would sometimes try to make up for the lack of sleep by stealing little catnaps here and there. Sometimes, Ali and Amir would get into noisy arguments, and I'd hiss at them to quiet down. "Try to be more considerate! Mom is napping!" They would continue to argue, but in pantomime now, their eyes angry, their mouths contorted in soundless screams, and Mom would enjoy some badly needed rest.

Mom never complained, no matter how tired she was. There were times when she needed a few minutes of sleep before going off to work, and she'd plead with us to wake her at eleven-thirty sharp. The plant was only ten minutes away, so she didn't need much time to get ready, but she didn't want to risk being late for work. At the exact time, one of us would go into the bedroom and call out, gently, "Mom, it's eleven-thirty." And she'd pop up in bed like a jack-in-the-box, exclaiming: "Eleven-thirty?! Is it really?" It became something of a joke in the house. "Eleven-thirty! Impossible! You must be mistaken!"

I don't know how Mom did it. She even found time for a bit of socializing with her new friends in the Persian community. They would have us over for dinner, and she would reciprocate as soon as she could manage it. She would always put on a good show. She never skimped on food—not in Iran in the days when she could afford it and not here in America where she couldn't. She took great pride in what she served. She would rather serve no meat at all than a mediocre cut that was unworthy of her guests.

On one or two occasions, when the evenings went on longer than expected, Mom would note the time and beg off, saying she was tired. But she was only hurrying away because it would soon be time for work. She'd change into her cotton shirt and her khaki pants and off she'd go, only to return several hours later, her clothes stained black with ink.

She told no one about the job, of course, just as she told no one about the babysitting. She always looked cheerful and happy, her face reddened with slaps. And perhaps she looked *too* healthy. At one point one of the Persian couples took her aside to let her know that they were investing in a store in a strip mall and that for a very modest $180,000 she could become a partner. It was kind of sad, really. Here she was, living hand-to-mouth, and they assumed she had money to burn.

"It's best to keep your problems to yourself," she explained. "No one wants to hear about them, so there's really no point in whining. And what can anyone do for you, anyway? Most people have problems of their own."

And she really truly believed she had nothing to complain about. "Look at us. We have a house. The boys are in a good school. You two are studying hard and building a future. What could be better?"

It amazed me. Not one word of complaint, *ever*. She was putting in fifty hours a week with the neighborhood kids and another twenty at the plant, and she prepared meals for the family every day of the week, but there was never even a peep of protest.

In fact, it was quite the opposite. She found humor in every situation. "The poor creatures who can't show their faces in the daytime, among regular people—those are my coworkers at the plant," she said, laughing. "They are all a little strange, and I guess I'm one of them."

She would tell us about some of the characters at work: the man with very bad skin, the woman who never smiled, the drunk who had trouble standing by the end of the shift. Mom was curious about all of them—*Who were they? What kinds of lives did they lead? Did they have families?*—but she never approached them, not even during the short breaks. She was shy, she didn't speak English, and she always found a stack of papers near her station and sat there by herself, sipping her coffee. One night, as she was perched there, alone, deep in thought, pondering her past, thinking about Baba Joon and Iran and the life she'd left behind, she was approached by Davie, the night manager. He was a very short man, and Mom was under the impression that his name was *Baby*. "Good evening, Mrs. Latifi," Davie said, startling her. "Why aren't you joining us?"

Mom looked up at him, still lost in thought, and for a moment she had no idea where she was. "*Salam arz meekonam*," she said, bowing politely. "I offer you my greetings." Then she realized she was at the plant, not in Iran, and she added a single word to this very formal greeting: "Baby."

Davie looked at her, understandably confused, then turned and walked off without another word.

When I got out of bed that morning, I found Mom in the kitchen, getting breakfast ready, as usual. She poured me a cup of coffee and told me the story, and I laughed so hard I spat my coffee across the table.

Whenever we socialized—and we made an effort to do so at least once a month, for Mom's sake, if not our own—the Persian women always talked about their favorite subject: their children. I remember one couple in particular—an ear, nose, and throat specialist and his wife, a gynecologist—who were very worried about their two young daughters. There was so little parental control in this country, they said. The boys became involved with drugs. The girls turned into "hoochie mamas," party girls. And you could always spot the hoochie mamas a mile away: They dressed so trashy!

I am pleased to say that Afsaneh and I were not considered hoochie mamas. On the contrary, people went out of their way to praise us—"They are such good girls. So well-behaved! So polite!"—and my mother accepted the praise with little show of emotion, as if to say that she expected no less from her daughters.

Afsaneh was twenty-one at this point, and I was nineteen. Most girls our age were into serious partying, but not us. We were proper young ladies. When we had people to the house for dinner, we helped serve each dish, and, when they were done, we cleared the table. And we always addressed our elders formally: We used the word *shoma*, the equivalent of "thou;" never *toh*, the informal "you," which was reserved for one's peers. We probably overdid it. Whenever we would reach for a drink, we would always look at our elders and sometimes address them with the formal phrase *ba ejazeh* (with your permission). This was very old-school, but we couldn't shake it, nor did we want to. There was nothing wrong with good manners.

"I don't know how you do it!" the mothers would exclaim.

"They do it themselves," Mom would reply. "They are good girls."

During these get-togethers, the adults would talk about the old days, and the memories were often painful, but there had been many good things in Iran, too. Some of the Persians felt that good things would come again in Iran, and they longed to go home. But not Mom. She saw the possibilities here; she saw good things happening. She missed her aging mother, certainly, and I know she missed her garden, but America was home now. She was determined to rebuild here.

One Saturday afternoon I returned from work to find Ali standing at the railing, halfway up the stairs, crying.

"What's wrong?" I asked.

"Grandma died," he said, crying harder.

I hurried through the house and found Mom on the couch, convulsed by sobs. I tried to comfort her, but to no avail. The words came out of her in bits and starts: Mammon was dead, and it was all her fault. She had left her behind in Iran, old and sick and with those terribly gnarled fingers. "But what could I do?" she wailed. "How could I choose between my mother and my children?! I have four children! My children needed me!"

I assured her that it wasn't her fault and that she'd had absolutely no choice in the matter, but she was inconsolable. When night fell, I told her I was going to call the newspaper plant to say she was sick, but she would have none of it. She pulled herself together and went to work, and on Monday she was back to double duty: babysitting from eight to six and off to the plant before midnight. Still, for the next few weeks, she padded around the house like a lost soul, and from time to time, without any warning whatsoever, she would burst into tears: "It was my fault! I let her die! And I couldn't even go back to bury her!"

There was nothing to do but let her work through the pain, and that's what we did. We waited. And before long Mom was back.

Then it was March. I got up one morning to find Mom cleaning the house with great vigor. "What are you doing?" I asked.

"It's almost Norouz," she said. "Or had you forgotten?"

I had indeed forgotten. She was referring to the Persian New Year, which on the Gregorian calendar falls in late March. About two weeks before the start of Norouz, many Persians take part in something called *khane tekani*, which literally means "shaking your house." You will see people painting their homes, washing their carpets, sweeping out their attics, cleaning their yards. One could say it is a form of spring cleaning, but that is only a very small part of it. In Persian, *no* means "new," and *rouz* means "day." The last Wednesday of the year is known as *chahaar shanbeh suri*. At dusk, with the cleaning over, people light small bonfires and sing traditional songs, and those who can manage it are urged to jump over the flames. Fire, too, is seen as a cleansing, purifying agent: It burns away all the negative things in one's life—the bad habits, the misfortune, the sorrow. It's all about cleanliness: clean house, clean soul, new beginnings.

On the "new day" itself, people focus on family and friends, and, for the next two weeks, there is much visiting back and forth. In each house, one finds a *sofreh eid*, a variation on the engagement cloth used during wedding ceremonies. Laid out on this garment, one will find  the *Haft Seen* (Seven S's,) comprised of seven items that begin with the letter S. These are *sabzeh*, or sprouts (representing rebirth); *samanu*, a pudding (for sweetness in life); *senjed*, the sweet, dry fruit of the lotus tree (representing love); *serkeh*, or vinegar (for patience); *seer*, or garlic (for its medicinal qualities); *somaq*, or sumac berries (for the color of sunrise); and *seeb*, or red apples (symbols of health and beauty). In addition, there are candles laid out on the *sofreh eid*, one for each member of the household. The lit candles represent the goodness and warmth that enter life with the coming of spring.

Now here we were, in America, these many years later, hugging, kissing, and wishing one another a happy new year. Mom sprinkled rose water on our hands and told us to take our seats at the table. She had prepared the traditional Norouz meal of *sabzi polo va mahi*, a fish and rice dish infused with fresh green herbs. It was even better than I remembered.

We didn't have much family in America, so there wasn't going to be any visiting back and forth, so when Afsaneh suggested we go to Tampa to see Nasser and Angie, we all jumped at the idea.

Two weeks later, at the beginning of spring break, Afsaneh got a deal from Dollar-Rent-a-Car, and we piled into a new Dodge and roared away. This time, we didn't take a butter knife for protection. We didn't need one; we had one another.

When we crossed into Florida, I could almost feel the collective relief. We were on vacation, a *real* vacation.

By that point, Nasser and Angie had had a second child, another little girl, and they had abandoned the restaurant, which had been a struggle from the start. They had invested in a car dealership instead and were beginning to have some real success with it. "Business is good," Nasser said. "So I have a surprise for you."

The following morning, he took us to Disney World—something I'd been dreaming about for many years. He really went all out. We saw Epcot Center. The *Jaws* show. We went on every ride imaginable. We ate vast amounts of junk food (which didn't mix well with the rides). And, at long last, I met Mickey Mouse. I even went up to him and shook his hand. I, Afschineh, age nineteen, grinning from ear to ear and shaking the hand of the elusive Mr. Mouse. It wasn't the earth-shattering experience I'd been expecting, but then again, I wasn't the same girl.

At the end of the week, we were on our way home. Mom returned to work, the boys returned to school, and Afsaneh and I took up where we'd left off. As yet another academic year drew to a close, I began preparing for the LSAT, the test that would determine whether I was going to get into law school. I discovered that you could practice for the test, and that sample LSAT books were available at the college bookstore. I would take these to Benetton with me and work on them during my breaks.

Summer came and went, uneventful in the extreme. Even now, as I rack my brain to remember it, I'm at a loss. Mom worked, Afsaneh worked, I worked. The boys whiled away their days playing tennis, swimming, and watching television, and the Elvis impersonations gave way to renditions of the Bobby McFerrin hit, "Don't Worry, Be Happy."

In September, Afsaneh and I were back at ODU. This was her final semester. She would have graduated the previous spring, but she'd been so busy trying to make money that she was still a few credits shy. Unfortunately, she was having serious second thoughts about medical school. She shared these misgivings with me, but not with Mom. I had no such misgivings about my own future, however. I knew I was going to become a lawyer.

A month later I went to take the LSAT, and I was very nervous. When I arrived at the auditorium, the girl at the next desk turned to me and asked, "Did you take Kaplan?" I had no idea what she was talking about and learned only much later that there were dozens of preparatory courses designed to help students improve their scores. It was a good thing I didn't know about them since I couldn't have afforded them anyway, though I must say I was disappointed with my results. I had done fine, but I had hoped for more. I knew I wasn't going to be getting a personal call from the Dean of Harvard Law School. But no matter. In November, armed with my middlingly respectable test scores, I applied to three law schools: William and Mary School of Law in nearby Williamsburg, California Western School of Law in San Diego, and Wake Forest in Winston-Salem, North Carolina.

Something else happened that November that I will never forget: Our family celebrated Thanksgiving for the very first time. We loved the whole idea behind the celebration. It wasn't about religion, and it wasn't about gifts; it was about people sitting down to enjoy a meal together and acknowledging everything they had to be thankful for. And we had a lot to be thankful for.

Mom was in charge of the turkey, but she created her own recipe, and our poor, all-American bird emerged from the oven with a distinctly Persian flavor. I was in charge of both the mashed potatoes and the sweet potatoes, and Afsaneh was responsible for the pies, which entailed getting into the car and driving to the local supermarket. She returned with three types of pie: pumpkin, pecan, and apple. "The man at the bake shop told me it wasn't a proper Thanksgiving without at least three pies," she explained.

That first year, our unofficial Thanksgiving debut, we invited anyone who had no other place to go, which ended up consisting of five fellow Persians from ODU, some of the same ones who had helped us paint the house. To this day, Thanksgiving has become a family tradition at the Latifis, and it is my favorite American holiday by far.

‧ ✿ ‸

In December, Afsaneh graduated, and Mom told her not to let it go to her head. "This is only the beginning," she said. Alas, Afsaneh was still torn about medical school and still wary of broaching the subject with Mom.

In January 1989, I turned twenty, and we celebrated quietly: the five Latifis, together again. Then in March I began hearing back from the law schools. I'd been accepted at both Wake Forest and at the school in San Diego, and I'd been wait-listed at William and Mary.

One weekend, shortly before classes ended at ODU, I went to visit William and Mary, which was a short drive from home. I found it a little stuffy. Two weeks later, I drove to Wake Forest, four and a half hours away. It was a glowing day in early spring, and I remember getting out of the car and seeing the stately law school building made of ancient brick and the equally beautiful Wait Chapel and thinking, *This is the place for me. This is where I belong.* But after taking a look around, I thought that perhaps the school was too small and that I'd feel like too much of an outsider there, too noticeable, and on the drive home I was suddenly less sure about my little epiphany.

When I got home, I discovered that a videotape had arrived from the California Western School of Law in San Diego, and I immediately sat down to watch it. The campus didn't amount to much, but when I saw footage of all those cute guys on surfboards, I was pretty well sold on the place. I guess deep down I was a party girl, but I didn't really know how to party, so, technically, I was actually a party girl manqué.

"I'm curious about this school in California," I told Mom.

"If you think it's a good school," she said, "maybe we should take a look."

We bought some inexpensive tickets and flew out to Los Angeles. One of my mother's cousins picked us up at the airport and gave us a tour of the city. Mom was deeply impressed by the many Persian stores. They were filled with fresh *sabzi, safran,* turmeric, *kashk,* peas, prunes, dates, almonds, etc., and she said we would stop by and stock up before we returned to Virginia Beach.

We stayed with Mom's cousin that first night, and the next day we rented a car and drove to San Diego. The weather was beautiful, the air smelled of the sea, and there were many vacant apartments near the school, which were both attractive and reasonably priced. "I think this might be it," I told Mom.

We gave the school a five-hundred-dollar deposit to hold my place, then got in the car and decided to visit Tijuana. We had never been to Mexico, and we were curious, but we found the place too intimidating, and—without ever having stepped foot outside of our locked car—we were soon on our way back to L.A.

We spent another night with Mom's cousin, and the next day we went shopping at some of the Persian stores in Westwood. On the flight back to Norfolk, I began to have misgivings about San Diego, and, in the days and weeks ahead, I became less and less enchanted with the idea of moving that far from home. I wasn't ready to leave my family. I didn't have it in me. Still, I had to make a decision. The deadline was approaching.

"I don't think I can do it," I finally told my mother. "San Diego is practically another country."

"Well," she said. "What do you want to do?"

I called Wake Forest and asked them if it was too late to reconsider. Their deadline was that afternoon, at three, but they told me they'd hold my spot if I would overnight a check. Afsaneh wrote a check to the school, and I rushed over to Federal Express and sent it off. Two months later, I found myself in Winston-Salem for orientation. I took Mom and Afsaneh with me, of course, which was probably a mistake. The point of the visit was to mingle with your fellow students and to look for a place to live. Most of the students were older than me and were better at mingling, and the vast majority paired up and found housing. I paired up with no one, however, and ended up renting a modest one-bedroom apartment near the school. Afsaneh wrote out another check—the deposit on the apartment—and we drove home.

Toward the end of August, we borrowed a big pickup truck and went back to Hanes Furniture to buy some "slightly distressed" items for my new pad. When the truck was fully packed, off we went. I will never forget the way my mother looked, sitting behind the wheel of that truck, with her elbow out the window and her eyes on the road ahead. I half-expected to see her reaching for some chewing tobacco.

When we got to Wake Forest, we drove directly to the apartment building and moved in. We must have been quite a sight: three Iranian women, struggling, hollering, and laughing under the weight of our new purchases.

Mom and Afsaneh spent the weekend with me, and on Monday morning, bright and early, it was time to say good-bye. We all started crying. I thought back to that horrible day at Sacré Coeur, when the cab came to take Mom away.

"You are the children of a soldier," she had said. "And soldiers are brave. They don't cry."

It had been a clear, sunny day, just as it was now, and I had started crying, just as I was crying now. "I'm not crying, Mom," I had said. "It's the rain." But this time I didn't blame the illusory rain; I wasn't a child anymore.

"This is for the future," Mom said, trying to console me. "And remember: I'm only a phone call away."

I kissed her, and I kissed my sister, then I hurried off without looking back. I didn't want to watch them pull away. I'd been through that too many times already.

(۱)

وزارت کشور
شهربانی کشور
(تلفن: ....)

شماره
تاریخ ۲۳ ۳ ۵۸
پیوست

از :
به :
موضوع:

دوست عزیز برادر عزیزم

۲۴ ۳ ۵۸

اینجانب دوهفته است را امتحان از اسلام عزیز که برکت ایزدی ببیند نام الهی نمودم

حال من غیر از شما لطفاً دانستم تا حد لیاقت نیز سلامت بودم روبشتم راست بیمار بودم

دیشب مرا از نقطه اندر شهربانی در الهیجار خوراک دادند این در کار نقطه نیم مردم راه هل سپردم که

دانستم تا من تقدیس خودی برای کسی که کشتی خود را به صرف می دهم است تمام آن را که توانستیم

در مقابل این دست تو امای ست نداشتم گردن ابیدلام می را مورد عمو قرار دهی دانا

این راه هر حال لستمان می دهیم از حمین طلب لشکر می کنم دل لباس انتخاب را با تمام عیده میندل

آن زیاد می بدل نمیکند دومی دیدم که بعد است می آمدی سیج در حال میلین دانشم دل نمیخواد

وگیشه نباید از راحت فدری آنکه مرباری می کردم راهی دارو دگیلم که حال می خوب است نمیدانم

چیو تورن؟ آن رحتی می کردند که بیمار دارو وطیف از هدایم نیز گردن سیو کتب را دهی آن را

دنبال کار بودم گفتم گردم کنه برای می لباسی داده اند میچ کسی نداندامی مال غیر نزدیکم لطفاً لدهرا که دی

نماید سیورگفتم ها که مقنع کند در مراه در خوردنه بیرمی دانشته این نباید هتم دل خوکنم که کسی دارد

سیج تا میتیم مردی نداشت درانی اننا سب بنسی دیوال فرم اهلی می کنم که باید سب محن دعایی داد ما

CHAPTER FOURTEEN
Law School

ONE OF THE FIRST PARTIES I GAVE DURING LAW SCHOOL

AT THE END OF THE FIRST WEEK of law school, after I got my first, terrifying taste of the tremendous workload ahead of me, there was a party to celebrate the fact that we had survived those first five days. I poked my head inside but didn't stay. For one thing, it was a little too intimidating. For another, Mom was en route. We had been together only the previous Monday morning, but already I missed her, and she was uncomplainingly making the four-and-a-half-hour drive to see me.

"All the students are so much older than me," I told her late that night. "I feel like the dorky little sister."

"You're not dorky," she said. "Even your braces are beautiful."

Wow. Talk about a stretch.

Mom spent the entire weekend cooking up a storm and freezing meals for me in little plastic containers. She would put a strip of tape on each container, and make a note of what was inside with a black Magic Marker. While she cooked, I studied, and, when my eyes got bleary, we'd go back to the grocery store to shop for the next round of cooking. Late Saturday afternoon, when I was too tired to crack another book, we found time for a bracing walk around the campus.

My mother left early Sunday—she had to work at the plant that night, and she wanted to spend some time with Afsaneh and the boys—and on Monday I was back in class. I remember running into the Dean of the Law School that morning. "Miss Latifi," he said dryly. "I just found out you're only twenty years old."

"Yes, sir?"

"I hope you won't be attending any of the Friday parties," he said, smiling. "Underage drinking in a law school would not be a good thing."

As I found out, the Friday parties were a regular event. The mere fact that you were still standing at the end of another tortuous week was cause for celebration.

I knew from the start that law school had been the right choice for me. I loved studying, I loved the intricacies of the law, and I loved the idea of justice. The only downside so far—besides the intense pressure to get good grades— was the fact that I desperately missed my mother. When we spoke on the phone the following Wednesday, I cried, so on Friday, when she was done with her babysitting job and had no weekend duties at the printing plant, she again drove four and a half hours into the night. The moment she arrived, she looked in the freezer. "What? You don't like my cooking? You haven't touched any of the meals I made you!"

We had a four-course meal for dinner that night.

The next morning I stepped out of the shower and found her in the living room, poring through the White Pages.

"What are you looking for?" I asked.

"There must be some Iranian families in Winston-Salem," she said.

Suddenly a name leaped out at her, and she reached for the phone.

"Mom! This is crazy. Put the phone down this instant!"

She ignored me and dialed, and a woman picked up at the other end. "Khanoom, I'm sorry to bother you," my mother said in Farsi, plunging right in, "but my daughter just moved here from Virginia, and she's going to law school. She doesn't know a soul. She's very lonely, and . . . and come to think of it, I don't really know *why* I'm calling."

And the woman said, "Well, we're having a dinner party tonight. Why don't you and your daughter come over? You can meet some nice people."

Mom was immensely grateful. She took down the directions, again thanked the woman, and hung up. She was beaming, very proud of herself, but I felt otherwise. "This is totally embarrassing!" I said. "We're not going!"

"Embarrassing?" she replied. "When it comes to the well-being of my children, I have no shame whatsoever."

"Well, I'm sorry," I said. "Count me out."

"You're going," she said. "I can't keep driving down here every weekend. I'm falling asleep behind the wheel. Even the lemons aren't working anymore." She was referring to the cut lemons she kept in a plastic bag on the seat next to her. Whenever she got sleepy, she would reach for one of them, and the sour taste helped keep her awake. "Now they just make my gums sore."

So we followed directions to the home of these strangers, whom I'll call the Sobhanis, and found ourselves in a tony section of Winston-Salem. Mrs. Sobhani welcomed us as if we were old friends, and she brought us inside and introduced us to her husband, Mohammad, to their son, Massoud, and to Massoud's beautiful wife, Sepideh, who wasn't much older than me. There were a few other guests, all of them Iranians, and before long we were directed to the dinner table. The main dish was *ghormeh sabzi*, which brought back memories of home—of my own family, gathered around the dinner table in the house on Saltanat Abad. It was the first of many meals I was to enjoy at the Sobhanis's. They virtually adopted me, and, over the course of the next three years, I was at their house, or at Sepi's house, at least once or twice a week. It got to a point where I felt like a total freeloader, but they never took no for an answer, and they always sent me home with leftovers, which I would put in the freezer, next to Mom's carefully labeled containers.

When I wasn't at their home, I was either in class or in the library, studying. Many of the students had already begun to form study groups, but I had never studied in a group, and I was a little worried about relying on other people for information. I wanted to cover everything myself so that I would have no one to blame but myself. Toward the end of that first semester, however, I became friendly with a fellow student, Leilani Hamilton, and we began bouncing ideas off each other, sometimes for hours at a time, and this became our very own ersatz study group.

I tried to make more friends. There were two very nice guys in my apartment building, and from time to time we would go out for pizza or even throw a little dinner together at one of our places. But other than that, I was still a bit shy and dorky. I was younger than everyone else, I was wearing braces, and—let's face it—I was different. The law school was as lily-white as any place I'd ever seen. There were no Asians, no Indians, no Middle Easterners, and very few blacks. To me, most of the students looked as if they had just stepped out of the pages of a Ralph Lauren catalog. I didn't. And it struck me: I had been in America since August of 1982, more than seven years, and I only had one or two American friends. There was a reason for this, of course. Like many foreigners, I tended to gravitate toward my own people because these were the people with whom I had something in common—even if it amounted to no more than a shared heritage. I wanted to make American friends, believe me, but I simply didn't know how to go about it. I thought I would be perceived as an outsider, and, rather than risk rejection, I kept to myself. But in law school, beginning with my friendship with Leilani, this began to change. By the end of that first semester, I was no longer making my way along the school corridor with my books clutched to my chest and my eyes on the floor. I was no different from anyone else. We were all struggling to survive our first year.

❦ ❀ ❧

One night in early October, shortly after I'd gone to bed, I heard faint footfalls in the corridor. They stopped in front of my door, somewhat abruptly, and my heart leapt into my throat. My bedroom had a long window that faced a balcony, and the balcony butted up against the corridor. As I looked up, I saw an ominous shadow fall across the window. Now the shadow reached up and knocked on my door, and I was so paralyzed with fear that I couldn't even scream or reach for the phone to call for help. The shadow knocked again, more persistently this time, and suddenly it occurred to me: *What kind of burglar knocks?* So I got out of bed and wrapped a blanket around my shoulders and tiptoed out of the room, toward the front door. "W-who is it?" I stammered.

"Ma'am," the shadow answered. "It's the police."

"How do I know you're really the police?" I replied. I had watched enough American television to know exactly what to say. I was nobody's fool.

"Would you please look through the peephole, ma'am?" the shadow said.

I looked. There was a police officer outside, in uniform, and he was holding up his badge, but everything was distorted by the tiny, fish-eye lens.

"How do I know that's a real badge?" I asked.

"Do you have a mother and sister in Virginia?"

I threw the door open, practically tearing it off its hinges. "W-what happened to them?!" I shouted. "Are they okay?!"

"They're fine," he said. "It's you they're worried about. They've been trying to get through for hours, and the line's been tied up, so they called us."

The next day, the whole law school had heard the story. People kept coming up to me, grinning: "Open the door! Police!" It was quite embarrassing.

Ironically, as a result of this mild humiliation, I found myself chatting with a fellow student I'd never met before, and he asked me if I'd met Leila.

"I know Leilani," I said. "But no Leila. Who's Leila?"

"She's a first-year law student," he said. "She's from Iran, too."

I found this hard to believe. As it turned out, however, there were *four* foreign students at Wake Forest that year, and all of them were from Iran. I sought Leila out, and we hit it off immediately. And in fact by the end of the semester, I gave up my place, and we moved into a roomy, two-bedroom apartment in the same complex. It was great. I had a new friend, I was doing well in school, my braces were about to come off, and I was saving money—and saving money had become a huge concern.

At Old Dominion, as you may recall, I'd gotten by on grants and scholarships, but in law school everything was based on loans. I wasn't happy about going into debt, but apparently that was the American way. Still, whenever one of my checks arrived, I'd immediately run down to the bank to deposit it, then send a portion of the money home. I know the school would have frowned on this, but my family desperately needed it.

At Christmas, when I went home for the holidays, I realized how much my life had changed in just four short months. Sitting there, surrounded by my family, it struck me that I *almost* felt like an adult. I'd been relying on Afsaneh since I was ten—an entire decade—and I was finally learning to take care of myself. When I returned to school for the second semester, I didn't even cry. (Well, maybe a little.) I buckled down and hit the books, and by the end of January I was out interviewing for clerkships. One of my early interviews took place at a prominent firm in Charleston, West Virginia. They offered me a job, starting in June, right after school, and even found a place for me to stay. I immediately signed on.

As soon as classes ended, I went home. I had three weeks before the start of my clerkship, and I wanted to spend the time with my family. That second week, Dai'e Hossein came to visit. As you may recall, Dai'e Hossein's daughter, Mojdeh, my cousin and best friend, had been killed many years earlier in a terrible car accident, and Dai'e Hossein had moved to Sweden with his family and disappeared from our lives for a while. But here he was again, standing in front of me, in tears.

A few days later, I was navigating the churning waters below Niagara Falls, aboard the *Maid of the Mist,* with Dai'e Hossein, Mom, and Afsaneh, and the following night we were pulling into Times Square, the blazing, pulsing, neon heart of New York City. I had been to New York once before, but never in this part of it and certainly not at midnight. And the one thing that stays with me to this day—beyond the crowds, the noise, the energy, the excitement, the shops, the food—is the fact that no one even noticed us. And I mean this in the best possible sense. In New York, I didn't stand out; I wasn't different. New York made me feel as if I *belonged.*

A week later, I arrived in Charleston for my clerkship, and you would think that I had just stepped off a spaceship. Everywhere I went, people stared at me, and they stared shamelessly. I'd felt so at home in New York, but here, in the lily-white American heartland, I'd become the worst kind of interloper. And I wasn't imagining it, either. Not two weeks into the internship, a local newspaper sent a reporter to the law firm to interview me. They wanted to do a little story about me, he said, a human-interest story: the Iranian-girl-in-Charleston-for-the-summer type thing. I should have declined, but I thought that that would be impolite, and the following week there it was on the front page, below the fold. People kept stopping by to tell me how much they had enjoyed the story and what an *interesting character* I was. But I didn't want to be an interesting character. I wanted to be a regular person, like everyone else.

On the heels of this, the partners asked me to come along on one of their high-profile cases, and we drove out to the airport and got into the firm's private jet. We flew off to meet with the clients, a group of Hare Krishnas who were facing a number of heinous charges, including kidnapping, rape, and child abuse, and all I could think was, *Why are we representing these people?* I was still in dreamland. I had just finished my first year of law school, and I still believed that law was solely about justice.

Things went downhill from there. I was hopelessly lonely in Charleston, and I found the place depressingly provincial. Everywhere I went—to a movie, to a coffee shop, for a walk in the park—people stared at me as if I were a freak. "Yes!" I wanted to scream. "I'm different! So what? You're not that cute yourself!"

Eventually, I broke down. I went to see one of the partners and told him how unhappy I was. I was friendless, isolated, and had never felt so out of place in my life. "I'm pretty miserable," I said, just in case I hadn't made myself sufficiently clear. "I'm sorry. I want to leave."

"I don't know what to say," he replied, stymied. "Isn't there something we can do?"

"No," I said. "I can't think of anything."

"I wish I could make you change your mind."

But he couldn't. I thanked him, went back to the apartment, packed up, and left. My family was only too thrilled to have me back. This was the summer of 1990, right after the July Fourth weekend. By this time, Afsaneh had left the rented car business and was working for the Iranian ear, nose, and throat doctor we'd met socially. She remained undecided about medical school. The boys played tennis, swam, watched movies, came home, and acted out the fun parts. They were really looking forward to *Goodfellas*, which hadn't yet been released, but they'd seen the trailers, and they took to walking around the house, talking out of the sides of their mouths like gangsters. "What's for dinnah? You know what I'm sayin', Joey?" As for Mom, she was just being Mom: babysitting all day, then putting in five backbreaking shifts at the printing plant. I would come down to breakfast, and she'd greet me with that little hula number.

"I don't know how you do it," I said.

"Life is good," she said, laughing. "I have my family back."

That was the summer Iraqi troops invaded Kuwait, setting off the Persian Gulf War. Saddam Hussein was back in the news, and President Bush—the *first* one—decided to go to war. In a matter of days, in what became known as Operation Desert Shield, almost a quarter of a million American troops were en route to the Persian Gulf. Now when people asked me where I was from, I would tell them I was Iranian, and I was quick to point out that Iranians didn't like Saddam Hussein, either. I wanted them to know that I wasn't the enemy.

In August, I went back to Winston-Salem for my second year. My Iranian friend Leila had met a third-year student in her environmental law class who was looking for a couple of roommates. The woman's name was Beth, and we went over to see her. She was a lovely, red-haired girl, though a bit of a tree hugger, and the place was a huge, beautiful Victorian house near campus. Needless to say, we moved in.

The second year was much easier, both academically and socially. I was tutoring first-year students and enjoying it immensely, and I was making new friends. I also continued to see the Sobhanis and had become very close to their daughter-in-law, Sepi.

Mom still came to visit every second or third weekend, depending on her schedule, and we always spent at least one of those nights with the Sobhanis. One Saturday they invited us to a concert in Greensboro, North Carolina. It was a very posh affair, featuring a well-known Persian singer, and it was held in the ballroom of a fancy hotel. Mom helped me dress for the occasion, and she may have done too good a job because the following day the Sobhanis received a call from an Iranian woman who'd also been at the concert. She was from a very prominent Persian family. "I understand you're very friendly with that attractive young lady," the woman said.

"Afschineh?" Mrs. Sobhani replied. "Why yes! Absolutely. We're very close to her."

"Well," the woman said. "My brother is looking for a wife."

This was serious. Mrs. Sobhani immediately began singing my praises. "Oh, Afschineh is terrific! We adore her. She's so well-mannered and so bright and just a delight to have around!"

The woman felt much the same way about her brother. He was terrific, brilliant, handsome, deeply charismatic, and *an engineer*. He had seen me at the concert, too, and he very much wanted to get to know me better, but he wanted to do it *properly*.

Mrs. Sobhani was very excited. "Afschineh, you should really meet this boy! These are good people from a good family. This could be a very nice thing for you."

I really wasn't interested, but I was too polite to decline, so I went along with it. The guy called to make a date, and we agreed to have dinner the following Saturday. Shortly before the appointed day, however, I started to get cold feet. I called Sepi and asked if she and her husband would join us because I didn't want to be alone with this stranger. She told me that she'd be delighted and we could simply have dinner at her house. When I called the guy to tell him, he was instantly amenable, and he told me he would come by beforehand to pick me up and drive me to Sepi's.

On Friday, the night before my Big Date, I got back to the house and discovered that two dozen peach-colored roses had been delivered in my absence. There was a little note from the engineer: "I am really looking forward to tomorrow evening." I was very moved. The roses were beautiful, the note was very sweet, and nothing like this had ever happened to me. I was being *romanced*. This was the stuff of Jane Austen novels. I couldn't believe it. I was twenty-one years old, and for the first time in my life a man was showing serious interest in me. I didn't know whether to be thrilled or frightened, so I called Sepi, a woman of experience. "He sent me two dozen roses!" I said. And Sepi said, "That's *good*. That shows he is a good and proper man. He has good manners."

When I got off the phone, I heard noises in the living room, and I went downstairs to investigate. It was Friday night, and I had completely forgotten that Beth was going to be hosting a party for the environmental law students. I thought it was going to be a little party, but they were moving all the furniture aside. Suddenly a truck arrived to deliver a dozen kegs of beer, and a moment later a bunch of guys showed up with musical instruments and began to set up a makeshift stage. *Wow*, I thought. *I'm cool. Party at my house.*

It was turning into quite the day. I had come home to two dozen peach-colored roses, and it looked like I was in for an evening of big fun. But a few hours later, with the house full of drunk students, the music blasting at earsplitting levels, and *two* visits from the police, asking us to keep the noise down, it didn't seem like that much fun anymore. I began thinking, *Boy, I'm in trouble now. This isn't proper for a nice Persian girl. How will I ever get this mess cleaned up before my date shows up?* He wouldn't be showing up till six the following evening, of course, but I was already worried. I was cool, but I was screwed. I kept going up to Beth and Leila, badgering them in mid-party. "You guys are going to help me clean up this mess tomorrow, right? And you'll help me put the furniture back where it belongs, right?"

Unlike me, they were having fun. "It'll be fine, Afschineh. Have a beer. Relax."

I went to bed, and I was so tired that I managed to fall asleep despite the noise. When I came downstairs the next morning, my jaw dropped. The place was a complete shambles.

"Shit," I said aloud, "I'm in trouble."

I began to clean up, but I really didn't know where to start. I felt the first stirrings of panic. I looked out the window and noticed it was raining, and I went outside and saw that the front yard was littered with cigarette butts, crushed plastic cups, and mud. If these were the people who were going to be caring for the environment, the environment was in serious trouble.

I began picking up cigarette butts by hand. I picked them up for more than an hour. Then I turned my attention to the empty beer kegs and dragged them to the rear of the house. That took another hour. Then I went inside and started moving furniture. Finally, Beth and Leila stirred to life, and they saw that I was in a bit of a panic. They made some coffee and pitched in.

At six o'clock that evening, with the house looking almost presentable and myself fresh out of the shower, my date arrived. He was a very handsome and sweet guy. We got into the car and drove to Sepi's place. He had brought a nice bottle of wine, and we had a great dinner. He was easy to talk to and had a nice smile and a good sense of humor.

After dinner, he drove me home and asked about my plans. I told him I wanted to get my law degree, practice for a couple of years, then maybe go back to school for a teaching degree.

"North Carolina's great," he said.

"I'm not sure I want to stay here," I said. "I might want to move to D.C. I think I'd be happier in a bigger city." New York wasn't even in the realm of possibility at the time.

"I love D.C.," he said.

I could see he was trying to be accommodating, and sweet as he was, I just couldn't get interested. He wasn't even thirty, but he was already a man, a *serious* man, and he was looking for a wife. I was suddenly reminded of the opening line from one of my favorite novels, *Pride and Prejudice* by Jane Austen: "It is a truth universally acknowledged that a single man in possession of a good fortune must be in want of a wife."

Alas, I wasn't looking for a husband. I was only twenty-one. I was afraid that if I got involved with him, my life would be over.

When we got back to the house, he walked me to the door and shook my hand. "I had a wonderful evening," he said. "I'll call you."

I didn't know how to respond. I didn't want him to call me—I didn't want to lead him on—but I didn't want to be mean or hurtful, either.

The next morning, bright and early, the phone rang. I was worried that it might be him, but it was Sepi. "So?" she asked. "What did you think?"

"He's nice," I said. "But I don't know. I just don't think I'm ready."

"I liked him," Sepi said. "At first I thought he was too serious and mature, but he's sweet and has a nice sense of humor."

He called on Monday. He said he had been talking to the people at his office, and they had a branch in D.C. "I could transfer at the drop of a hat," he told me. That was a little scary. We'd had one dinner together, and he was already mapping out our entire future. I called my mother the moment we got off the phone. "I don't know what to do," I said. "I don't want to get married."

"It's up to you," she said. "But first, you finish law school."

Thanks, Mom. Big help.

The following week, Mom and Afsaneh came to Winston-Salem, and we went to another concert in Greensboro. The Sobhanis met us there, and this guy and his family were also there. At one point, he came over to our table to say hello, and I introduced him around. He made a very good impression on everyone, including Mom, but I told her that I definitely wasn't interested in getting serious and that I was worried about leading him on. "Could you do me a favor?" I asked her. "Could you please tell him, on my behalf, that I don't want to pursue this? That I'm not ready for marriage."

"No," she said, "you're an adult now. You have to do it yourself."

I couldn't believe she was expecting this of me, but I knew she was right. I didn't have a choice. I waited for an opportune moment, and, when I saw him alone, I approached and suggested we go for a little walk. As we turned toward the exit, I realized that he had probably misread my intentions, and the moment we stepped outside I felt compelled to blurt it out. "I'm not ready to get married," I said. He stopped and turned to face me. It was a cool night, and he removed his jacket and draped it over my shoulders. He was sure making this hard for me. "I just don't think I'd make a good partner right now," I went on, fumbling. "Not for you or anyone else." He looked very sad, but he smiled and said he understood. That was the end of our little walk.

Late in the evening, when we were leaving the concert, Mom saw him sitting on the far side of the lobby, alone, looking absolutely crushed. And the next day, at lunch with the Sobhanis, this became the subject of our conversation. "I am so mad at you," my mother said.

"*Me?* What did I do?"

"I hope he finds a girl a thousand times better than you!"

Everyone at the table laughed. My mother had spoken in Farsi, and she had delivered the line with such conviction that it sounded like a curse. I couldn't believe it. My own mother! "Thanks a lot!" I said.

"Well, I'm sorry," she said. "You should have seen the look on that poor man's face. It was enough to break my heart."

That was it. Men and me, we were history. You couldn't win.

A week later, I was walking across the campus and ran into Leila. She was carrying a small booklet that contained brief biographies, as well as photographs, of all of the incoming first-year law students. "I saw the cutest One-L I've ever seen!" Leila gushed.

"Me, too!" I said, having just pored through the booklet myself.

As it turned out, we had both singled out the same guy, and, unbelievable as it seems, he was gliding toward us—in the flesh—at that very moment. He smiled—he had a great smile—and floated past. He was tall, at least six-one, with dark hair and brown eyes. I thought I would die. I was almost sure he'd heard us.

"That was certainly embarrassing," I told Leila. "Thank you for including me."

A few days later, I saw him at the cafeteria at the Benson Center. I thought he was so cool. Most of the guys in law school wore T-shirts and tennis shoes, but he was wearing dress pants and loafers, looking absolutely perfect. I was sure I was going to swoon, but then he crossed the room and planted a kiss on the cheek of a beautiful, dark-haired woman. *Oh, well,* I thought. *He has a girlfriend. What did I expect?*

It was odd. It's not as if I was genuinely interested in him—I didn't even know what that meant or what it might entail—but I was a little disappointed. Then I tried to look on the bright side, if you can call it that. What did I want with a guy, anyway? Who needed that kind of uncertainty in life? I was going to finish law school, get a good job, and make a career for myself. I wasn't going to depend on anyone but me. I was as hard as a nail. Nothing and no one would ever hurt me.

A few weeks later, I saw him again. We all had study carrels in the library, our own little cubbies, and I was studying at mine when he walked right up to me. "Hi," he said. "My name's Calder." He sat down, exceedingly self-confident, and proceeded to chat me up. "Who are you? I've seen you around. Why are all the One-Ls always coming up to your carrel and badgering you?"

"My name is Afschineh," I said. "And the One-Ls aren't badgering me. They come to me for help."

"So you're running a free tutoring service for first-year law students?"

"Not free exactly," I said. I was making eight dollars an hour.

"Oh, really?" he said. "I'll let you know if I can use your help."

I was nervous, but only a little nervous. After all, he had a girlfriend. Plus I was pretty sure he wasn't really interested in me. "Fine," I said, a tad smug, "though I'm not sure I'll be able to make time for you."

Two days later, I ran into him again. He had somehow finagled his way into the cubby close to mine.

"I got one of the other students to switch carrels with me," he explained.

"So I see," I said, and this time I was a little *more* nervous.

"I couldn't help notice that poster," he said. He was referring to the poster on the wall next to my cubby, a celebration of great women in history. "Are you some kind of feminist or something?"

"Feminist?" I shot back. "I appreciate all the great things women have accomplished. Does that make me a feminist?"

He smiled. He liked my spunk. I wasn't going to take any guff from him. When he found out I was from Iran, he said, "My girlfriend's mother thinks that the next big war is going to start in that part of the world."

I thought that had been very cleverly done. It was his way of telling me that he had a girlfriend. I respected him for his honesty, though I admit I was a little disappointed. I thought that maybe by now that dark-haired woman was history.

We kept running into each other in the days and weeks ahead, and he always had something to say.

"Where are you going?"

"Somewhere."

"What are you doing?"

"Something."

He started calling me "Miss Something-Somewhere."

"Why are you so evasive? Why can't you be more specific?"

And all I could think was, *Why does this charming, handsome man—this charming, handsome man with a girlfriend—keep torturing me with questions?*

It was strange. Whenever I approached the library, I would look for his red Honda in the parking lot. If I spotted it, I would get butterflies in my stomach. I finally decided I should keep my distance. There was someone else in his life, and the last thing I needed was heartbreak and disappointment. I didn't need romance, either. I hadn't experienced it myself, of course, but I'd heard that heartbreak and disappointment were a big part of romance.

※ ※ ※

That second summer, I interned with a local lawyer and stayed at the big Victorian house with Beth, who was also studying for the North Carolina Bar. Leila found a clerkship out of state.

From time to time, when I could get away, I'd go home for the weekend. Things hadn't changed much, which wasn't good. Mom was still working two jobs, for a *third* straight year; Afsaneh remained employed at the doctor's office, though none too happily; and the boys were struggling to fill the long, hot summer days.

The biggest problem was financial. There was a mortgage to pay, as well as property taxes, which were unexpectedly high, and the family cars were forever breaking down. In addition, there were two growing boys in the house, and they could eat their way through a hundred dollars worth of groceries at the rate of about twenty dollars an hour. Whenever I made it home, we never went anywhere. Even McDonald's was too much for a family of five. "For the same money," Mom would say, "we can eat like kings at home." And that's what we did.

That summer, the summer of 1991, Afsaneh finally decided that she was going to go to medical school after all. She had applied to a podiatry school in Manhattan—maybe it was all those years of forcing people into shoes that didn't fit—and had found a reasonable sublet in New York, on East Eighty-second Street. On a sweltering day in late August, I drove to New York with Afsaneh and Mom, to help her move. If I had known it was a fifth-floor walk-up, I might not have been so quick to volunteer.

Afsaneh had applied for a loan, and she got it, and once again we were amazed at the way this country worked. The opportunities were there, if you had the will to pursue them—and we had the will to pursue them.

In the fall, I went back for my third year of law school, but I found a new home. A prominent local family had a beautiful carriage house on their property, and, in exchange for two nights of babysitting, they waived the rent. It was an incredible deal.

My friend Leila, meanwhile, had become engaged to an Iranian guy, and one weekend they came to Virginia Beach with me for a short break. We were sitting around that first night, laughing and joking—Leila, her fiancé, Mom, Afsaneh, me, and the boys—when the conversation took a serious turn. Leila's fiancé, like his father before him, was a member of one of the world's largest independent religious organizations, the Baha'i faith. Shortly after Khomeini swept to power, his father was executed for his beliefs.

"My husband was also executed," Mom told him, "but for very different reasons."

Suddenly, Ali broke in. "Wait a minute," he said. "I thought Dad died in an accident?" He was confused and upset, and Amir, sitting next to him, was equally upset.

"I'm sorry," Mom said. "I probably should have told you a long time ago, but you were too young to understand, and I didn't want you to grow up with hatred in your hearts."

She left the room and returned a moment later with a copy of Dad's will. Neither Afsaneh nor I had ever seen it, except for that one time, briefly, when we were detained at the airport in Tehran, before we left for Vienna. But Mom had told us what it said: how Baba Joon had expected us to study hard, be brave, and make him proud. Now we looked at it for the first time. "*To my beloved wife,*" my father had written. "I am writing this letter and last will and testament before I am innocently executed. I am not sure if you know how much I love you. You have always been in my thoughts and I have never lost sight of your generous and beautiful soul and selflessness. You are worthy of worship."

There was a great deal of crying in the house that night. Mom repeated what Baba Joon had said the last time she saw him—"You know I've done nothing wrong. Please make sure the children know I was guilty of nothing"—and we wept even more. I could see, from what was said that evening, and from what was left unsaid, that there had been a brief period of time following my father's death when my mother had been very angry with him. He had refused to listen to his friends or his family, had refused to see the warning signs, and he had left her widowed with four children. But she had made peace with her anger a long time ago. "Your father was an honorable man," she told the boys. "He believed in his country, and he gave his life for his country. He was a soldier in the truest sense of the word. You should be proud of him. I know I am proud of him. And even though our life together was cut short, I am very happy to have been married to a man of such character and honor."

I think Ali and Amir were extremely moved by her words and extremely proud of Baba Joon. Especially Amir, who was too young to have any real memories of him.

Back in Winston-Salem, I continued clerking at the same law firm. I still sent a little money home from time to time, whenever I could spare it, but with Afsaneh in New York, and such limited help from me, it was turning into a very tough financial year for the family.

Amir went to work at a one-hour-photo place, and Ali got a job as a bagger at the local Farm Fresh market. I remember being home one cold winter weekend and riding along with Mom to pick him up at work. While we waited for him in the parking lot, Mom went around collecting shopping carts and putting them in their proper place. Ali emerged from the store and was absolutely mortified. "Mom! Stop! That's *my* job. You're embarrassing me!"

The truth is, there were times when there literally wasn't any bread in the house. This was the year the family went into serious credit card debt. It seemed to be a fairly common way to keep one's head above water, and it's not as if we had a choice. The car broke down: credit. We needed groceries: credit. Not enough to cover the mortgage this month: credit.

Mom remembered one bleak afternoon when she was home with the boys, feeling overwhelmed. The minute they left the house, en route to visit a friend in the same complex, she allowed herself to burst into tears. But she was barely getting started when Amir came rushing back inside. "Look what I found!" he exclaimed. "A fifty-dollar bill! Right on the street!" When he held the money out to her, she cried even harder.

"What's wrong, Mom?" he asked.

"Nothing," she said, wailing. "I'm ecstatic."

"And that's why you're crying?"

"You obviously don't know your mother very well," she said, still sobbing. "I'm being happy in my own way. Sometimes, when I'm very happy, I cry."

BY THAT POINT, MOM HAD DECIDED THAT BECOMING A
LAWYER INSTEAD OF A DOCTOR WAS OKAY, AFTER ALL.

LEILA, AFSANEH, AND ME

CHAPTER FIFTEEN

The Graduate⁓

ON GRADUATION DAY AT WAKE FOREST LAW SCHOOL

My third year of law school was a breeze. I was living in a beautiful carriage house, babysitting in lieu of paying rent, and happily neglecting my studies. When the weather was nice, Leila and I would skip class and go hiking. There were hundreds of miles of trails in the surrounding mountains, and we never got tired of exploring them. If the weather wasn't as nice, I'd check in with Sepi, and we'd go window-shopping and have lunch at the Village Tavern, a little café with great sandwiches. Sometimes, the weather notwithstanding, I knew I absolutely had to study, and I'd make my way over to the library, park myself at my carrel, and bury my nose in my books.

"Let's go to the med school library," Leila suggested one afternoon. "There are some really cute guys there."

It turned out she was right. There were lots of cute guys there, and one of them, clearly Persian, seemed to think *I* was pretty cute. He came over and asked if I was from Iran, and we started talking. I was my usual circumspect self. But I later found out that he knew the Sobhanis—and that they'd heard good things about him—and we went for dinner at the Village Tavern. He was a very nice guy and easy to talk to, but he seemed a little too flirtatious and informal. The next time I was over at the Sobhanis for dinner, Mrs. Sobhani was less enthusiastic about my suitor. "I'm not sure he has the old-school values," she said. "He's not traditional enough for my liking." I was so impressionable that I stopped seeing him.

A few weeks later, I met an Iranian MBA student, and I'd heard good things about him, too. But he was a little too aggressive for my liking, so that went nowhere fast.

Meanwhile, I was putting in twenty hours a week at that local law firm and sending most of the money home. I didn't have any rent to pay, and Mom and the boys were still struggling to make ends meet, so I did what I could. Still, I knew this little arrangement wasn't going to last forever. At this point in my studies, I was supposed to find a permanent job and take the bar exam in the corresponding state. I had been offered a full-time position by my employers in Winston-Salem, but I didn't want to settle in North Carolina. My dream had been to move to a big city, and I was leaning toward Washington, D.C. New York was wonderful, of course, but I felt it was out of my reach.

"That's crazy," Afsaneh told me on the phone. "*I'm* in New York, and it's great. We could live together."

"You really think so?"

"It would be great," she said. "We'll be together again, and I know you'll love it here."

Emboldened by my sister's enthusiasm, I sent several resumes off to firms in and around New York and even included one to the office of the Bronx District Attorney. To my great surprise, I got a call a few weeks later from the D.A.'s office, and they scheduled an interview for December. The day before my interview, I took a train from Winston-Salem to New York City. It left shortly before midnight and got in early the next morning. Afsaneh had left the keys to the apartment with the super at her building, and I made my way up five flights of stairs, dumped my things, took a quick shower, and went off to the Bronx on the subway.

Unfortunately, I managed to get lost. I remember stepping out of the dank shadows into a neighborhood that was somehow darker and more terrifying than the underground world I'd just left behind, so I turned around and went back, and a kindly gentleman pointed me in the right direction.

When I got off at the right place, up at 166th Street, I was still disoriented. I was wearing a suit, which made me feel very out of place among the few people I saw on the street, and it was so windy that I kept losing my balance. To compound matters, my long hair kept blowing in my face, and I could hardly see where I was going. And the garbage! Plastic bags and old newspapers were blowing everywhere, slapping up against my legs. I felt like I was in a bad western: At any moment, the windstorm would break, and the bad guys would come riding into town. Fortunately, no bad guys came, and I arrived at my appointment without further incident. I was interviewed by an assistant district attorney, who told me a little about the inner workings of the office and about the various departments: Domestic Violence, General Crimes, Narcotics, and so on and so forth.

"I know you're from a small town," he said. "How do you think you'd do here in the Bronx?"

"I think I'd do very well," I said. "I want to live in a big city."

"Well, you certainly pass muster with me," he said. "Let me see if I can get you a few minutes with the person directly above me, so that you don't have to come all the way back for your second interview."

"That's very thoughtful," I said. "I really appreciate it."

I went back outside to wait, and I noticed this Chinese man making the rounds of the offices with food. Suddenly I realized I was very hungry. "Excuse me," I said. "Is there anywhere to eat around here?"

"Are you kidding?" he said. "Have you seen this neighborhood? Leave the building at your own risk."

A moment later, with my stomach still grumbling, I was summoned for my second interview. This woman worked for the Narcotics Division, and I was very interested in her department. I asked so many questions that I felt as if I was doing the interviewing. I think I made a good impression, though, and I certainly hoped I had—I really wanted the job. The salaries were fairly modest at the D.A.'s office, but I had heard that this was the best way to get trial experience and that if you did well there, you'd be scooped up by one of the big firms in no time at all.

About two months later, I was called back to meet with the district attorney himself. I was a little nervous because I knew that they interviewed more than three hundred applicants to fill thirty positions. The interview went well, although he seemed a little concerned about my ability to handle life in the big city. I assured him that this would not be a problem.

"I lived in Norfolk for many years," I said.

"Why the prosecutor's office?" he asked, changing the subject. "Why not the public defender?"

"Oh, I could never work for the public defender," I said. "I might be putting people back on the street who perhaps don't deserve to be on the street. As a prosecutor, I have to make my case beyond a reasonable doubt, and this appeals to me. It means that anyone I put behind bars almost certainly deserves to be there."

I went back to Winston-Salem feeling very good about the whole experience. I felt a little cocky, even. *Look at me*, I thought. *A little girl from Iran, and I was walking around the streets of the Bronx like I owned the damn town.*

The moment I got back to Winston-Salem, Calder reappeared. I hadn't seen him in many months, but one afternoon he showed up in the library and started chatting me up again. He let it slip, casually, that he had broken up with his girlfriend, and asked if I'd like to see a movie with him. The following weekend, we went to see *The Commitments*, he took me back to my place, and we shook hands good night. As I've said, I was a very traditional girl.

When he called the next day, I didn't know what to think. To be completely frank, I was a little nervous. I'd never had a real relationship, and I didn't know exactly what that might entail. During my three years at Wake Forest, I'd seen plenty of students drift in and out of relationships. Some of them seemed to do so effortlessly, but others seemed to have a hard time dealing with their broken hearts. I knew that I'd be in the latter group. On the one hand, I didn't want to find myself crying in the school corridors or listening to people whisper behind my back: "Poor Afschineh! Did you hear? She got dumped. Her boyfriend fell in love with that tall blond."

On the other hand, Calder seemed like a very nice guy, and I'd be graduating in a couple of months, so it wasn't as if we were in it for the long haul. I thought I should throw caution to the wind and try to find out what this boyfriend-girlfriend business was really all about. After all, if it didn't work out, I wouldn't have to deal with the repercussions for very long.

Calder called shortly after I had made this monumental decision. He had tickets for a Wynton Marsalis concert, which was being held on campus the following week. I told him we should invite Leila and her fiancé and that everyone could come to my little carriage house for dinner before the concert. On the appointed day, I stood in my tiny kitchen and cooked up a storm. I made *zereshk polo*, rice with sour red currants, served with chicken, and it was a big hit. Then we went to the concert, which was quite wonderful, and Calder and I returned to my place for my first kiss. That was pretty wonderful, too.

A few days later, in March, I went home for Norouz. The Iranian community in Virginia Beach had rented a huge hall for the occasion, and they threw a big party. Afsaneh came down from New York, and we piled into the car with Mom and the boys and went off to celebrate the New Year.

I remember being very happy at the party, and I know Calder was a big part of it, even in absentia. For the first time in my life, I understood what it meant to have someone in my life who wasn't a member of my family, someone I'd *chosen*, someone who had chosen me, and it was a very good feeling.

Afsaneh also had a suitor, though she didn't meet him until that night. He was a Persian doctor, living in D.C., and he was known to the Kareemzadeh family through one of the sons. He was a respectable man, in search of a wife, so at their urging Mom invited him down to meet Afsaneh. Alas, Afsaneh wasn't exactly bowled over. She was very pleasant to him, however, and everyone enjoyed the party, but it clearly wasn't meant to be.

When I returned to Winston-Salem, I finally told Leila about my first kiss. "After the concert, when Calder and I got back to the house, he said he'd like to come in and help me do the dishes," I confessed. "And after we did the dishes, he kissed me."

"And?"

"And nothing," I said, blushing. "It was very nice."

"That was your first kiss?"

"Yes," I replied.

"Wow," she said, trying hard not to look too shocked.

"I was nervous, and Calder could tell I was nervous, but I liked it."

"Well, thank God for that!" she said.

"It's not a big deal, anyway," I said dismissively. "I'm not taking it seriously."

"Why not? Everyone loves Calder. He's a great guy."

"I know he is, and I like him, too, but this isn't going anywhere," I replied. "I'm graduating in two months. It's perfect. This will never get complicated."

In retrospect, I think that sounds cold and a little calculating, and perhaps it *was* cold and calculating. Calder was like an experiment to me. I had never been in a serious relationship, and this was my first stab at one. At the age of twenty-three, with the end of law school only weeks away, I was finally coming into my own. For years on end, other people had been taking care of me. In Austria and later in America, Afsaneh had usurped the role of mother. And when we were finally reunited with Mom, Afsaneh didn't immediately relinquish the position. Suddenly I had two mothers, but I didn't complain. I let them take care of me. It was easier than taking care of myself. But it wasn't particularly healthy, and as a result I was emotionally backward. That part of me had never developed properly. Now, at long last, after three years at Wake Forest, things were beginning to change. I was living on my own. I was paying my own bills. I was making my own decisions. I was actually cooking for myself from time to time. And I was even learning how to socialize (a little). I *almost* felt like a real adult.

"If you ever have a problem," my mother had always said, "you come to the family first." And that's what I had done; it's what the Latifis had done their entire lives. And while it was nice to know we had a family that was always there for us, that intense closeness also worked against us. It made us less needy. It made us less eager to look for relationships outside the family. We wanted nothing from other people. We had one another. Our family had been torn apart, but it remained a source of great strength to those of us who had survived. That strength was also a handicap, however, and I became aware of this only as I began taking those first tentative steps toward independence. I found the experience both thrilling and terrifying. I was on my way to becoming an adult, whether or not I wanted to. Before long I'd be graduating and setting off to find my way in the world.

For the time being, though, I still had my family, and I still had Calder. At this point, Calder and I were going out two or three nights a week, and we'd see each other at the library almost every day. When he wasn't there, he'd usually leave a little surprise on my desk. A packed lunch, say—a salad and half a sandwich. Or a favorite chocolate. This went beyond the "thoughtful boyfriend" stuff. Calder understood that in many ways I was still a child, and he made every effort to make me feel safe. He succeeded. Now when I had news to share, whether good or bad, I didn't automatically call my mother and my sister. I called Calder. It was a little confusing. I had gone into the relationship thinking I could keep it simple and brief, but I found myself growing very attached to him. By the time May rolled around, with graduation only a couple of weeks away, I was more confused than ever. I began to tell myself, quite convincingly, that the relationship was over and that soon it would be time to move on.

A few nights before graduation, Calder took me to a nice restaurant for dinner, and we both tried to pretend that everything was fine. I imagined that he was ready to move on, too, and that, like me, he hadn't expected the relationship to last beyond the end of the year. We said good-bye at the edge of campus—I asked him not to walk me home—and I was a real stoic. Not a single tear, not even a tiny crack in my voice. I didn't think Calder wanted me to get emotional, and I certainly didn't want to make a fool of myself.

"Let me have your number in New York," he said. "I'll call you."

I didn't think he meant it, but I gave him my number anyway. The Bronx D.A.'s office had not offered me a position, but I had decided I would try my luck in New York anyway. I had a sister there and a place to live, and there was really nothing for me in D.C. Maybe New York was a fairy tale, but I'd heard that fairy tales sometimes came true.

"I'll be there most of the summer," I told him, "preparing for the bar."

"I'm going to call you," he said, taking the phone number, and I guess he saw the doubt in my eyes. "Honest."

We kissed good night and I went off, telling myself that I'd never again hear from Calder and that most likely he'd return as a third-year student and find himself a loose sorority girl. This wasn't a very pleasant thought, but it helped me deal with the pain.

Though not really. By the time I got back to the carriage house, I was sobbing. I went inside, shut the door, and tried to pull myself together, reprimanding myself for being such a wimp. Then I noticed that my answering machine was flashing. I dried my eyes and hit the replay button, and Calder's voice came over the tinny speakers: "I will miss you. . . . I just called to talk to you one more time. . . . Please call me back. . . ." We hadn't been apart ten minutes, and I already had four messages from him. He was leaving the next day—there was no reason for him to stick around and watch the graduation ceremonies—and there was a great deal that remained unsaid.

"It's me," I said.

"How are you?"

"Oh, you know. Hanging in."

"I'm very proud of you," he said.

"For what?"

"You know. Everything. Who you are. What you've accomplished. This big step you're taking by going to New York."

"It's not such a big step. My sister will be there to take care of me."

"You don't need anyone to take care of you. You do a very nice job on your own. But do me a favor."

"What?"

"Stay away from those New York City boys."

"Don't worry," I said. "I hear they're not that interesting anyway."

I don't remember the rest of the conversation. I think both of us wanted to say things we were too afraid to say. I knew I cared for him, but until that moment I didn't realize just how much. Still, I didn't think sharing this with him would do either of us any good, so, once again, I kept my feelings to myself.

"Have fun at the graduation," he said.

"I will," I said. "Thanks. Have a safe trip home."

And that was that. I put the phone back in its cradle and said aloud: "Get over it, Afschineh. You're never going to see him again."

I woke up early the next morning, started packing my things, and getting ready for my family. Mom, Afsaneh, and the boys arrived a few days later for graduation. The Sobhanis came, along with a few friends. My mother sobbed during the entire ceremony. Afsaneh joined in before long, and a few moments later I was sobbing, too. The boys, however, were *not* sobbing. They were rolling their eyes and wondering what all the sobbing was about.

"I am so proud of you," my mother said when it was all over. "My little girl is a lawyer."

"Not quite, Mom. But I'm one step closer."

"Look at you! Your father would be so proud. He might have liked it better if you were a doctor, but they say being a lawyer in this country is not so bad."

Ah, mothers! How would we survive without them?

We went to dinner at the Sobhanis, which was fun and very festive, and the following morning, bright and early, Afsaneh left for New York. She still had another week or two of classes. The next day, Mom and the boys helped me pack, and I gave away most of the "slightly damaged" furniture that had served me so well for three years. Then we were in the car, on our way home, and two days later I was on my way to New York to begin studying for the bar. I had registered for a preparatory course at New York University, and it started on May 19, so I didn't get any break at all. I arrived and crashed with Afsaneh, and the next morning I was on the 6 train on my way downtown. The course was called the Bar/Bri. *Everything You Need to Pass the Bar*, the ads claimed. This was good. I needed all the help I could get.

The course turned out to be even more intense than I'd imagined. I was there from nine to two, Monday through Friday, and off to the library directly afterward to review what I'd just learned. But I loved it. And I loved the city. From that very first day, when I bought my subway tokens and asked the clerk how to get to New York University, I fell in love with the place all over again. I loved the sounds, the smells, and the people on the busy streets. And I loved the anonymity. Nobody stared at me. Nobody wondered who I was. Nobody sent reporters along to do "human interest" stories on the odd-looking girl from Iran. I was free. I would make my way along the teeming sidewalks, thinking, *Here I am, where I belong.*

Even though the D.A.'s office had not offered me a position, it wasn't enough to dampen my spirits. This was New York. I'd find a job. And why take it personally? I wasn't the only one without a job. Thanks in large part to Robert Redford, the legal market was completely saturated. A few years earlier, back in 1986, he'd appeared in the film *Legal Eagles*, with Debra Winger and Darryl Hannah, and suddenly everyone wanted to be a lawyer. But it wasn't just the lawyers. The whole country was in bad shape. The year 1992 had started out inauspiciously, with George H. W. Bush vomiting on the lap of Japanese Prime Minister Miyazawa Kiichi, and things had gone downhill from there. I tried to pay attention to all the newspaper articles about the faltering economy and such, but there was more entertaining fare in the daily press. John Gotti was convicted of murder that year. Amy Fisher went to prison for the shooting of Mary Jo Buttafuoco. Mike Tyson was sentenced to six years behind bars for the rape of Desiree Washington. This was a lot more interesting than facts and figures about economic indicators and what have you, and—from my point of view—much more *important*. After all, I was on my way to becoming a lawyer. These sordid tales were part of my education.

When class let out at two, I'd make my way to the library with some of the other students. One of them was this guy who'd graduated at the top of our class at Wake Forest. I didn't know him well, but he seemed nice enough, if a bit socially awkward, and, when he invited me for coffee one afternoon, I didn't want to hurt his feelings by refusing. As we were crossing the street near campus, a loud wolf-whistle pierced the air. I turned to look and saw a group of construction workers grinning at me. "Don't worry," my friend said. "Those guys will whistle at *anything*."

"Thanks a lot," I said.

"No, no," he stammered, "that's not what I meant."

I usually took a short break from the library at four-thirty and grabbed a little take-out snack at one of the many neighborhood delis, then went back for two or three more hours of studying before heading home. Sometimes I'd cut across Washington Square Park on my way to the subway, and I'd always find these guys gliding past me, mumbling, "Nickel, dime, nickel, dime."

"I'm sorry," I'd say. "I don't have any change."

One night I told my *one* Manhattan friend about it—a girl I knew from Winston-Salem who was living on the Upper West Side and working as an analyst for Morgan Stanley—and she burst out laughing. "You idiot," she said. "They're trying to sell you pot."

"Pot?"

"Yes," she said. "Marijuana. A nickel bag is five dollars. A dime is ten."

I didn't ask her how she knew this.

In the mornings, I was always up early, off to the subway, and on my way downtown. And in the evenings, I'd head home, exhausted, my head swimming with legalese. "Okay, elements of first-degree murder," I'd begin, talking to myself over the din of the roaring subway. I began to notice people moving away from me and realized that in the space of a month I had turned into that special breed of New Yorker: a crazy woman who talks to herself on the subway.

In mid-June, Calder called. He was clerking in Atlanta for the summer, but he was thinking about making a trip to New York. He could only get away for two nights and seemed eager to come.

"What are you going to be doing here?" I asked.

"Seeing you," he said.

I was ecstatic. I called Mom and told her Calder was coming to see me.

"Where is he staying?" she asked.

"I don't know," I said. "Here."

"With you?"

"Well, no," I replied. "I guess I can go stay with my friend from Morgan Stanley."

"That's a good idea," my mother said.

Calder and I had the best time together. It was right around his birthday, so I greeted him with a birthday cake made from store-bought cupcakes. I would have made a real cake, but I was too busy studying, and I knew I wasn't going to get much done for the next couple of days.

"I have to spend the night with my friend on the West Side," I told Calder after that first night. "I promised my mother."

He was a perfect gentleman. He walked me downstairs and put me in a cab.

The next day we walked around SoHo enjoying the good weather and went for dinner in Little Italy. I acted like a real New Yorker and pretended I knew my way around, even when it was obvious that I was hopelessly disoriented. After dinner, he dropped me at my friend's house on the West Side, and the following morning we again met at the apartment. "I'd like to come back to see you again," he said. I couldn't believe it. I was thinking, *I have an actual boyfriend, and he really cares for me.* It didn't seem possible. But he came back three weeks later, and we had another whirlwind of dates. After he left, however, with the course slowly drawing to a close, I buckled down and began to study in earnest.

In July, I took the bar exam. It was excruciating: two hellacious days of testing. It was held at the Jacob Javits Center, over on Twelfth Avenue, and when I walked out, exhausted, I felt completely crushed. I knew I had failed. I was in such a daze that I just started walking, and I walked all the way home. It must have been five or six miles, all the way across town, then north to the Upper East Side, and it was dark by the time I reached the building. I don't know how I made it up those five flights of stairs; my legs were killing me, and my head was throbbing.

"I think I failed," I told my mother.

"Did you eat anything?" she asked.

"No."

"Eat something."

"I can't," I said. "I'm too tired."

I collapsed on the futon in my clothes, and I didn't wake up till noon the following day. I felt as if I'd been hit by a truck, but I pulled myself together, showered, dressed, and got something to eat. When I felt sufficiently fortified, I called my one lead in New York City, a Persian attorney whose name had jumped out at me in the Martindale Hubbell book of lawyers.

I went to see him at his office the next day. His father had been a lawyer in Tehran, but had moved to Paris in the early 1980s, shortly after the Shah fled the country. He had started a practice there, and he had sent his son to New York to open a branch office. He told me that they practiced international commercial litigation, and I nodded wisely though I had no idea what this entailed. Still, I was genuinely interested—and not simply because this was my only lead. I spoke Farsi, English, and German, and I assumed my talents would be very useful *on an international level*. I was also curious about the rest of the world, and I had visions of myself jetting from one exotic location to another, my leather briefcase tucked smartly under my arm.

"We don't have anything at the moment," he said, interrupting my reveries. "Why don't you take the month of August off—St. Tropez is wonderful this time of year—and call me when you get back."

Yeah, right. All Persians are millionaires. I wonder if they have any seats on this afternoon's Concorde.

Instead of going to St. Tropez, I went to Virginia Beach. Ali had just finished a year at Tidewater Community College, and both he and Amir were now headed for Virginia Commonwealth University in Richmond. Mom was still working at the newspaper plant and still babysitting, but it was clear the family was at a crossroads. It didn't make sense for Mom to stay at the house by herself, especially from a financial point of view, so she would either have to move to Richmond with the boys or come to New York to stay with Afsaneh and me. Mom didn't know what to do. She didn't want the boys involved in any bad business, or in *rah'e bad*, as she put it—the bad road. She had heard many stories about drugs, and she understood enough English to pick up tidbits here and there from the papers and the TV newscasts. Many of America's young people were clearly going down the bad road. This was not going to happen to her children.

Although still undecided, Mom knew she had to move out of the house, and we made plans to rent it. At about the same time, we heard from Khaleh Mali, who was still in Iran. The tenants at our old home in Saltanat Abad had long since overstayed their tenancy, and they were refusing to pay any additional rent. Khaleh Mali had tried to talk to them, but she said there was no reasoning with those people. They took the position that Mom had moved abroad and abandoned the property, and they said the house now belonged to them. It was very scary. There were rumors that the government would confiscate your property if you left the country for a given period of time, and Mom's tenants were threatening to go to the local authorities about her. Mom didn't know what to do. Toward the end of August, we drove the boys to Richmond, put them in the dormitory, signed them up for a meal plan, and took Mom back to New York with us.

279

The boys hated the dorm, and they especially hated the cafeteria-style food, but there was nothing to be done. Mom, however, fell in love with New York at first sight. It was late summer, and the weather was fine. Before long Mom was wandering the streets and marveling at the city. "They have such nice fruit! And flowers on every corner! And the stores are so big! And the people on the streets look so interesting!"

I think she enjoyed the freedom. She had been working so hard for so many years that it must have felt as if she'd just been released from prison. She even loved the apartment, small and cramped as it was. She slept on a futon in the living room, and Afsaneh and I shared the twin bed in the little bedroom.

A week after we arrived, I went back to see that same Persian lawyer about a job. I half-expected him to ask me about St. Tropez, and I was ready to regale him with stories, but he just welcomed me back and said he had nothing but a clerical job. "And I know you wouldn't want a little clerical job," he added.

"You're wrong," I said. "I want it. When can I start?"

I started the following week. I hated it, but I didn't complain. I was making twelve dollars an hour, and the family needed the money.

In November, Khaleh Mali called again. She was at the end of her rope with Mom's tenants, and she felt the only recourse was to begin legal proceedings. This meant that Mom would have to return to Iran, and she wasn't exactly keen on the idea. She said she would think about it and did her best to *not* think about it.

A week after that phone call, at about four on a Thursday afternoon, I was tending to my clerking duties when the secretary buzzed to tell me I had visitors in the lobby. I was very confused. I went outside to find Mom and Afsaneh waiting for me, both of them grinning from ear to ear. Mom was holding a big bouquet of flowers.

"What happened?" I asked.

As it turned out, a letter had arrived at the house from the New York State Bar Association, addressed to me, and Mom, with her usual tact, had taken it upon herself to open it. I had passed the bar. The list was subsequently published in the *New York Law Journal*, and it was easy to find my name.

Afschineh Latifi Moghadam Tehrani. I had the longest name on the list and probably the worst job.

The following week, we went down to Winston-Salem to celebrate Thanksgiving with the Sobhanis. We stopped en route to visit Shamsi, and I asked my mother to please cook up a large, take-out order of *zereshk polo*.

"For whom?" she said. "We are dining with the Sobhanis."

"For Calder. He's still at school, preparing for finals, and he won't be going home for Thanksgiving. I thought it would be nice to stop by and say hello."

Mom got busy in the kitchen. She wondered aloud if she was finally going to meet "this Calder boy." She had heard a great deal about him by now, and she was looking forward to seeing him in the flesh. Alas, it didn't happen. We drove down to Winston-Salem the next morning, and we stopped at the Sobhanis first. Mom and the boys stayed there, and Afsaneh and I went off to see Calder and deliver his *zereshk polo*. It was pretty awkward. Calder and I said hello at the door and hugged briefly—I guess I was a little self-conscious in front of my sister—and he invited us in and introduced us to his brother, who had come down to spend Thanksgiving with him. We chatted for a few minutes—about school, about my lousy job, etc.—then Afsaneh and I had to rush back to the Sobhanis. It was unsatisfying in the extreme.

"He's even better looking than I remembered," Afsaneh said as we drove off. She had met him once before, briefly, in Winston-Salem, when she'd come to visit. "Where's he going to settle after he graduates?"

"I'm not sure," I said. "I think Atlanta."

The Sobhanis put on an exquisite Thanksgiving dinner, though it wasn't exactly traditional: There was no turkey at all. It reminded me of those amazing dinners Mom would whip together back in Tehran, when Dad showed up unexpectedly with guests. She would serve one course after another, each more complicated and delicious than the preceding one.

Then it was back to New York and to my grind of a job. I was still clerking, but now they actually had me preparing various documents that called on my legal talents, limited as they were. Still, I liked the place less and less. I thought the company was ethically shady. It seemed to me that everything they did was designed to *skirt* the law, not uphold it. It's as if they went through the books to find out how much they could get away with.

To compound matters, I wasn't making enough money. America had been very good to me, as they say, but I'd amassed a mountain of debt, and the banks were eager to be repaid. One weekend, I saw a Help Wanted sign in the window of Maryann's, a Mexican restaurant near the apartment. I went in to inquire and got a job as a hostess. I worked Fridays, Saturdays, and Sundays, and occasionally they'd ask me to fill in for someone during the week. It wasn't very demanding. I would smile a chirpy smile and say something profound—"How many in your party?"—then lead the patrons to a table and tell them to enjoy their dinner. But I genuinely liked the job. I didn't have any friends in New York, and it was nice to be out of the apartment, nice to have somewhere to go. The staff at Maryann's was young and friendly, and most of the patrons were college-age kids, so I fit right in. That's what I told myself, anyway.

Meanwhile, I kept looking for a better legal job. I checked the law journals without much success, and even went to see a couple of headhunters. But the news was grim: The legal market had never been this bad, and it was almost impossible to find anything without at least six or seven years of experience. I took comfort in knowing that I was probably the only restaurant hostess in Manhattan who had passed the bar, but then I realized that Manhattan was a very big place and that there were probably plenty of law school graduates waiting tables or worse.

I got home late one Friday to find my mother still awake. "What's wrong?" I asked.

"I have to go to Tehran," she said.

It was those pesky tenants again. Mom had to go back to see what she could do. The house was all we had in the world.

"I still remember the day your father and I drove up to that house for the first time," she said, fighting tears. "Do you remember our beautiful garden? Baba and I planted that garden together. I thought I would see my children married in that garden. I thought Baba and I would grow old together in that house. I thought we would be there for the rest of our lives."

Two weeks later, Afsaneh and I took Mom to Kennedy Airport. We were very worried about her. The Khomeini government was fanatical about keeping track of its enemies, and Sarhang Latifi had been one of its enemies—one of *God's* enemies, to hear them tell it. His name would appear on a list. There was no telling what might happen when Mom landed in Tehran.

But nothing untoward happened. She called the moment she arrived and said she had made it through immigration and customs without incident. "They interrogated me for three hours, and they asked me to fill out one form after another, but I didn't complain. I knew they were just goading me."

A few days later, she called again. The tenants were impossible, she said. The man appeared to be a devoutly religious person, and Mom had tried to appeal to that side of him, but he ignored her entreaties. "You live in the West, lady. You are no longer part of this culture. You have turned your back on your country. I have lived in this house since 1986, more than six years, and it belongs to me now. You have no rights in this country." My mother saw it differently. She hired a lawyer to commence eviction proceedings. He took the case, but he wasn't exactly brimming with confidence. The government did not look kindly on people who had moved to the West, he said, echoing what the squatter had told her. She had relinquished some of her rights by abandoning her homeland.

"You should see the poor country!" my mother said. "It's terrible. It doesn't feel like Iran anymore. Pollution, noise, inflation. Everyone is working two jobs to make ends meet. The people have lost their warmth. They seem tired, wary, hostile, suspicious."

That Christmas, while Mom was off in Tehran fighting court battles on an almost daily basis, Calder invited me to visit his family in Fort Wayne, Indiana. I had met them briefly a year earlier, shortly before I graduated, but this was much more serious. We stayed in their home, in separate bedrooms, and celebrated Christmas together. They turned out to be the nicest, most generous people in the world, and Calder didn't do too badly himself: He gave me a pair of sapphire earrings with diamonds in them. I was literally struck dumb. I had imagined a brief, two-month liaison, and it was turning into something else entirely.

I went back to my job in New York, my head spinning. Afsaneh was bowled over by my earrings and asked me all about the trip. It was great. What could I say? I was pretty crazy about that boy.

Afsaneh was still making her way through podiatry school and enjoying it, but she didn't have much time for men. The boys were plodding through college, in Richmond, and *not* enjoying it. We would hear from them from time to time, and it was always a variation on the same refrain.

"We are definitely not living in a dorm next year," Ali told me. Normally he would reserve such complaints for Mom, but Mom was still in Tehran, trying to push her case along.

"We'll talk to Mom when she gets back," I said.

By the end of May, Mom still wasn't back, and the boys were done with college for the year. They were getting booted out of the dorm, so we had them come to New York to stay with us for the summer. It was just like old times: the four of us crammed into a space that was barely large enough for one normal person.

Ali found a job at the B. Dalton bookstore at 666 Fifth Avenue. We tried to meet up for lunch two or three times a week, schedules permitting. Amir looked for a job but couldn't find anything, so he slept a lot and watched too much television.

Mom returned from Tehran in July. Nothing much had happened. The tenants had refused to move, and she had begun eviction proceedings, though she'd been warned it could take years before anything happened. She now turned her attention to the boys. They were adamant about not returning to a dorm and to another year of terrible food, so Mom decided to move to Richmond and find an apartment big enough for the three of them. Our house in Virginia Beach was still rented out, and we were actually making two or three hundred dollars profit each month, and I had two jobs, so I would be able to send money from time to time. Afsaneh, struggling through medical school, couldn't contribute to the family finances, but Mom was sure she'd find work in Richmond.

"We'll be all right," she said. "We're hard as nails."

They found a two-bedroom apartment near campus in a building that was occupied largely by students.

"It's great," Ali said, oozing sarcasm. "In every other apartment, there's a party every night. And here we are living with our mother. We're the biggest nerds in town."

Mom got on the phone. "It's fine," she said. "He's exaggerating. But the neighborhood *is* a little strange. There's a 7-Eleven down the street, and every time I walk past I can see men picking up transvestites."

"How do you know they're transvestites?" I asked.

"No woman could be that ugly or that muscular," she said.

Before the end of the month, Mom found a job babysitting for a young American couple with two kids. The wife was in medical school, and the husband was studying law. They were very accommodating and glad to have Mom in their lives. The biggest problem was geography. Mom needed a car to get to work, and the boys needed a car to get to class, and in the space of a week they bought two beat-up cars at auction. This was becoming a Latifi family tradition.

Mom made the boys take premed courses, and she spied on them to make sure they were going to class. If she didn't see their rattletrap of a car in the school lot, she would cruise by the basketball courts and find them there. She didn't confront them, though. She would drive home and wait for them to return. "How was your premed class today?" she'd ask. Both boys would hang their heads in shame. They couldn't lie to her. None of us could ever lie to "Big Moms."

After they went to bed, Mom would go through the boys' pockets, looking for anything untoward. I don't know what she expected to find—drugs? money? mash notes from girls?—but she never found anything.

"Don't you think it's wrong to invade their privacy like that?" I ventured on the phone one night.

"No," she said. "It's for a good cause."

"And what cause is that?"

"To keep my sons on the straight and narrow."

"You may be overdoing it, Mom."

"A mother can never do enough," she said. "One day you'll have kids of your own, and you'll understand."

"Don't hold your breath," I said.

"I want to be a grandmother," she replied, ignoring me.

"I'm still working on finding you a little garden," I replied. Then I told her I loved her, wished her good night, and went to bed.

CALDER AND ME ON OUR PARIS TRIP, IN FRONT
OF NOTRE DAME

CHAPTER SIXTEEN

Family Ties

ALL THE GIRLS FROM THE KOOCHEH: ME, HALEH, MAHSA, AND
AFSANEH AT HALEH'S BRIDAL SHOWER

EVERY SATURDAY MORNING, Afsaneh and I had an early breakfast at the Seventy-ninth Street Diner, a few blocks from our apartment. We were generally the only patrons who weren't nursing a hangover, and it was fun to watch the bleary-eyed customers stumbling through the door in search of sustenance.

After breakfast, if the weather was good, we'd behave like typical tourists. We might go to the Metropolitan Museum of Art, for example, or the Frick Collection, and we often went window-shopping in SoHo, oohing and aahing over all the beautiful things we couldn't afford.

By late afternoon, we'd work our way back to the apartment, and I'd get ready for my evening job at Maryann's, leaving my sister to her own devices. Later in the year, however, one of the hostesses left unexpectedly, and Afsaneh applied for the position. From then on, we worked together every Saturday night. It was our favorite night of the week. We felt we ran the restaurant, and we had an exaggerated sense of our own power. Anyone who came in with attitude didn't get a table, even if there were plenty of tables available. We were determined to educate the world. Our motto was "Be nice or be gone." It was my first experience with the corrupting influence of power.

Later that year, I went to see Calder in Winston-Salem, and the following month he again came to visit me in New York. Then in May 1993, right after he graduated, his parents bought him a round-trip ticket to Paris, where they were living at the time. The ticket came with a terrific bonus: It included a companion ticket for me. We went in early August, right after Calder took the Georgia State Bar. It was a wonderful present and an unforgettable vacation. We started in Paris, hitting all the requisite sites—from the Louvre to Notre Dame to the Sacré Coeur Cathedral, my hands-down favorite—then stopped to visit Sabi before driving to southern France and through the Loire Valley. One afternoon, I was trying to take a picture of Calder and his parents in front of a spectacular chateau, but there was an old woman with a horrible blue hat in the background. "This picture would be perfect," I hollered, "if only that woman with the ugly blue hat would get out of my way."

The woman turned to look at me, managed a pained smile, and addressed me in heavily accented English: "Which way would you like me to move?" she asked, unable to keep the sarcastic edge out of her voice. "To the left or to the right?"

I was completely mortified.

Otherwise, the trip was a dream come true. Calder and I were together twenty-four hours a day, seven days a week, for two weeks, and we never had a single argument. You'd think we would have found an opportunity to get on each other's nerves, but it didn't happen. I was so happy, I was almost giddy. I couldn't believe it. This guy was my boyfriend and my best friend. Who could ask for anything more?

When we returned to the States—he to Atlanta, I to New York—I began to analyze and overanalyze the relationship. I was crazy about Calder, but I was afraid of moving to the next level. It was my first serious relationship, and I wasn't in a big rush to settle down. I certainly wasn't interested in anyone else, and I know Calder wasn't, either, but I felt I had to do *something*.

"If you are dating this boy, you should be thinking about the future," my mother said. She wasn't judging me—Mom never passed judgment—but I understood her concern. I *did* have to think about the future. But what was there to think about? Was I supposed to move to Atlanta, take the Georgia State bar, and start again? No thank you. That wasn't for me. I hated my job in New York, but I loved New York. Calder, meanwhile, seemed very happy in Atlanta. He went to work for a prestigious local law firm and settled in. Three or four nights a week, we'd burn up the phone lines, and from time to time, money permitting, we would take turns flying back and forth to visit.

That Thanksgiving, our family congregated at Shamsi's place in Virginia Beach, and I asked if I could invite Calder, his brother, and his brother's girlfriend. Shamsi thought this was a terrific idea, and Mom spent two days puttering around Shamsi's kitchen, getting ready for the main event. She made her usual Persian-style turkey, I was again in charge of the potatoes, and Afsaneh went off to the store to fetch the "homemade" pies. The party was a huge success. I remember looking around the table and thinking that at one time all of our guests had been Persians. That year, we had three genuine Americans at the table—Calder, his brother, and his brother's girlfriend—and it felt absolutely right. It didn't hurt that I was pretty crazy about one of them, mind you, though you wouldn't know it to look at us. When it came to displays of affection, I was very cautious in front of Mom. No, that's not entirely accurate. It went beyond caution. There were *no* displays of affection. In fact, at one point during the evening Calder unthinkingly gave me a peck on the cheek, and I almost died. "Please," I whispered, "not in front of my mother."

"I'm sorry," Calder replied, visibly flustered. "Is she going to hate me forever now?"

"No," I said, "but keep your distance."

It was ridiculous. Here I was, a grown woman, and I couldn't hold my boyfriend's hand in my mother's presence. This was particularly strange because everyone absolutely adored Calder, including Shamsi, who kept getting his name wrong. "Afschineh," she said, taking me aside for a moment in the kitchen. "I must tell you: I really like Carlos." When I told Calder that she kept referring to him as Carlos, he seemed to like it. "That's my Latin side," he said. "Maybe if you're lucky, you'll get to see it one day."

When Afsaneh and I got back to New York, we found a bigger apartment in the same neighborhood. It was also a walk-up, on a more manageable second floor, and the single biggest disadvantage was that it looked out at the brick facade of the building next door. As a result, I never knew what the weather would be like till I walked outside, so I resorted to wild guesses. I invariably guessed wrong. If I emerged from the building in my raincoat, the sun would be shining. And if I showed up expecting sunshine, I'd find myself in the middle of a snowstorm.

Mom and the boys came up for an uneventful Christmas, and after they left I finally began to grapple with the fact that I was seriously disenchanted with my job. My bosses had rented several offices to independent attorneys, and every once in a while I'd visit with one of the friendlier attorneys and whine about how much I hated my job.

"I know a guy who's looking for someone," he said. "He's involved in a big litigation case, and he needs full-time help. Why don't you go see him?"

That's how I met Robert Tucker. I called him up and introduced myself, and he invited me over for an interview. He was a handsome, buttoned-down man in his late thirties, fit and trim, and he looked very professional and very conservative in his pinstriped suit and polished loafers. If you went to central casting and said you needed a lawyer, you couldn't have done better than Robert Tucker. He worked out of his apartment, and he explained in a clear, distinct voice what he did for a living: "I practice intellectual property and corporate law," he said. "Things like trademark infringement. I go after counterfeiters. My clients are mostly fashion designers—jewelry, handbags, watches, that sort of thing—and some of them conduct business in Europe and Asia, where we have very serious problems with counterfeiters. I see you speak German. That could be very useful."

Unfortunately, the practice was still relatively small, and he needed someone who could be part of the legal team as well as run the office. That didn't appeal to me. I'd been doing clerical work for a long time, and I'd had enough of it, so I called him the next day, thanked him for his time, and politely declined the offer. He couldn't have been nicer about it. "I can understand your concern," he said. "But please don't hesitate to call me if you change your mind."

This was in early June of 1994, and I remember that over the course of the next few days everything at work seemed to go from bad to worse. By Friday, I decided I couldn't take it anymore, and, with the exception of my Saturday shift at Maryann's, I spent most of the weekend moping. On Sunday night, at around ten o'clock, I went to look for Robert Tucker's phone number. "Mr. Tucker," I said, meek as a mouse, "I'm sorry to bother you at this late hour, but I was wondering if that job was still available?"

"Yes," he said. "When do you want to start?"

"I'd like to give two weeks' notice, but if you need me to come in beforehand, to familiarize myself with the operation, I'd be glad to do so."

"No. Two weeks is fine. See you then."

"Thank you, Mr. Tucker."

"My name is Robert," he said, "and I'm glad you changed your mind."

When I told my employers I was leaving, they were totally shocked. "You're unhappy here?! What do you mean? We thought you loved it!"

"Well, no," I said. "I'm afraid it's not working out."

I felt guilty about giving notice, and on my last day I half-expected my employers and my colleagues to come by and wish me well in my new endeavors. But no one said so much as a single word, which went a long way toward dissipating the guilt.

Two weeks later, on a Wednesday, I showed up at Robert Tucker's apartment to start work, but he was leaving for a full day of meetings and was in a bit of a frenzy. He had set up a makeshift office in the dining room, and he asked me to please take care of some of the clerical things while he was away. "When I get back, we'll get into the legal stuff," he promised. "Here's a key to the apartment. Just come and go as you please."

His wife, Jennifer, wasn't around—she was a flight attendant—and I felt a little odd, being in his home alone, so I took off at five, thinking I shouldn't be there when she returned. The next morning, I arrived to find Robert already at his desk. He had reviewed my work and said he was very pleased, and true to his word he handed me a file and asked me to read the correspondence and draft a complaint. The case involved trademark infringement, which was a whole new world to me, albeit an interesting one, and Robert told me not to worry. "We'll go over it when I get back," he said. It turned out that he was leaving town that day for an entire week. He was going to a summer camp that catered to children with cancer, something he'd been doing for several years. I must admit that I was pretty astonished by this. I didn't know too many attorneys who would exchange a full week of billable hours to entertain kids with cancer. I didn't know too many attorneys, period, but there was something really special about Robert.

"I don't want to screw anything up for you while you're away," I said.

"You won't. There's nothing here you can screw up. Just take it easy. Read through some of these files. Familiarize yourself with my caseload."

"I feel so useless," I said. "I feel I should be doing more, keeping busy."

"Believe me, you're doing plenty," he said. "Anything you learn while I'm gone is going to prove helpful later, so just learn and have fun."

The man was unreal. I thought I was dreaming. How did I get a boss like this? What had I done to deserve him?

I sat around reading all day, day after day, and I found the cases so interesting that I actually took some of the files home with me and looked through them until I fell asleep. I never realized that intellectual property law was so interesting. It went well beyond some fly-by-night operation knocking off a Rolex watch that was being peddled on a New York City street corner. People spent many years building a company, a brand, and a reputation, and someone could come along and quickly destroy their good name and their livelihood, along with the livelihood of the workers in their employ. If you created something—a unique handbag, a signature belt buckle, a pair of forged steel cufflinks—you had a right to protect it. That was the heart of copyright and trademark law: creation, source, and ownership. It wasn't solely about giant, Goliath-like corporations, pushing the "little guy" around, but about the artists behind the products and about the people who depended on them. And in fact, most of Robert's clients were artisans—jewelers, leather smiths, sculptors, clothing designers, etc.—who were only just beginning to experience a small measure of success. For them, the battles were about survival.

When Robert came back, we sat down and reviewed the work I'd done, and he was always highly complimentary. Even when I'd completely missed the point, he would find a gentle way of steering me in the right direction. I remember telling Calder about him on the phone one night, and I guess I must have sounded like a smitten schoolgirl.

"So," Calder said, a slight edge creeping into his voice, "he's kind, brilliant, generous, a marvelous teacher, gives his time to needy children, and fights for little guys across the globe. I didn't realize you were working for Indiana Jones."

Now that my professional life seemed to be falling into place, I turned my attention to my family. It's not as if I had ever neglected them—we spoke on the phone every day, sometimes two and three times a day—but I began to miss them in ways I hadn't previously allowed myself to miss them. Mom and the boys were still in Richmond, but they didn't love it, and Mom kept talking about how much she had enjoyed New York. But she wasn't going to leave the boys to their own devices. She was going to make sure they both became doctors. "We are so uncool," Amir told me on the phone one day. "Everyone in our building is under the age of twenty-one, and they party every night, and we're the two Persian guys who live with their mommy."

It was nice that the boys could confide in me. In a strange way, with Afsaneh focused on medical school, I had usurped her role as head of the family. I had become the focal point. I was the one everyone called with their problems, large and small, and I found that I enjoyed the responsibility. This was my family, I loved them, and I began to wish with all my heart that we could be together again, like a real family. I wanted us all under one roof, near at hand. I didn't feel complete without them.

Of course, I was also trying to figure out how Calder fit into my life. We continued to visit back and forth, and this became a source of some minor friction. Neither of us had any money, travel was expensive, and it was certainly easier to have the other person make the trip. But it went beyond that: We had reached a point in our relationship where we both began to wonder where it was going. We began to have conversations about the future and what it was we expected from each other, and this added a seriousness and an intensity to our lives that complicated everything. I didn't know if I wanted to settle down with Calder. He was a great guy, but what did I know about guys? I wasn't interested in anyone else, mind you, and I couldn't even picture myself having dinner with another man while he was my boyfriend. But there was a whole world out there, and I knew almost nothing about it. How could I judge whether he was the right man for me? And how would I ever be able to judge if I had no interest in other men?

All of this was further complicated by the distance between Atlanta and New York. The relationship didn't have a foundation. We would spend a weekend together and have a great time, but it's easy to enjoy each other in small doses. It's not real. We wondered what life would be like if we lived in the same city. How would we deal with the small, mundane problems of everyday life? Would we grow closer than ever, or would the relationship fall apart?

These questions gnawed away at both of us and at Calder in particular. At one point he even asked me to move to Atlanta. But I didn't want to move to Atlanta. I didn't want to take the Georgia State Bar and start again. I'd already thought about this, and it wasn't for me.

"We have to spend more time together," Calder said. "We can't go from seeing each other every couple of months to settling down."

"I can't live with you, Calder," I replied. "Maybe I'm old-fashioned, but I couldn't live with a man if I wasn't married to him. My culture won't permit that, and morally I can't accept it, either."

"We'll find you an apartment, and I'll help you with the move and the rent," he said. "I think it's important that we get to know each other better."

"What else do you want to know about me?" I shot back.

"Come on. You know what I mean. We have to see if we're really compatible, if we can deal with each other on a daily basis. If I come home from work angry or vice versa, we need to make sure we can handle it."

He was right, of course, but what was the solution? I wasn't moving to Atlanta as a single woman, and he had absolutely no interest in coming to New York. We had reached an impasse, but it really didn't bother me. In a strange way, I was quite comfortable with our situation. I had a boyfriend, yes, but he lived far away. What could be easier? Calder, however, was deeply frustrated by the fact that I was willing to let things drift along. He felt I wasn't sufficiently committed to the relationship, that I didn't want to move to the next phase, and he wasn't far wrong. What he didn't seem to understand, and what I myself didn't understand at the time, is that I couldn't handle the risk. I wasn't equipped to handle it. I had lost my father at age ten, and a piece of my heart went with him. I wasn't ready to be vulnerable again. I didn't want to be left behind. I would depend on myself and only myself, and on my direct family in a pinch. I would be like a soldier, hard as a nail. In some ways, I was *too* tough, and I didn't always behave well. If I felt Calder pushing me, demanding more of me, I could turn on him in a flash. There is a not very complimentary Persian saying: *Mesle sag pacheh meegeereh* (She'll bite your leg like a dog). It's not as if I'd snarl and nip at Calder, but I know I tended to pull away, and I could be difficult (to put it mildly). I was confused and conflicted, and I was tired of trying to figure things out, so I focused my energies on my work.

Unlike my personal life, that part of my life was going exceedingly well. With me in the office, Robert had the freedom to go out and drum up more business, to be a rainmaker, as they say in the legal profession. Before long, the practice began to flourish. Robert found another apartment in the building, turned it into an office, and hired a secretary. True to his word, he was going to turn me into a full-time lawyer.

In February 1995, a few months after we made the move into our new quarters, Robert went out and splurged on new computers. He told me to take the old one home and offered to set it up for me, and he came over the following Saturday to help me do it. Although he said nothing about our dark, dingy apartment, he went back to the building and spoke to the super about the next vacancy. Apparently, it broke his heart to think of my sister and me living in that tiny space with nothing to see from the windows but a brick wall. A few months later, a one-bedroom apartment became available on the twenty-first floor, and Robert urged us to take it.

"We can't afford to live in that building," I said.

"Yes, you can," he said. "It's rent-stabilized. Plus you're getting a raise."

When we went up to look at the apartment, I almost wept. You could see all the way to the Empire State Building from the living room. I didn't know what to say. I didn't know how to thank Robert. I felt as if God had sent me an older brother, someone to watch over me and help me on my way. "It's too much," I said, fighting tears. "You're too good to me."

"Afschineh," he said, "this is only the beginning."

The summer of 1995 was fabulous. We lived in a doorman building, with a spectacular view of Manhattan. The doormen always welcomed us with a smile and a pleasant word. "Good morning, Miss Latifi. Beautiful day, isn't it?" We felt like real New Yorkers.

This was also the summer Afsaneh graduated from medical school as a Doctor of Podiatric Medicine (DPM). Mom, the boys, and Shamsi came up for the ceremonies, and they seemed more impressed by the apartment than by the fact that we had a doctor in the family. Robert invited the whole clan out to Southampton for the weekend: It was his gift to the family. He had a beautiful house there, which he had pretty much renovated himself. When it came to construction, Mr. Indiana Jones was second to no one. On Sunday, before we returned to the city, I couldn't find Mom. I finally spotted her outside, admiring his garden, and I went out to join her.

"It's beautiful here, isn't it?" I asked.

She just nodded. She was too choked up to answer.

As soon as we returned to the city, just before Mom and the boys returned to Richmond, we heard from Khaleh Mali, back in Tehran. There was good news and bad news. The good news was that Mom's case against the tenants was moving forward, and there was a chance she would be able to evict them. The bad news was that the case could not go forward without her presence in Tehran.

Afsaneh traveled to Tehran with her in August, excited about the visit, and returned alone after three weeks, deflated by the experience. The city had seemed drab to her, the people joyless. And while the wheels of justice were creaking slowly forward, everything was taking longer than had been anticipated. Afsaneh told me that they had gone to the courthouse three or four times a week to push things along. "Every time we made a little progress—every time we moved up the ladder, as it were, to the next bureaucrat in line—the clerk would always begin by saying, 'Well, how fast would you like to see this case get settled?' At which point he or she would open the desk drawer, waiting for Mom to drop a bribe inside." Afsaneh shook her head sadly, thinking back on her brief visit. "They've made a mess of the country, Afschineh. You wouldn't recognize our old *koocheh*. I hardly recognized the house. And all the old neighbors are gone."

Afsaneh had just begun her residency at a hospital in Brooklyn, and the boys were back in Richmond, free of Mom and probably thankful for the break. But there was no escaping her. She called every week: "Are you keeping an eye on the boys? How are things at work? At the new hospital? How's Calder? Say hello to Mr. Tucker for me."

Finally, in October, after two and a half months in Tehran, a verdict was rendered in Mom's case: She had won. She called me, ecstatic, and told me she needed my support. "You're the lawyer in the family," she said. "I could use your help."

I made arrangements to return to Iran, but not without great trepidation. I hadn't seen the country of my birth in fifteen years.

AFSANEH AND MOM IN ESFAHAN

A MOSQUE IN ESFAHAN

OUTSIDE A PUBLIC BATHHOUSE IN ESFAHAN

SHIRAZ

CHAPTER SEVENTEEN

The Journey Back

PERSEPOLIS

IN LATE OCTOBER 1995, I flew to Tehran to help my mother settle her affairs at the end of her long legal battle with the tenants. I hadn't been back since 1980, and I was nervous about what I would find. As the plane began its descent, I could feel knots in my stomach, but I knew I had to pull myself together. I could not afford to be weak in front of these people. I was the daughter of a soldier.

By the time I got off the plane, in my long coat and head scarf, I was feeling confident, almost cocky, and the feeling was fueled when I caught sight of my mother in the waiting area, high overhead. She was in the company of a dozen relatives, peering down at me through the floor-to-ceiling windows, and the moment they spotted me, they all waved madly. I waved back and disappeared toward one of the immigration kiosks.

As soon as I reached the front of the line, the questions began.

"So you're a resident of the United States?" the immigration officer asked me.

"Yes," I replied.

"Why?"

The answer should have been self-evident. *America had welcomed me with open arms. It was my home now. I was happy there.* But I had to be diplomatic. "The actions of my government forced me to flee," I said, "and America provided me with opportunity."

"And you are here why, exactly?"

"To visit my family," I replied. And then added, pointedly: "There must be two dozen people waiting for me in the terminal. I saw them a moment ago. They were all waving as I came through."

This irritated the immigration officer. He saw it as a warning, and he didn't like it. I was told to step to one side and await further instructions. I did as I was told, and he turned his attention to the next passenger. Suddenly I was a little worried. I had heard plenty of stories about people who never made it out of the airport. I didn't think I would be one of them, however: Too many people had seen me already.

A moment later, a woman came and led me down a small corridor and into a narrow room. Two immigration officers, both male, both unsmiling, were waiting for me behind a long table. "So, Miss Latifi," said the first, "why don't you tell us where you've been all these years?"

"I've been in America," I said.

"And what do you do in America?"

"I'm a lawyer."

"A lawyer. Is that a respectable profession for a woman?"

"Yes," I said, unable to hide my frustration. "In America, women are treated as equals."

"Really? Then why did you come back? If it's so wonderful in America, what are you doing here?"

"As I told your colleague, I'm here to visit relatives. I haven't seen most of them in fifteen years."

"Hmmm. Very interesting. After fifteen years, you remember that you have a home and a family."

"I have a family, yes," I replied, "and I was born in Iran. But I have not been welcome here in many years."

I didn't feel quite as tough as I sounded, but I wanted these men to know that they couldn't push me around. They tried, though. They questioned me for four hours, and the questions seldom varied. "Why was I really there? What, precisely, had I been doing in America? What did I really want in Tehran? Did I think I was fooling anyone?" As dawn broke, they finally gave up. I had nothing to hide, and there were people waiting for me in the terminal. There was nothing to be gained by questioning me further. I made my way to the baggage claim, empty at this hour, found my bags, and stepped outside. My mother and my many relatives let out a collective cry that must have carried clear across the city. For the next ten minutes, I was hugged and kissed by my welcoming committee, many of whom I didn't even recognize. Complete strangers were throwing their arms around me and weeping.

At long last, we made it out of the terminal. The welcoming committee had come in four cars, like a caravan, and, like a caravan, we began the journey home. I traveled in the first car, with Mom and some second and third cousins.

"What did those men want from you for four hours?" one of the cousins asked.

"I think they wanted to make me feel as unwelcome as possible," I said.

The moment we got to my cousin's house, before I'd even unpacked, I said I wanted to see the old neighborhood. Everyone tried to talk me out of it, telling me to get some rest, that there would be plenty of time for that later, but I can be pretty stubborn when I want to be.

I went with Mom and my cousin. My cousin drove. The neighborhood didn't look anything like I remembered it—it was ordinary, unimpressive— and when I first laid eyes on the house I refused to believe that this was the "palace" of my childhood. It looked shabby and small, easily half the size I remembered. I wanted to go inside, but Mom had already sold the place—a buyer had been patiently waiting in the wings—and there were a number of construction workers getting the house ready for the new owners.

"I used to live here many years ago," I told one of the workers. "Would you mind if I had a look around?"

"You can't go inside the house," he said. "There's too much construction. But you can look from the yard."

I went through the creaky gate and noticed that the fruit trees were gone. All the apple and cherry trees, gone. The vegetable garden—also gone. But what had I expected? That life would stand still?

The next thing I knew, I was crying. I wasn't making a sound, but I could feel the hot tears spilling down my cheeks. Everywhere I looked, I saw my father. I saw him near the entrance, in his crisp uniform, returning home from the barracks. I saw him moving toward me on the little path that led to the back of the house, and I saw myself running to greet him and jumping into his outstretched arms. I saw him hovering over the barbecue, grilling kebabs, and I saw him at the bedroom window, looking down at me, smiling, overflowing with love. The memories played in my head like home movies, and they were as choppy as home movies. I saw myself as a child, in that very yard, picking apples. And I saw myself on my knees, helping Mom and Dad tend to their vegetable garden. I saw myself leaving the house with my father, my small hand dwarfed by his large one, on our way to run errands. And I saw myself on the street, playing with the neighborhood kids, running, joking, and laughing with all the self-confidence of a child who knows that she leads a charmed life and that nothing bad will ever happen to her or her family.

Now I was crying in earnest, and I felt my mother's hand reaching for mine. I couldn't stop crying. This was where my family had been torn apart. This was where my life had been interrupted.

"Let's go," my mother said gently.

I turned, and we left the property. As we moved toward the car, I wiped my tears and looked at the neighboring houses. Nothing looked the same. Nothing looked even remotely as I remembered it. It didn't even feel like my life. For a moment I wondered if I'd imagined my entire history, though I knew this was impossible. Then other memories raced toward me. I remembered visiting Baba Joon in prison; remembered telling him not to worry, that we'd get him out of there. And I remembered my cousin coming home with the newspaper the day my father's so-called trial and subsequent execution was made public. It had happened *right there*, where I was standing at that very moment. I looked up and saw Maryam's house, directly across the street. It didn't look like Maryam's house, but I could see the kitchen window, and I remembered sitting there with Afsaneh and watching the mourners file in and out of our house. I began to hyperventilate. If Mom hadn't been there to support me, I'm sure I would have collapsed. She got me into the car and held me until I had calmed down.

"Let's go home," she said.

"No," I said. "I want to see Baba's grave."

"That's out of the question," she said.

"Mom," I said firmly. "I've never seen my father's grave, and I want to see it now."

My mother knew she had no choice. I have inherited some of her stubbornness, and I was determined. We stopped for flowers en route. "You know," she said, "people who were executed were not supposed to get proper burials.

BABA JOON'S GRAVE

303

But I bribed a doctor to say that Baba had died of a heart attack, and we were able to bury him in the family plot."

"Does anyone ever visit his grave?" I asked.

"Yes," she said. "Our relatives have been taking care of it over the years, and we give the groundskeeper a little extra to keep it nice and clean."

When we reached the cemetery, my mother led me toward the grave. "That's it there," she said, pointing it out. "I planted that little tree to give him some shade." It was a small tree, but it looked healthy, even now, with winter just around the corner and half of its leaves gone. I knelt at the grave and began to brush the fallen leaves aside.

"I just want to talk to him for a minute," I told my mother. She obliged me and moved off, and once again I began to weep. "*Salam*, Baba Joon," I said. "I'm here, and I am missing you more than ever. I did everything you asked. I studied hard, and I am a lawyer now. Mom made sure we made something of our lives. She took good care of us. She respected your wishes." I was crying so hard that I could hardly talk, but somehow I managed. I told him about the school in Austria and how Afsaneh and I had blown all the money Mom had left at the local bank. I told him about moving to the United States and how hard it had been to live with a family that didn't want us. I told him about the day Afsaneh had to walk to work at McDonald's and how her plastic shoes had practically melted in the heat. "Isn't that funny, Daddy?" I said, sobbing. "Afsi was so proud of those cheap shoes."

I told him that Afsaneh was a doctor now. "Isn't that something? Not all that long ago, she was serving burgers and fries in her little uniform, with her silly little hat, and now she's Dr. Latifi."

I told him about Ali and Amir and how well they were doing at school, despite the fact that they occasionally skipped class to play basketball. "They are young men now," I said. "Both of them are so handsome. And they're good boys, too. You would be so proud of them. I wish you could see us, Baba Joon. The family. Your family. We have tried so hard to be the good people you always wanted us to be, and I think in some small way we've managed it. I'm just so sad you're not here to share it with us."

By this time I was on my knees, doubled over his grave, sobbing inconsolably. I had learned to cope with his absence a long time ago, but now, kneeling on his grave, I missed him more desperately than ever. My heart ached. It felt as if a stone had lodged there.

I don't honestly know what I had expected from that visit to the cemetery. If I thought it would provide some sort of closure, I couldn't have been more wrong. There was no closure to be had. On the contrary, I'd opened up the floodgates. I was drowning in sorrow. I was crying about everything I'd missed by not having a father, and everything I would miss in years to come. One day, God willing, I would get married. But my father wouldn't be there to give me away. And one day, God willing, I would have children. But my father wouldn't be there for that, either, and my children wouldn't meet their grandfather. God, how I missed him! To have had him at my side so I could watch him growing old. To see him surrounded by small children that looked a little bit like me. He would have made a wonderful grandfather.

When I tried to get to my feet, I couldn't manage it. For the second time that day, Mom had to help me to the car. We drove back to the house in silence, and I went to bed and slept for eighteen hours straight.

For the rest of the trip, I could feel that stone in my heart. I felt that nothing or no one could ever make it go away.

We visited relatives and were treated to elaborate meals, and during the day we drove through a city I didn't recognize. Tehran was still a beautiful place—the bazaars teeming with life; the mosques with their cool, blue tiles; the towering, snowcapped mountains in the near-distance—but I didn't know where I fit in. It was very confusing. Back in America, I would tell people I was from Iran. But now that I was home, as it were, I didn't really know what that meant. Yes, this was the country of my birth, but how much did I know about it? When you're eight years old, nine, even ten, your street is your whole world. I knew almost nothing about my culture or my people.

"Why don't we go to Esfahan?" my mother suggested. Esfahan is two hundred and fifty miles from Tehran. It is one of the most beautiful cities in the world and an important cultural center in Iran. "It will help you understand where you came from," she said.

We went to Esfahan and spent the first two days at Hotel Shah Abbas, an institution in Iran. It is a very old hotel with traditional Persian wall paintings in every room and a sprawling garden with its own teahouse. The hotel

GARDENS IN ESFAHAN

306

had become somewhat run-down, but I loved every inch of it—from the tiles underfoot to the creaky elevator and the even creakier man who operated it. We spent those first days walking through the streets of Esfahan, marveling at this ancient city. We visited the Chehel Sotun palace and the Imam Mosque, one of the most stunning buildings in Iran, with its two turquoise minarets. We walked through the neighboring bazaars, surrounded by pleasant, smiling people. I would look at them and think, *These are my people. We share the same history. The same blood runs through our veins.*

On the third day, eager to know more, we hired a knowledgeable guide to take us through some of the sites. He talked about Iran's history: the Elamites, the Aryans, and Alexander the Great, who invaded Persia in the fourth century B.C., destroying Persepolis, in Shiraz, and crippling the Persian Empire.

He talked about the Arabs, who ruled till 1050 and converted the bulk of the population to Islam. He talked about the various dynasties that followed—the Safavids, the Afshars, the Zands, the Khans, and the Pahlevis—and I found myself feeling very proud of my heritage. I was part of a rich culture with rich traditions. Iran was in my blood.

That evening, we checked out of our hotel and went across town to stay at a modern, more luxurious hotel we'd heard about from our guide. When we arrived at the front desk and turned in our passports, as required by law, the clerk informed us that he wouldn't be able to give us a room.

"But we called," my mother said. "You told us you had plenty of rooms."

"It's not that," he replied. "You're traveling without a man, and we can't give rooms to unaccompanied females."

"But that's ridiculous," my mother replied. "I'm traveling with my daughter. We are visiting from Tehran. It's ten o'clock at night, for God's sake."

"I'm sorry, ma'am," the clerk replied. "I can't let you check in without a letter from the police department. If it were up to me, I'd be more than happy to give you the room, but I would lose my license."

We were exhausted, but we didn't have any choice. We took a cab to the police precinct and were dropped at the main gate. We walked through, past knots of armed guards who stared at us—two unaccompanied women—with undisguised hostility, and were finally led into the office of the man in charge. My mother was very polite. She said she'd been told that she needed a letter to register at the hotel.

"You've been well-informed," the man said. "You *do* need a letter to register at the hotel. That's the law."

"Well," my mother said, "can you give us one?"

"I'm not sure," he replied. "What are two women doing out alone in the middle of the night?"

"This is my daughter. We're from Tehran. We're visiting this beautiful city."

"And where is your husband?"

"He's at home," my mother lied. "He couldn't get away. He's a businessman."

"At home, is he? Why don't we call him and ask him how he feels about his wife and daughter parading around the streets at this hour? Give me his number."

She gave him the old number at the house in Saltanat Abad. The phone line was still connected, and she knew that no one would be there to answer it. The man dialed and listened to the ringing phone. "Your husband's not home," he said finally, hanging up. "Where could he be at this time of night?"

"I don't know. He's probably having dinner with friends."

"Well, give me the names of his friends, or of some other relatives."

"What more do you want from me?" my mother said, getting angry now. "How dare you treat us like this in our own country? We are respectable women, and all we want is a room for the night. I've done everything you asked. Now, please, I've had enough of this charade."

The man looked at her and said nothing for a long time. Then he reached for the appropriate form, had her fill it in, and grudgingly signed it.

"Thank you," she said.

The man said nothing.

On the way back to the hotel, I was livid, but I didn't want to talk in front of the cabdriver. The moment we stepped into the room, however, I fell apart. "These people have ruined Iran!" I said. "I spent the morning learning about our culture, our rich history, and our ancient traditions, and in the evening I am reminded that barbarians have taken over the country."

"You're right," my mother said. "It's all politics. These people are destroying Iran."

"What good is any of this if you can't be free?"

The next day, we went back to Tehran, and two days later I was on my way to New York. I had seen enough. I was ready to go back.

AFSANEH AT BABA JOON'S GRAVE, ON HER TRIP BACK TO TEHRAN

CHAPTER EIGHTEEN
Home

ALI'S LAW SCHOOL GRADUATION

TOP: AMIR, ALI, JENNIFER, HARRISON, ROBERT.
BOTTOM: ALLISON (DAUGHTER), MOM, ME, TRISTAN, KASPER.

In the summer of 1996, my brother Ali graduated from Virginia Commonwealth University and came to stay with us in New York. He was having serious misgivings about medical school, and it had become a source of friction with Mom.

"Do you want me to be unhappy?" he asked her.

"No. I want you to go to medical school."

"But I don't think I want to go to medical school."

"You're too young to know what you want," she replied.

"What is it with you and doctors?" he shot back. "Afschineh went to law school, and she's doing fine. I think I'm interested in psychology."

My mother reached me at work. "You have to talk to your brother," she said. "What is this psychology business? Is he crazy?"

I did talk to my brother, but, for the first time in my life, I approached him as an equal. I was done parenting him. He had a formidable enough parent in Mom. I was tired of being so serious and responsible. Up until that point, our lives had been largely about financial survival—the mortgage, the rent, the student loans—but we seemed to be emerging from that dark tunnel. This gave us room to breathe.

"You're interested in psychology?"

"I don't know," he replied. "I want to make Mom happy, and psychology seems almost doctorlike, but that's probably not it, either. I need time to think."

He came to work for Robert, part-time, clerking and running errands, and we continued to explore other possibilities.

"What about law?" I asked.

"I don't know," he sighed. "Would I have to wear a suit all day?"

Robert became part of the discussions. He was like family to me, and I felt I could tell him everything.

"I'll speak to your mother," he said, and true to his word, he did. "Mrs. Latifi," he told her, "I have met your four children, and you've done a great job with all of them. They are amazing people. I know you want what's best for them, but maybe it's time to let them explore on their own. Being a doctor isn't the only job in the world."

My mother was stunned. She didn't know how to respond to Robert, and she didn't want to argue with him because in her heart of hearts she knew he was right. "I guess I'm afraid to let go," she said. "Is that such a crime?"

It wasn't a crime at all. Given what Mom had survived, it was easy to understand her need to keep her children close and to exercise as much control over their lives as she could—for as long as she could. Even parents who led charmed lives seemed to worry about letting their kids go. "Ali's a smart boy," I said, trying to reassure her. "He's come a long way from the days when he was wearing hot pants. He'll be fine. You'll see. I think he's actually getting quite interested in law."

I was right. Ali ended up taking the LSATs, and he did well enough to be admitted to Wake Forest. The Sobhanis were waiting for him in Winston-Salem, where they welcomed him like a son.

The following year, when Amir graduated, he and Mom gave up the Richmond apartment and came to New York to figure out their next move. Amir actually wanted to be a doctor, but he had a hard time finding a medical school he liked—or even one that liked him, to be completely honest. "Maybe I played a little too much basketball," he admitted sheepishly. He ended up going to Ross University School of Medicine, on the island nation of Dominica in the Caribbean, and called the minute he arrived.

"It's practically on the beach!" he exulted.

"You're there to study," Mom told him, "not surf."

Mom, meanwhile, was settling in with me and Afsaneh. "Two doctors in the family is not four doctors," she said that night over dinner, sighing loudly. "But I guess I shouldn't complain."

"Mom," I said, "you're incorrigible."

❧ ❦ ❧

In June 1998, Calder came to visit. He was a nervous wreck all weekend, not at all the Calder I knew, and I suspected he had something on his mind. Early on Monday, June 22, he was supposed to fly back to Atlanta. I was in the tiny kitchen, in my pajamas, fumbling with the coffeemaker, when he walked in and said he had something to tell me. "No," he corrected himself, looking a little flustered. "I have something to *ask* you."

He took a little box from his pocket and showed me the beautiful diamond ring he'd brought with him from Atlanta. I stared at it, not fully comprehending. I was still half-asleep.

"Wow," I said finally. "It's stunning."

"Well?" he asked.

"Well what?"

"I'm asking you to marry me, Afschineh."

I said yes, of course. I don't know why, exactly. I guess I thought this was the right thing to do—that it was the logical next step in our relationship—and I didn't want to fight it. Calder and I hugged and kissed. A normal woman would probably have cried, but I was too tough for that, so he settled for the hugs and kisses. Then I told him I would have to clear it with my mother.

"I already cleared it with her," he said.

"You're kidding? When?"

"Ages ago," he replied, "but I swore her to secrecy."

"Wow," I said, "a girl can't even trust her own mother."

In the weeks and months ahead, I turned into another person. I started planning my wedding. I looked at locations, studied menus, sifted through engraved invitations, worried about flower arrangements. I fell in love with a Vera Wang dress and took a mortgage out on it. (Well, not really. But you get the idea.) Alas, the day I went to be fitted for my dress, I started having doubts about this whole crazy undertaking. What was I going to do—become a housewife in Atlanta? What was expected of me? Did I even want to live in Atlanta? When was the earliest I could take the Georgia State Bar? Were there any jobs there?

Then Robert suggested we open a small office in Atlanta. "Why don't you fly down next week and start looking for space?" he said.

"Are you serious?"

"Absolutely," he said.

He liked Calder, too. *Everyone* liked Calder. *I* liked Calder. But the more I thought about leaving New York, the less it appealed to me. Ali was at Wake Forest at the time and Amir was in Dominica, but in my heart I knew that someday the entire family would be living in New York. Mom was living with us in New York and taking care of Robert and Jennifer's little girl, Allison, who had become like a little sister to us and a granddaughter to Mom. That was the dream, anyway. If I went to Atlanta, what would happen to us? I'd be living in a strange city, totally dependent on Calder. Did I even *know* Calder? And I had to think of my family. I was the breadwinner. If I left now, the result could be financially disastrous.

"It's strange," Calder confessed when I started expressing doubts. "I've been thinking about it, too. I was wondering if it wouldn't be better for us to live in the same city for a while."

So we were back to that. We were supposed to get married the following January, on the heels of my thirtieth birthday, and here we were, retreating. Before long, the wedding was off, then it was on again, then it was *definitely* off. One afternoon, during one of our increasingly frequent arguments, I snapped at him: "If you think this is painful, you don't know me at all. When I was a little girl, my father was executed. This is *nothing* to me."

The truth is, I found the idea of marriage absolutely terrifying. I didn't see how I could allow myself to get that close to another human being. There were too many risks involved. Instead, I would take care of myself. I was the daughter of a soldier. I was as hard as nails. That's what I told myself, anyway. It soon became apparent that I wasn't anywhere near as tough as I pretended to be. I was in fact devastated by the breakup, and it was months before I could bring myself to talk to Calder again.

"In many ways, we were married in our hearts a long time ago," he told me. "But we didn't work on the marriage. We let it fall apart."

I knew exactly what he meant. Distance had kept us together. Other couples met, married, and worked on their relationship, but we had never really worked on ours. We had coasted along for years and years, both physically and emotionally distant. But in some ways, if I'm completely honest with myself, I can see that that's the way I wanted it—that that's what made it work. To this day, I am still struggling to accept that loss as part of life. I simply couldn't cede that much of my heart to Calder or to anyone. My heart still ached for Baba Joon.

❦ ❧ ❦

Once again I escaped into my work. In November, 2000, I went to Bangkok on behalf of a client. Robert and I had spent months making a case against a ring of counterfeiters, and the Thai authorities invited me to take part in the actual bust. It was very exciting. I was jammed into the back of a van with six police officers. When we arrived at the suspect's warehouse, the officers climbed out of the van, removed their shoes, and entered the premises. (There were crooks beyond the front door, certainly, but in Thailand one respects a man's home and his property.) The suspect and his employees were quietly and politely rounded up. There was no shouting, no fanfare whatsoever, and no guns were drawn. But it was still a thrill. The officers seized bins of fake jewelry, the various molds, and even the company's many computers. The operation was successfully shut down.

Other counterfeiters came to take their place, of course. In the years since, I've been to Guam, Taiwan, Korea, Hong Kong, and Shanghai, and I always feel that sudden rush of adrenaline before we move in. It's as if I'm starring in my own television series: *Busted!*

AT AMIR'S MED SCHOOL GRADUATION

When Ali graduated from law school in 2001, Robert found him a studio apartment in the building and asked him to come to work for us full-time. The following year, Amir graduated from medical school and became a resident at Methodist Hospital in Brooklyn. He moved in with Ali, which I remember as a very happy day. The entire Latifi clan was finally together again, living in New York under one roof—albeit a very large roof. We began to refer to the building as The Dormitory.

That same year, Robert took me completely by surprise and made me a partner. Much as I hate to admit it, I cried—privately. Life couldn't possibly be that good, I thought. But it was that good, and it got better. Late one January night, Afsaneh and I found ourselves at an AIDS fund-raiser in Manhattan, talking to a terrific guy. His name was Ueli Laupper. He was from Lucerne, Switzerland, and exceedingly charming. The following year, Dr. Latifi was engaged.

In March 2003, feeling emboldened by our changing fortunes, the Latifi family pooled its resources and bought a modest little house in the Hamptons. It's on the wrong side of the highway and miles from the beach, but it has a nice backyard, and that's what sold us on the place.

Before we'd even signed the mortgage papers, I ordered roses from a Persian greenhouse in Los Angeles. They reminded me of the roses in Mom's garden in Saltanat Abad, and I wanted to surprise her. We planted them in early spring, and one weekend in June we arrived at the house to find that some of the roses had bloomed in our absence. Mom had tears in her eyes. It took her a long time to pull herself together.

She planted vegetables that first summer, as well as all sorts of herbs. She can spend hours on her hands and knees in the dirt, digging, clearing, and pruning. She loves the feel of the cold, damp earth between her fingers; it reminds her of the old days. On weekends, she and Baba Joon would spend hours in the garden, planting, digging, and marveling at the earth's bounty, and she remembers those days as some of the happiest of her life.

❀ ❀ ❀

At the age of thirty-five, my age today, my mother was already a widow with four children. There were times when she felt she couldn't go on, but she had made a promise to my father, and she was determined to keep her promise. She would see to it that we studied hard, made something of our lives, and became good, decent people. That had been my parents' most ardent wish: to educate their four children and to give them the tools to make their way in this uncertain world. At the end of the day, that's what it was all about. You

317

did the best you could; you put a little goodness out there so that it would live on after you were gone. That was your job: to make the world a better place.

My mother never imagined that she would have to raise us on her own, and there were times when she wasn't sure she'd manage, times when she wasn't sure she would survive another day. At those times, she would reach deep into her heart, where Baba Joon still lived and lives to this day, and she would tell him, "I will not let you down."

When people hear our story, they often remark that my mother must be very proud of us. We came to this country with nothing, and now there are two doctors and two lawyers in the family.

I hope she is proud of us because she made us who we are. She never wavered. She would not be broken. She put our family together again.

Sometimes, even after all this time, I think back to the small notes my father smuggled out of prison during those last weeks of his short life: "*Mommie joon'e azizam ghorbanat.* My beloved for whom I would give my life . . . please don't worry about me. Please make sure the children don't feel lonely. . . . Never forget: You are the wife of a soldier."

She never forgot, Baba Joon. She is a soldier herself.

Acknowledgments

Writing this book and reliving so many memories would have been impossible without having been able to tap into my father's courage and sense of honor and without having been nourished by my mother's love, devotion, and never-ebbing confidence in me. I have no words to thank you!

I am forever grateful to my sister, who throughout my life has been and continues to be a source of support and strength. Thank you for fixing my hair; for holding a seat on the school bus for me; for letting me cry so many times on your shoulder; for helping me take those first, unsuccessful attempts at dressing with style; and for raising me. You still complete my thoughts and sentences. Most importantly, I am thankful that you have been here to share this journey with me.

I am thankful to my brothers, Ali and Amir. Ali, your kind heart and gentle spirit, which you try to hide, are an inspiration to me. Amir, your contagious sense of humor and ability to brighten up a room are a priceless gift to our family. Your stage awaits you. Baba Joon would have been incredibly proud of the men you have become. There is so much of him in each of you. His sense of honor, strength of character, goodness, and generosity of spirit live on in the two of you.

To all three of my siblings, who are in many ways extensions of me, thank you for helping me capture our lives in this book, and thank you for letting me share your photos, even the embarrassing ones—notably Afsi's prom photo and Ali and Amir doing their Moon Walk.

Many thanks to my Khaleh Mali, who treated all four of us Latifi children as if we were her own. You have created an unbreakable bond, and we will forever be a part of you.

To Mom's best friend, Sabi, who is a sister to her and an aunt to us. Thank you from the bottom of our hearts for being Mom's friend, confidante, and such an unflagging supporter over the span of these many years. Also, thanks for being her coconspirator in making "how to raise our daughters" decisions.

Special thanks to my friend, brother, and law partner, Robert Tucker. You are an angel in our lives. So many things would have simply been impossible without your support and guidance. You are truly an Indiana Jones to the Latifis.

Thanks to my brilliant and talented coauthor, Pablo Fenjves, who made the process of writing this book effortless. Also thanks for *almost* making me believe that Afsi and I weren't the complete, hopeless nerds that I know we were.

Most importantly, thanks to my publisher, Judith Regan. I would not have written this book if it weren't for your faith in me and insistence that I could do it. You were right—it has been a cathartic experience.

Also, special thanks to the staff at ReganBooks, especially my editor, Aliza Fogelson, and our art director, Michelle Ishay. Your assistance and remarkable direction on this book are truly appreciated.

There have been so many wonderful and kind people in our lives, back in Iran, in Austria, and in the United States, who have enriched our lives and confirmed our faith in the goodness of humanity. Some of these people were practically strangers, like the Iranian woman who accepted our guardianship in Vienna; some were mere acquaintances, like Mr. Owens; and some—such as Sabi, Haleh, and the Tuckers—have become friends for life.

We are so fortunate and blessed to have all of you in our lives!